STREET *by* STREET

NORWICH

STREET *by* STREET

NORWICH

PAMELA BROOKS

breedon **books**
PUBLISHING

First published in Great Britain in 2006 by
The Breedon Books Publishing Company Limited
Breedon House, 3 The Parker Centre,
Derby, DE21 4SZ.

ISBN 1 85983 469 8

Printed and bound by Cromwell Press, Trowbridge, Wiltshire.

CONTENTS

For Gerard,
Christopher
and Chloë,
with all my
love.

Acknowledgements

I owe a great deal to my husband, Gerard, for looking after our children while I was doing research and writing the book – and for putting up with all the maps that were spread over the house at one point! I should also mention my two small research assistants, Chris and Chloë, who helped me to explore some of the streets and yards of the city on foot, put up with me taking endless photographs and didn't complain when whatever I said would be a 15-minute walk turned out to be rather longer than that.

Thanks also to the staff of Norfolk County Library (particularly Costessey branch and the Local Heritage section, who were incredibly helpful in giving me access to the books and documents I needed) and to Stephanie of Dragon Hall, Clare Agate of Norfolk County Library and Richard Powell of Norwich City Council for being generous with photographs.

Introduction

Norwich grew from a simple crossroads in Saxon times to a warren-like city by the end of the 19th century. Much of the development took place via the yards – a large house would be extended and eventually the new buildings would enclose a courtyard. The yards became narrow passages with around 10–15 houses in them, and the houses were often built back to back. In some parts of the city they were even below street level – unsurprisingly, those areas were known as 'holes'.

At one point, the city had a church for every week and a pub for every day, and all of them had yards or alleys. The names of the streets and yards changed over the centuries to reflect the change in pub names or ownership of the buildings, or even the occupations of the inmates. In March 1771 the city ordered that the names of streets should be put up; *Chase's Directory* of 1783 says that the city has 'long laboured under great inconvenience on account of the difficulty of ascertaining, precisely, the address of inhabitants'. The street names had been put up 'in a few of the parishes: but even this has been done in so partial and improper a manner that little benefit can accrue'. At that point, most of the shops and trades were found by hanging signs – which Chase lambasted as 'very dangerous and disagreeable in windy weather' as they 'interrupt the view, and impede the free circulation of air'.

But the street names were still in a state of flux more than 60 years later. *White's Directory* of 1845 says that putting up street names 'was recently done afresh' but added that 'the numbering of doors is still very imperfect and in many streets there are no numbers at all'. Towards the end of the 19th century the council decided that there were too many streets with similar names – so the street names changed yet again. And so did the numbering!

Researching the history of the streets of Norwich has been like putting together tiny strands of a puzzle – and it's been absolutely fascinating, trawling through old street directories and learning more about the people of my home city and their daily lives. Because this book has quite a broad canvas, I haven't been able to give an in-depth picture of all the people and the events, but I hope I've given you a flavour of the people who lived here and the events that shaped their lives – from the heart-warming to the tragic, by way of the bizarre.

How the book is set out

Each street or yard is listed alphabetically, together with its location and information about how it got its name, who lived there, notable buildings and major events. Buildings and people are listed in alphabetical order; events are listed in date order within theme and – in the cases of roads which have streets and yards leading off them – streets are listed in numerical order, odd numbers first. Anything with an asterisk is a 'lost' yard or street.

I had hoped to place every single yard and every single derivation, but soon discovered that was a tad overambitious! Firstly, the street directories have different layouts – some give a 'street order', some give an alphabetical list of people and some give a list of streets (but without street numbers). Therefore, although I was able to work out which street a particular yard was on, I haven't always been able to pin down the exact location. (I checked the remaining yards myself on foot – and some of them still don't have a nameplate!) Secondly, because Norwich 'does different', names often linger for years after a resident or business has moved on (for example, where Marks & Spencer's is now was called 'Bunting's Corner' for years after Bunting's moved) so I haven't been able to trace back every single derivation, either. And finally, there are large time lags between some of the existing directories, so there are bound to be some yards which sprang up and vanished in those 'missing' years. However, I hope you'll enjoy dipping into this book as much as I've enjoyed researching and writing it.

CHURCHES

1	All Saints Westlegate
2	Christ Church Holy Trinity (Cathedral)
3	St Andrew
4	St Augustine
5	St Benedict
6	St Clement Colegate
7	St Edmund
8	St Etheldreda
9	St George Colegate
10	St George Tombland
11	St Giles
12	St Gregory
13	St Helen
14	St James
15	St John de Sepulchre
16	St John Maddermarket
17	St John Timberhill
18	St Julian
19	St Laurence
20	St Margaret Westwick
21	St Martin-at-Oak
22	St Martin-at-Palace
23	St Mary the Less
24	St Mary Coslany
25	St Michael at Pleas
26	St Michael Coslany
27	St Michael-at-Thorn
28	St Paul
29	St Peter Hungate
30	St Peter Mancroft
31	St Peter Parmentergate
32	St Peter Southgate
33	St Saviour
34	St Simon and Jude
35	St Stephen
36	St Swithin

GATES

I	Ber Street
II	Brazen
III	St Stephen's
IV	St Giles'
V	St Benedict's
VI	Heigham
VII	St Martin's
VIII	St Augustine's
IX	Magdalen
X	Pockthorpe
XI	Bishopgate
XII	Conesford

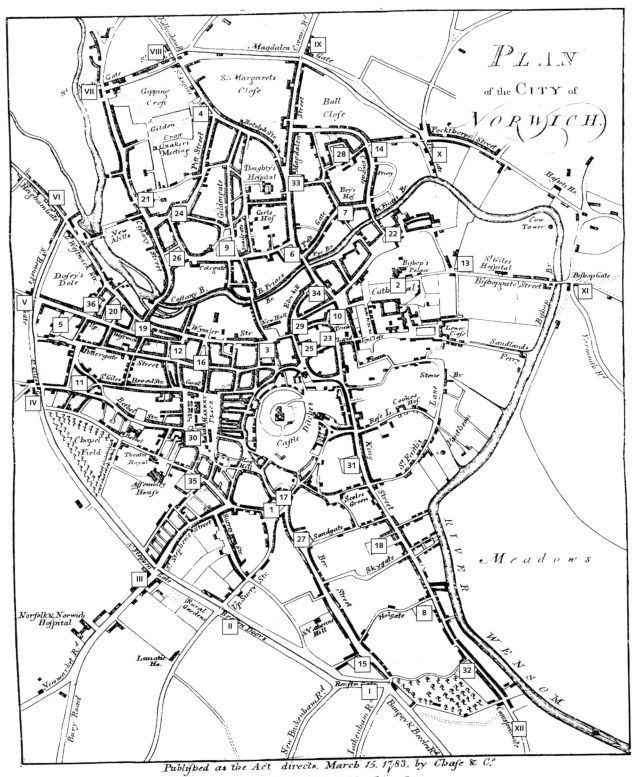

PLAN
of the CITY of
NORWICH.

Meadows

RIVER WENSOM

Published as the Act directs, March 15. 1783, by Chase & Cᵒ
Engraved by T. Smith, White Lion Lane.

ABC YARD
Fishergate, was next to Porter's Sawmills and was gutted by fire in 1900.

ABBS' COURT
1–5 Coslany Street, was known as Gent's Yard or Upper Yard by 1883. *Pigot's Directory* of 1830 lists Zachariah Abbs, boot & shoe maker, in Coslany Street.

ABBEY LANE
Runs from 137 King Street to Bracondale. It contained the Church of St Clement at the Well, which was named in records before the Conquest. The church was added to the parish of St Julian in 1482; the church and churchyard were sold in 1560, and the church was used as a barn until the 18th century. The city mortuary was next to Abbey Lane in 1925.

ABEL'S COURT OR YARD
65–67 Magdalen Street.

ABORNE'S YARD
Was located on Lower Westwick Street, precise location unknown.

ADAM & EVE YARD
17 Bishopgate, was named after the Adam and Eve pub, which is thought to be the oldest pub in Norwich, recorded at 17 Bishopgate in 1249 when it was used by workmen building the cathedral. Elizabeth Howes, the landlady from 1845–60, used to transport sand from Yarmouth in her

Adam & Eve pub, Bishopgate. (Photograph by author)

wherry and sold it to local pubs for their floors and spittoons – but she also used the sand to hide contraband booze!

ADAM & EVE YARD
84–86 St Benedict's Street, was named after the Adam and Eve pub, which is recorded at 106 St Benedict's Street between 1760 and 1856.

ADDISON'S YARD
117 Magdalen Street. *Harrod & Co's Directory* of 1877 lists Benjamin Addison, carpenter and wheelwright, at Magdalen Street. The yard was lost by 1964.

ADELAIDE COURT
51–53 Pitt Street. See Adelaide Yard.

ADELAIDE YARD
57–59 Pitt Street, was named after the Queen Adelaide pub, which is recorded at 57 Pitt Street from 1836. It was badly damaged in the Baedeker raids of April 1942, though the skittle alley survived and was used as the pub! The pub was closed in 1965 and demolished in 1967.

AGRICULTURAL HALL PLAIN
Agricultural Hall Plain runs from the junction of Castle Meadow and Market Avenue to the top of Prince of Wales Road; Bank Plain runs off it.

Buildings on Agricultural Hall Plain
The Agricultural Hall was designed and built by John Pearce. The foundation stone was laid on 25 March 1882 by the Earl of Leicester – but controversy raged. In April 1882 Philip Back tried to stop the hall being built, on the grounds that the land had been used since time immemorial for fairs and markets, so the Corporation didn't have the authority to build the hall. However, the court refused his application for an injunction, Back withdrew his application and the hall was opened by the Prince of Wales (later Edward VII) on 16 November 1882. The hall had removable iron pens and was the venue for livestock shows, public meetings, fairs and circuses until World War Two. The first exhibition there was held by the Norfolk and Norwich Christmas Show Association, and in May 1990 Gladstone visited the city and gave an address at the Agricultural Hall. In January 1894 the French acrobat Charles Blondin – whom the *Norfolk Chronicle* called 'the most famous and intrepid of all rope walkers' – performed there two weeks before his 70th birthday, and in October 1894 Jerome K. Jerome, the author of *Three Men in a Boat*, gave a lecture at the Agricultural Hall on 'Humour, Old and New'. After the war, the hall became part of the Norwich postal sorting office and then

Agricultural Hall. (Photograph by author)

became the headquarters of Anglia TV. In 1979, during excavations on the site, the remains of an Anglo-Saxon timber church and graveyard were found.

The Boer War memorial is the winged figure of Peace, made from bronze, and was designed in 1903 by George and Fairfax Wade at a cost of £1,600. It's set on the top of a column of Portland stone and Aberdeen granite, and it contains 300 names of people who died in the South African wars. The memorial was restored in 1988–89.

Hardwick House was designed by P.C. Hardwick and built in 1865 by Sir Robert Harvey as the Crown Bank at a cost of £13,000. Its doors opened on 1 January 1866, but four years later it went bankrupt, owing £400,000, and there was nearly a riot when the depositors wanted their money back. Sir Robert Harvey, unable to face the shame, shot himself in July 1870. In 1875 postmaster Benjamin Viny Winch moved the post office from Exchange Street to Hardwick House, and it remained the post office until 1969 when the Thorpe Road sorting office was built. The building is now part of Anglia TV.

The Royal Hotel was designed by Edward Boardman and built in 1896 as a replacement for the old Royal Hotel in Gentleman's Walk. The architectural detail is in Cosseyware – a soft red brick made by Guntons of Costessey, also used on the old Norfolk and Norwich Hospital. It was renamed Henry's in 1989, then became the Chicago Rock Café.

ALAN ROAD
252–254 King Street. It was built 1925–35.

ALBION YARD
64 Peacock Street.

ALDEN'S COURT/YARD
Was located just after the Black Swan Yard at 23 Ber Street. *White's Directory* of 1883 lists Chas F. Alden, boot tree and last maker. The yard was lost 1896–1900.

ALDEN'S COURT
St Stephen's Plain, precise location unknown. *White's Directory* of 1845 lists Robert Alden, brazier and tinplate worker, at St Stephen's Plain.

ALDERSON PLACE
St Catherine's Plain (the triangle between Finkelgate, Ber Street and Queen's Road), consists of flats built in 1959. It was named after Dr James Alderson, who was the father of Amelia Opie (see Opie Street). In 1925 the area was known as Alderson Street, at 7–9 Finkelgate.

ALEFOUNDER'S YARD
83 Westwick Street (off Browne's Yard), is believed to take its name from a pub. It was lost by 1941.

ALLCOCK YARD
45 King Street, took its name from Trivett Allcock, head of the Presbyterian School on King Street. Allcock was known as a strict disciplinarian but had a kind heart; pupils later remembered him reading *The Old Curiosity Shop* to them in the evenings and giving them sausages that had been cooked in a dustpan and potatoes roasted in the fire. Just to the left of the yard was a 15th-century house, which became a slum in the 19th century; in 1851 57 people were recorded living there! The house was demolished some time in the late 1960s, and the area lies beneath buildings of the Cotman Housing Association, which were put up in 2001.

ALL SAINTS' ALLEY
Runs from 20–22 Westlegate to Lion and Castle Yard, and took its name from All Saints' Church (see All Saints Green).

ALL SAINTS' GREEN
Runs from the junction with All Saints' Street to Queen's Road; it's bisected partway through by Surrey Street. The street takes its name from All Saints' Church. According to Blomefield, the road was called All Saints' by Timberhill. It became known as All Saints' in the Old Swyne-market in the 13th century, as the swine market moved to Orford Hill some time around 1270. It became Allderhallen (All Saints) Green by the mid-16th century and was briefly known as Winnalls Street in the 18th century after Winwaloe's (St Catherine's) Church. The area was densely populated until the slum clearances of the 1930s, when many of its residents moved to the new Lakenham estate. According to Blomefield, the street also had a common well and a pit called Jack's Pit, which was filled in by 1744. Part of the street was known as Rodney Street in the mid-1800s, and the section between Surrey Street and Queen's Road was known as Upper Surrey Street by 1783.

Streets off All Saints' Green
East:
Franklin's Court*
Carter's Yard (11)*
Maltster's Yard (15–23)*
Bull Lane (21)
Rifleman Yard (29)*
Saint's Court (43–45 – runs to 30–40 Surrey Street)
Surrey Street (51–53)
West:
All Saints' Yard (24–26)*
All Saints' Street (runs to Ber Street)
Exact location unknown:
Browne's Yard*

Buildings on All Saints' Green
Churches
All Saints' Church dates from 1320. It's now redundant and in the care of Norwich Historic Churches Trust; in 1976 it became an ecumenical centre.

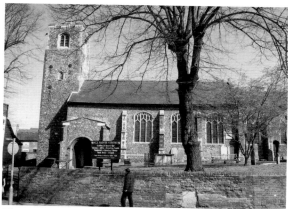

All Saints' Church. (Photograph by author)

St Winwaloe's or St Winwaloy's Church was originally dedicated to St Winewaloci but by the time of the Domesday book had been rededicated to St Catherine. After the plague in 1349, the parish was united to St Stephen's; the building was demolished in the 16th century.

City Wall
Brazen Door was one of the gates in the City Wall (see Barn Road), located at the entrance of All Saints' Green (formerly Upper Surrey Street). It was called Brazen Door because the tower had brass posterns; it wasn't wide enough to allow carriages to pass, so it was widened in 1726 and became known as New Gate. When the gate was replaced by a single large door, it was known as the Iron Door; it was also known as Swinemarket Gate, as it was near the old swine market. It was the last of the city gates to be built; on 19

December 1770 part of the wall fell down, demolishing two houses, but nobody was hurt. The gate was finally demolished in 1792.

Other buildings of note
Carlton Cinema, All Saints' Green, was the first cinema in Norwich designed for 'talkies', according to cinema historian Stephen Peart. It opened in 1932, changed its name to the Gaumont in 1959, but closed in 1973 and became the Top Rank Bingo Club (now the Mecca Bingo Club).

Ivory House, 52 All Saints' Green, was built by architect Thomas Ivory in 1771. It became the Militia Barracks in 1860 (known by 1912 as the East Anglian Brigade Royal Artillery Territorial Forces Barracks). It was restored in 1971 and converted to offices by the city council.

Ivory House. (Photograph by author)

The Thatched Assembly Rooms, at 15–23 All Saints' Green, became the Thatched Cinema in 1915 and closed in 1930. Bonds used it as a ballroom; then it was gutted during an air raid on 27 June 1942.

People linked with All Saints' Green
Edward Temple Booth, mayor in 1826, lived in the Militia Barracks. He was a manufacturer of crape, bombazine and camlets (his business, Temple and Theobald, was located in Muspole Street) and was also the chair of the Norfolk and Norwich Joint Stock Bank.

Events at All Saints' Green
In July 1862 there was a tragic accident in the street. Newspaper proprietor Henry Stevenson was driving in a phaeton with his wife when the horse became frightened and rushed off at full speed. The phaeton was tipped over near All Saints' Church, and Mrs Stevenson died from her injuries within the hour.

ALL SAINTS' STREET
Runs from the end of All Saints' Green to the end of Ber Street.

ALL SAINTS' STREET
Former name for Cowgate.

ALL SAINTS' YARD
24–26 All Saints' Green, takes its name from the church. Lost 1896–1900.

ALLEN'S YARD
St Benedict's Street, precise location unknown. *Harrod & Co's Directory* of 1877 lists Mrs Allen, butcher, at St Benedict's Street.

ALMARY GREEN
Runs through the Close; it took its name from the mediaeval 'almonry'. The remains of St Ethelbert's Church, destroyed in the 1272 riot (see the Close), lie under Almary Green. The parish was added to the Church of St Mary in the Marsh in the late 13th century.

ALMS LANE
Runs from 9 Muspole Street to 88 St George's Street. It takes its name from the almshouses in Muspole Street and was known as Alms House Lane in 1845. Alice Crome paid for the houses in 1516 for seven poor widows to live in.

AMISS COURT
See Armis Court.

ANCHOR CLOSE (also ANCHOR STREET)
102–104 Barrack Street, was renumbered 128–30 in 1964.

ANCHOR QUAY
Is a new development between Westwick Street and Coslany Street; it's on the site of the old Anchor Brewery and takes its name from that and the fact that it's on the river.

ANCHOR YARD
103–113 Barrack Street, took its name from the Anchor pub at 1 Silver Road (which was also known as the Blue Anchor in 1822–63, the Golden Anchor in 1850 and the Anchor inn in 1888). The pub was closed in 1945 and the yard was lost by 1964.

ANCHOR YARD
98–102 Calvert Street to 107 St George's Street, took its name from the Crown and Anchor pub at 119 St George's Street. It was known as the Crown and Anchor yard at the St George Street end and as the Anchor (of Hope) Yard in its Calvert Street location. The Crown and Anchor in St George's closed in 1936, and the yard was lost by 1964.

ANCHOR YARD
King Street. The yard was listed in *Chase's Directory* of 1783 and was lost by 1830. Yarmouth Barge Master John Livock was listed as a resident in 1783.

ANCHOR YARD
18–22 Surrey Street, took its name from the Anchor pub at 16 Surrey Street, recorded there from 1760. The Anchor was known as the Golden Anchor in 1822 and was closed in 1913. The building was used as an estate agent's and demolished in the 1990s.

ANDREW'S YARD (or COURT)
Was located on the north side of St Stephen's Street. *Kelly's Directory* of 1912 lists Sidney Charles Andrews, confectioner, at 49 St Stephen's Street.

ANGEL YARD
140–146 Oak Street, took its name from the Angel pub, which is recorded at Oak Street by 1806. The Angel was closed in 1910, and the yard was lost by 1964.

ANGEL STREET OR YARD
Off Castle Street, took its name from the Angel inn at 16 Market Place (also known as 16 Gentlemen's Walk). The Angel is mentioned at the trial of the Royalist rioters in 1648 (see Bethel Street) and was the headquarters of the Whig party in the 1830s. The Angel became the Royal Hotel in 1840 when Queen Victoria married, and the name of the street changed to Royal Hotel Street. In 1897 the site became the Royal Arcade and Arcade Street. Newspaper advertisements for exhibitions at the Angel include a pair of elephants in 1685, 'dancing on the rope and vaulting' by Daniel von Straven in 1693 and Monsieur du Pain immersing his feet in boiling lead in 1815. According to *Chase's Directory* of 1783, the freemasons lodge met at the Angel on the fourth Wednesday of the month from May 1747. In January 1819 Madame Tussaud exhibited her touring waxworks of 'compositional figures of 90 public characters'. In a separate room (and for an extra 6d admission fee) people could see the display of heads of aristocrats who had been guillotined in the French Revolution – casts that had been taken just after the heads had been chopped off! Other exhibitions at the Angel include Miss Biffin, who was 'deficient of arms and legs' but showed her miniature painting and needlework at the Angel, and the giant Monsieur Louis in 1827 – he was a 26-year-old from Lorraine who was 7ft 6in tall. James Webb, the 'benevolent stranger', distributed considerable sums of

money among 'the public institutions and the necessary poor of Norwich' in February 1813, and the Angel yard was packed for three days.

ANGLIA SQUARE

Is the shopping development between Botolph Street, Upper Green Lane and Magdalen Street. Sovereign Way and Anne's Walk lead from Magdalen Street to the shopping precinct. The Odeon Cinema opened here in 1971.

ANNE'S WALK

Is a footpath that runs from the west side of Magdalen Street to Anglia Square.

ANNISON'S YARD

18 Bull Close. The yard was lost 1935–41.

APPLETON'S COURT

111 St George's Street (and Yard at 168). *Harrod & Co's Directory* of 1877 lists John Appleton, fish curer, at 'Middle Street' (aka St George's Street), and *White's Directory* of 1883 lists William Appleton, fish curer. The court and yard were both lost by 1960.

APPLETON'S YARD

Cowgate, precise location unknown.

ARABIAN HORSE YARD

70a Oak Street, took its name from the Arabian Horse pub at 72 Oak Street, recorded in the 1830s and closed 1908; the yard was lost by 1960. See also Little Arabian Horse yard.

ARCADE STREET

Runs from Castle Meadow to 6–7 Castle Street and Back of the Inns, was formerly known as Royal Hotel Street and

took its name from the Royal Hotel. It became known as Arcade Street when the Royal Arcade was built on the site of the hotel by George Skipper in 1899.

ARCHER'S YARD

36 Muspole Street. *Harrod & Co's Directory* of 1877 lists John C. Archer, engineer and boiler maker; his private address is also listed as 'Rosemary Lane, Muspole Street'. The yard was lost 1935–41.

THE ARCHWAY

120a Magdalen Street, is a new development.

THE ARCHWAY

25–27 St Stephen's Street, was formerly Hunt's Yard and King's Head Yard; it was lost by 1947.

ARMIS'S COURT

Also known as Amiss Court, 91 Barrack Street. *Kelly's Directory* of 1912 lists Mrs Ellen Armes, shopkeeper, at number 87. The yard was lost 1935–41.

ARGYLE STREET

Originally ran from 204–206 King Street to the Wilderness in Bracondale; nowadays it runs from the south side of Rouen Road to Southgate Lane.

ARNOLD'S YARD

St Margaret's Plain, precise location unknown. *Harrod & Co's Directory* of 1877 lists Alfred Robert Arnold, brewer, wine and spirit merchant, at St Margaret's Plain.

ARNOLD'S YARD

St George's Street (Middle Street), precise location unknown. *Robson's Commercial Directory* of 1839 lists George Arnold as the landlord of the William IV pub, located at 108 St George's Street. It may be that Arnold's Yard is an alternative name for William the Fourth Yard.

ASHBOURNE STREET

Ran from 146–152 Ber Street; it was a dogleg road which led to Mariner's Lane and was known as Russell Street before 1900. It originally contained Lily Terrace, but nowadays Lily Terrace runs directly from Ber Street.

ARTHUR STREET

9–11 Mariner's Lane.

ASSEMBLY HOUSE YARD

Theatre Street, took its name from the Assembly House; it's listed in *Chase's Directory* of 1783 but was lost by 1830.

Royal Arcade. (Photograph by author)

ATKINS'S YARD

Ten Bell Lane, precise location unknown. *Peck's Directory* of 1802 lists William Atkins, Shawl Manufacturer, round the corner at 28 Lower Westwick Street (aka St Benedict's Street).

ATKINSON'S YARD

Formerly Newbegin's Yard, 18–24 St Mary's Plain. *Harrod & Co's Directory* of 1877 lists Thomas Atkinson, rag merchant, at St Mary's Plain. By 1925 the yard was under the site of Sexton's boot factory.

AUSTIN'S COURT

21–23 Bethel Street. The yard was lost by 1912.

AUSTIN'S YARD

Magdalen Street, precise location unknown.

AVEY'S YARD

13–15 Ber Street. *Kelly's Directory* of 1900 lists George Avey, grocer, at number 17. *Harrod & Co's Directory* of 1877 lists Thomas Avey, grocer, at Ber Street. The yard was lost 1912–25.

BACK OF THE INNS

Runs from Arcade Street (originally 11 Royal Hotel Street) to White Lion Street, and takes its name from the inns which used to back onto it; these included the Half Moon, the King's Head, the Bear, the Royal, the Star, the Castle and the Bell. Originally the street was called Cockey Lane, after the watercourses on the west side of the castle; it was formerly the outer bailey of the castle. According to *Chase's Directory* of 1783, the freemasons lodge met at the King's Head on the last Thursday of the month from 1736.

Streets off Back of the Inns

Half Moon Yard*

People linked with Back of the Inns

Sir Roger Kerrison, mayor in 1778 and 1802, was a banker in Back of the Inns (1938 site was Fletcher & Son). He was the Receiver-General for taxes in Norfolk for 30 years, although there was a huge scandal when he died in 1808 and the government couldn't recover the taxes he'd collected. He left debts of £580,000 with 3,600 creditors; the government made his firm bankrupt and the creditors got 16s 4d in the pound.

Events at Back of the Inns

The King's Head was a popular place for exhibitions. In November 1807 boxers John Gulley and Tom Cribb gave an exhibition of sparring at the King's Head to over 200 spectators, and in January 1809 Mr Lambert from Leicester exhibited there for an admission price of 1 shilling; he died in Stamford later that year at the age of 40, weighing an incredible 52st 11lbs.

BACK RAMPANT HORSE STREET

Ran along the back of Rampant Horse Street (hence the name) to the west side of Red Lion Street. It appears to have been lost by 1900.

BAGLEY'S COURT

6 Pottergate. *Kelly's Directory* of 1912 lists Charles Bagley, builder, at number 8. The court was restored in 1980–82.

BAILEY'S YARD

136–138 Magdalen Street, was formerly known as Royal's Yard in 1883.

BAKER'S ARMS YARD

9–11 Ber Street, took its name from the Baker's Arms pub, which is recorded at 9 Ber Street in 1760. The Baker's Arms was closed in 1914, and the yard was lost 1941–47.

BAKERS' ARMS YARD

Westwick Street/St Margaret's Street, took its name from the Baker's Arms pub, which is recorded at 45 Lower Westwick Street in 1839. The Baker's Arms was closed in 1895 and the building was demolished; the yard was lost along with the pub.

BAKER'S ROAD

192–194 Oak Street, runs to St Augustine's Street. *Harrod & Co's Directory* of 1877 lists James Baker as landlord of the Bess of Bedlam in Oak Street; *White's Directory* of 1854 also lists him as a butcher. However, this may be a coincidence – the street may take its name from any of the bakers that have lived on the street. The Bess of Bedlam pub is recorded at 80 Oak Street from 1806 and closed in 1907.

BAKER'S YARD

116–118 Barrack Street. James R. Duly, travelling acrobat, lived there in 1883. There was a frightening event at 18 Baker's Yard on 12 November 1925; the four rooms of the house were occupied by 22 people (including Ernico Diannunzio, his wife and their five children in just one room). A wall in one of the two lower rooms began to bulge – the occupants called to neighbours to get out, and they'd just evacuated the building when the upper part of the gable fell in. Some of them managed to shelter with friends, but one family had to go to the workhouse. The yard was lost 1935–41.

BAKER'S YARD

Fishergate, precise location unknown. *Pigot's Directory* of 1830 lists two bakers-cum-flour dealers on Fishergate: Samuel Rollings Abbott and George Jackson.

BAKER'S YARD

57–59 Pottergate. There seems to be a tradition of a baker's shop in the location. *White's Directory* of 1883 lists Henry Sullivan, baker; *Kelly's Directory* of 1900 lists Robert William Todd, baker, at number 57. The yard is now a modern development known as Colman's Court.

BAKER'S YARD

Is listed in *White's Directory* of 1883 as being just after Cowling's Yard on Westwick Street. *Kelly's Directory* of 1900 lists Marie Elise Cowling, baker, at number 68. The yard was lost by 1890.

BAKER'S YARD

12 Wellington Lane. Clearly there is a tradition of bakers in the area – *Kelly's Directory* of 1900 lists William Barber, baker, and *Kelly's Directory* of 1912 lists Frederick Girling, baker. The yard became known as Bailey's Yard by 1935 and was lost by 1941.

BALACLAVA TERRACE (or YARD)

35 Bishopgate.

BALDERSTON COURT

9 Calvert Street, is named after Matthew or Bartholomew Balderston, who was mayor in 1736 and 1751. He was a weaver, the captain of the Artillery Company and acted as His Majesty's Receiver-General for Norfolk for 35 years. He also founded a school in 1761 for 20 poor children who belonged to the congregation of Independents.

BALDREY'S (or BALDRY'S) YARD

Appears to have been located at 71 Barn Road.

BALDWIN'S YARD

49–53 Calvert Street. The yard was lost 1960–64.

BALDWIN'S YARD

Runs from 94–96 Oak Street to near 10 Quaker's Lane. Henry Baldwin, baker, is listed in *Harrod & Co's Directory* of 1877 and *White's Directory* of 1883. The yard was lost 1960–64.

BALLS' YARD

Located somewhere after 2 Bull Close. *Harrod & Co's Directory* of 1877 lists William P. Balls, umbrella maker, at Bull Close. The yard was lost 1890–1900.

BALLOON YARD AND WHARF

At 62 Lower Westwick Street, was named after the Balloon pub, recorded at 62 Westwick Street from 1830. The pub was renamed the Colchester Arms in 1914 and was closed in 1924. The yard was lost shortly after.

BANES' YARD

Ber Street, west side, precise location unknown.

BANK PLAIN

The street runs from the junction of Redwell Street and Queen Street to Agricultural Hall Plain and in the 18th century was the banking area of Norwich. The 18th-century historian John Kirkpatrick says that the road was originally called 'Motstowe' and was possibly the meeting place of the Anglo-Saxon burgh. It has also been known as Redwell Plain (see Redwell Street), along with Blue Boar Lane, London Street, Redwell Street and Queen Street. Bank Street runs off it.

Buildings on Bank Plain

Gurney's Bank House was founded by John and Henry Gurney in 1775 (later the site of Barclay's Bank).

Barclay's Bank. (Photograph by author)

People linked with Bank Plain

Ralph Hale Mottram, writer and magistrate, was born at Gurney's Bank House in 1883. He was encouraged to write by the author John Galsworthy, and his most famous book *The Spanish Farm,* written in 1924, was awarded the Hawthornden Prize; it was also filmed as *Roses of Picardy.* He was Lord Mayor in 1953–54 and was awarded an honorary degree, Doctor of Letters, from the UEA in 1966. After his death in 1971 a bench to his memory was set up on Mousehold Heath.

John Marsh, mayor in 1804, was an attorney. He lived at 3 Bank Place, which was eventually pulled down and used for Barclay's Bank. In 1805 he chaired a meeting at the Guildhall to re-establish the blind hospital.

James Poole, mayor in 1765, was a grocer and wine merchant. He built 3 Redwell Plain (which became Gurney's Bank House, pulled down in 1927 when Barclay's Bank was built). He was made bankrupt in 1773 and died in 1780.

John Steward, mayor in 1810, was a solicitor. He had an elaborate ceremony to celebrate his mayoralty, with 750 guests to his dinner and 400 to his ball at Chapelfield House; it's reported that guests stayed up until two in the morning! He lived in Bank Plain, somewhere between Gurney's Bank and Harvey and Hudson's Bank.

Events at Bank Plain
On 13 April 1856 there was a huge gas explosion at Gurney's Bank; Mr Utting, the clerk, smelled gas. He entered Mr Mottram's office with a lighted candle and an explosion inevitably followed; the windows were blown out and the *Norfolk Chronicle* reported that 'the ceiling was raised so that the gas escaped to the rooms above'.

BANK STREET
Runs from Bank Plain to Upper King Street. It was known as the Blue Boar Lane, then King's Arms Lane. It may also have been known as Excise Office Street (1783 until before 1830). The Excise Office was at number 11 in 1789, and John Snelgrove Esq was the collector of His Majesty's Excise.

Streets off Bank Street
Wade's Court (8)
Shalders' Court (location unknown)*

People linked with Bank Street
R.T. Culley lived on the street; he died there in 1883 at the age of 48, after being the deputy county coroner for 16 years and the coroner for five years.

BANTAM'S YARD
5 St Mary's Alley, was formerly known as Benton's Yard.

BARGATE COURT
34–36 Barrack Street, is a block of flats built in the 1930s. Bargate Court takes its name from Barre Gate, one of the gates in the City Wall.

BARKER'S YARD
57–59 Oak Street. The yard was lost by 1964.

BARKER'S OR BAKER'S YARD
West side of Rosemary Lane. *Harrod & Co's Directory* of 1877 lists Thomas Barker, hot presser, at Rosemary Lane. The yard was lost by 1890.

BARKER'S YARD
74–86 Westwick Street. The yard was lost by 1890.

BARLEY CORN YARD
Cowgate, was named after the Sir John Barleycorn pub, which is recorded at Cowgate from 1830. The pub closed by 1934 and the yard was lost.

BARLOW'S COURT
47 St Benedict's Street. The yard was lost 1890–96.

BARN ROAD
Barn Road runs from the junction of St Benedict's Street and Dereham Road to St Crispin's roundabout, Westwick Street. The name may have come from the Barn Tavern, which is recorded at 1 Dereham Road from 1859 and closed in 1991. Barn Road doubled in width when it became part of the inner ring road.

Streets off Barn Road
Lothian Street (just before Cushion's) and Heigham Street (both are outside the City Walls and, therefore, out of the scope of this book)
Cooper's Yard (after Cushion's)
Baldrey's Yard (71)

Buildings on Barn Road
City Wall
The City Wall was built between 1297 and 1334 to replace the ditch and bank around the city. Edward I awarded the city a grant of murage, which allowed the city to tax people to pay for the wall; the taxes were collected at the murage loft in the market place. Richard Spynke, a wealthy merchant, paid for large sections of the wall and for windows to be made in all the gates and towers. The wall itself was 20ft high and 3ft thick, and used 37,000 tons of

Section of the City Wall (from Wellington Lane). (Photograph by author)

masonry; there was also a ditch 60ft wide and 25ft deep in front of the wall. The wall ran for a distance of 2.5 miles and had 12 gates at major entrances to the city. It started at the boom towers near Carrow Bridge and followed a route along Carrow Hill, Bracondale, Ber Street, Queen's Road, Chapel Field Road, Chapelfield Gardens, Coburg Street, Wellington Lane, Barn Road, Bakers Road, Magpie Road, St Augustine's, Magdalen Street, Wall Lane, Bull Close Road and back down to the river. Spynke also gave enough money to pay for espringolds (used to cast stones), gorgions (the balls of stone used in the espringolds) and crossbows.

BARNARD'S YARD (formerly BARNES' YARD and BARNES' FOUNDRY YARD)

Runs between 60 Colegate and 30–32 Coslany Street.

BARNARD'S YARD

13–15 Fishergate. *White's Directory* of 1854 lists J. Barnard, game dealer, at Fishergate. The yard was lost 1912–25.

BARNARD'S YARD

Appears to have been located on the west side of Wensum Street. *White's Directory* of 1854 lists J. Barnard, game dealer, at Wensum Street, and *White's Directory* of 1883 lists Sarah Barnard, fishmonger, there. The yard was lost by 1890.

BARNES' (or BARNES' FOUNDRY) YARD

60 Colegate – now Barnard's Yard. *Harrod & Co's Directory* of 1877 lists John Barnes, iron founder, at St Miles Foundry, and the firm was still there in 1925.

BARNES' YARD

87–89 Magdalen Street. *Harrod & Co's Directory* of 1868 lists Benjamin Barnes, baker. The yard was lost by 1964.

BARNES' YARD/COURT

19–21 St Augustine's Street, former name for Nichol's Yard.

BARRACK STREET

The street originally ran from 45–47 Peacock Street to Bishop's Bridge. Since the building of the inner ring road, the part of the street between Cowgate and Peacock Street forms part of St Crispin's Road, and Barrack Street runs between the St Crispin's Road/Whitefriars roundabout to the Kett's Hill roundabout. It was originally called Pockthorpe Street (because it led to the hamlet of Pockthorpe), then Bargate Street (after the city gate), then St James' Street (after the church) from 1839–83 and finally Barrack Street after the Cavalry Barracks, which were built in 1791 and demolished in the early 1970s.

Streets off Barrack Street

South:

St Paul's Terrace (19–21)*

Cowgate (37)

Butcher's Yard or Butchery Yard (41–45)*

Mace's Yard (near 43)*

Nickall's Yard (45–47)*

St James' Palace Yard (44–54 or near 109 – though St James' Palace is listed in 1883 next to Nickall's Buildings)*

Priory Square (formerly Nickall's Buildings) (63–65)*

Patteson's Cut (The Cut) (70)*

Palace Yard (79)

River Lane (formerly Water Lane) (85)

Armis's Court (or Amiss Court) (91)*

Fairman's Yard (99–101)*

The Cut (103–105)

Anchor Yard (103–113)*

Dial Yard (113–117)*

Black Boy's Yard (127)*

Seven Stars Yard (139–141)*

Sportsman's Yard (141–143)*

White Horse Yard (145–149)*

Dun Cow Yard (149–151)*

Boddy's Yard (155)*

Light Horseman Yard (161)*

Marquis of Granby Row or Opening (165–171, renumbered 239 in 1964)*

North:

St Paul's Square (2)

Cowgate (22)

Bargate Court (34–36)

Rock Yard (34)*

Nickall's Yard (36)*

Say's Yard (42)*

Stewardson's Yard (formerly Crotch's Yard) (42)*

Wrestler's Yard (44–46)*

Dove Yard (62–64)*

Wall Lane (64–66)*

Silver Road (66–68)

Bird in Hand Yard (72–74)*

George Yard (92)*

Green Yard (96–98)*

Robin Hood Yard*

School Yard*

Anchor Close (also known as Anchor Street) (102–104)

St James' Close (112)*

Griffin's Court (114)*

Baker's Yard (116–118)*

Red Cow Yard, later known as Dun Cow Yard (118)*

The Lokes (after 128)*

Other streets whose exact locations could not be placed include:
Brenton's Yard*
Johnson's Yard*

Buildings on Barrack Street
City Wall
Barregate – also called Pockthorpe Gate – stood at the end of Barrack Street. It was removed in 1792. A polygonal brick tower called Pockthorpe Tower was joined to the gate.

Churches
St James' Pockthorpe Church was previously known as St James at Barr-gates and has also been known as St James Cowgate; it has an unusual brick tower. The roof was renovated in 1885 at a cost of £500. It was the first city church declared redundant and placed in the care of the Norwich Historic Churches Trust. It was excavated two years later in 1974 and was converted to a puppet theatre in 1980–82.

St James' Church, Barrack Street. (Photograph by author)

Other buildings of note
The Cavalry Barracks were built in 1971 on the site of The Lathes, formerly the grange of the cathedral. They were also known as Nelson Barracks. *Pigot's Directory* of 1830 describes them as 'the most considerable pile of modern architecture in Norwich', built of red brick; the boundary wall enclosed 10 acres of ground. The Cavalry Barracks were demolished in the early 1970s.

Events at Barrack Street
Barrack Street was the centre of a murder charge in August 1880, when William Davies and Alexander Browne of the Army Hospital Corps, together with orderlies Henry Prichard and William Solly, were charged with attempting to kill Private John Smith at the Army Barracks on 3 August. According to the *Norfolk Chronicle*, Smith was 'suffering from a loathsome disease'; the orderlies and Davies stuffed the fireplace with straw, closed the windows and door, and placed plates of burning sulphur on the floor to suffocate him. It didn't work, although Smith died a few days later. The prosecution claimed they'd just wanted to get rid of an unpleasant patient (and Smith had also made a will in their favour), but the case was heard on 12 November and they were acquitted.

BARRACK YARD
114–116 St George's Street. See also Little Barrack Yard. The yard was lost 1935–41.

BARTHOLOMEW STREET
Ran from 25–27 Thorn Lane to Horn's Lane. It was demolished by 1964.

BARWELL'S COURT
Runs from 10 St Stephen's Street to Malthouse Road, and was also known as Goodman's Yard in 1783. It took its name from the local wine merchant Barwells, listed at 12 St Stephen's Street in *Kelly's Directory* of 1900. There was an Elizabethan mansion at the court until 1915. John and Louisa Barwell organised the Polytechnic Exhibition (see Bazaar Court).

BATEMAN'S COURT
72 St Giles' Street, took its name from Frederick Bateman, JP and physician, who lived at 70 St Giles' Street in 1890.

BATH HOUSE YARD
97–99 Oak Street, took its name from the Bath House pub at 97 Oak Street, recorded there since 1797. It was called the Cellar House from 1830–36, renamed the Bath House in 1839 and was closed in 1869. The yard was lost 1960–64.

BATH HOUSE COURT/YARD
Botolph Street, precise location unknown.

BAXTER'S COURT/YARD
152–164 King Street. *White's Directory* of 1883 lists Miss Maria Baxter as a resident. The court seems to have been lost 1965–70.

BAXTER'S GARDEN

186–190 King Street, may also take its name from Maria Baxter (see Baxter's Court above) as it is referenced in 1883. The garden was lost by 1890.

BAYES' YARD

Ber Street, precise location unknown.

BAYFIELD YARD

146–152 Ber Street, appears to take its name from the Bayfield family. *Pigot's Directory* of 1830 lists Ann Bayfield, flour dealer; Henry Bayfield, baker, and William Bayfield, baker. The yard was lost 1947–60.

BAYFIELD'S YARD

57–59 Magdalen Street. *Pigot's Directory* of 1830 lists Gabriel P. Bayfield, ironmonger, at 34 Magdalen Street. *Harrod & Co's Directory* of 1877 lists Thomas Bayfield, ironmonger, at Magdalen Street. Bayfield made a valuable collection of fossils from chalk, which he gave to the British Museum. When he gave up his ironmongery business, he became master of the Blind School in Magdalen Street. The yard was lost 1970–75.

BAZAAR COURT

24–26 St Andrew's Street, takes its name from the Royal Norfolk and Norwich Bazaar, which opened in April 1832 for the 'encouragement of female and domestic industry'. Counters were let at small rents to 'respectable females recommended by the lady patronesses'. In November 1840 Norwich Polytechnic Exhibition opened at the Royal Bazaar; the exhibition included scientific objects, paintings, drawing and machinery such as steam engines and power looms – and 'shrunken heads'. In December 1843 Mr Beard was the first in the city to advertise 'patent photographic portraits' at the Royal Bazaar, at a price of one to two guineas. In January 1846 the Norwich School of Design opened there, and it moved to a new location on the top floor of the Free Library in 1857; the artist Alfred Munnings worked there in the evenings from 1873–98, although his 'day job' was as a lithographic artist for Page Brothers. The School of Art finally moved to the new Technical Institute buildings in St George's Street in 1901.

BEANEY'S GARDEN

186–190 King Street, is referenced in 1883; *Pigot's Directory* of 1830 lists Barnard Beaney, nurseryman, at King Street. The garden was lost by 1890.

BEAR YARD

In Gentleman's Walk, took its name from the Bear, recorded at 13 Gentleman's Walk from 1761. The Bear closed in 1877, and the yard was lost by 1890. In November 1788 a travelling menagerie was displayed at the Bear but terrified the audience when a tiger escaped – and the tiger ate two of the monkeys before it could be restrained!

BEAR AND STAFF YARD

In Fisher's Lane, took its name from the Bear and Staff pub, recorded there in 1806; the pub is listed as being in Roache's Court in 1839. The pub was also known as the Bear and Ragged Staff in 1822, named after the muzzled bear chained to a ragged staff shown on the arms of the Earl of Warwick; Warwick defeated Robert Kett in his rebellion of 1549 – see St Martin at Palace Plain. According to *Chase's Directory* of 1783, the freemasons lodge met there on the second and fourth Monday of the month from 1750. The pub closed in 1910; a report in the *Norfolk Chronicle* in 1908 said that the pub was used by 'women of ill repute' and convicted criminals.

BECKHAM PLACE

Edward Street.

BECKHAM'S YARD

91 Cowgate. *Pigot's Directory* of 1830 lists John Rix Beckham, baker and flour dealer. The yard was lost 1935–41.

BECKHAM'S YARD

116–118 Magdalen Street, was listed as Shrimpling Yard or Salter's Court in *White's Directory* of 1883. The yard was lost by 1964.

BECKWITH'S COURT

13–14 Quayside, took its name from John Christmas Beckwith (1750–1809), who was the conductor at the Norwich Festival; he was also the organist at St Peter Mancroft and the cathedral.

BEDDING LANE

Runs from 3 Palace Street to 25–26 Quayside. It was originally known as Badding's Lane, after a resident in mediaeval times; it was also known as Three Privy Lane in the 18th century, which Sandred and Lingström suggest may have been from the nickname of a pub. The tenements there were removed as part of the slum clearances.

Streets off Bedding Lane

Pye's yard (runs to 8–9 St Martin at Palace Plain)
Thoroughfare Yard (runs to Quayside)

BEDFORD STREET

Bedford Street runs from 23–25 Exchange Street eastwards

to 51–53 London Street. It took its name from the Bedford Arms pub at 13 Bedford Street (formerly the Duke of Wellington pub, 1822–1865), which was closed in 1975.

Bedford Street. (Photograph by author)

Streets off Bedford Street
North:
School Lane, formerly Hole in the Wall Lane (7)
Parsonage Square (which may also have been Duke of Wellington Yard, as the pub was sited there) (11–13 – runs to 35–37 Exchange Street)
Websdale Court (15–17)
Old Post Office Yard (19–21)
Bridewell Alley (23–25)
St Andrew's Hill (after 31)

South:
Little London Street (6)
Swan Lane (14–16)

People linked with Bedford Street
Sir Benjamin Wrench, who was a doctor in the city for 56 years, lived in a house on the corner of Bedford Street and Cockey Lane. His house was used by the Norwich Society of Artists (including John Crome), who met there fortnightly and held their first exhibition there in 1805.

Events on Bedford Street
There was a major fire at Hovell's basket makers in 1978, and much of the 16th-century house had to be rebuilt.

BEDFORD YARD
14–15 Scoles Green.

BEE HIVE YARD
65–67 St Benedict's Street, took its name from the Bee Hive pub, which is recorded at 67 St Benedict's Street from 1822. The Bee Hive was closed in 1935 and destroyed during air raids in June 1942, along with the yard.

BEEHIVE YARD
18 St Martin's at Palace Plain, took its name from the Bee Hive pub, which is recorded at 18 St Martin's at Palace Plain from 1845. The Bee Hive was also known as Erpingham House and Falstolf's House and was closed in 1922; it was demolished in 1968 and the yard was lost with it.

BELL AVENUE
Ran from Orford Street to the junction of Rose Avenue and Market Avenue, but it now lies under the site of the Castle Mall shopping development. It took its name from the Bell Hotel, which is believed to date from 1480 and may have taken its name from a bell foundry once located in Timberhill. Robert Aylemer, the mayor in 1481 and 1492, was a notary and grocer who owned the Bell messuage, which was probably the Bell Hotel. The Hell Fire Club met at the Bell in around 1754 – their aim was to crush the Methodists, particularly John Wesley. The Revolution Club (founded 1793 to embrace the views of French revolutionaries) also met there, while the anti-revolutionists moved across the road to the Castle pub. The Eldon Club was founded there in 1831. Playwright Arnold Wesker also worked here. From 1943–45, the Bell was used as the headquarters for the American Women's Army Corps. It closed between the mid-1960s and mid-1970s, reopened in 1976, was closed again in 1989 and opened again in 1994 as part of the Wetherspoon's chain.

BELL YARD,
3–4 St Mary's Alley, takes its name from the Bell at 2 St Mary's Alley; the pub became Smith & Carman beer wholesalers from 1880–1931.

BELL'S YARD
2 Wellington Lane. The yard was lost by 1941.

BELL'S COURT/YARD
29–31 Bethel Street – see Little Bethel Court.

BENNETT'S COURT
9–11 St Peter's Street, was known as Graham's Court 1883–90. *Pigot's Directory* of 1830 lists Edward Bennett,

grocer and tea dealer, near here. The yard was lost for the city hall development in the early 1930s.

BENNETT'S YARD
133–135 Ber Street. *White's Directory* of 1883 lists Mrs Maria Bennett, baker, at 133 Ber Street. The yard was lost 1935–41.

BENNETT'S YARD
98–104 Cowgate. *White's Directory* of 1883 lists Samuel Bennett, builder, at Cowgate. The yard was lost 1935–41.

BENNETT'S YARD
St Giles' Street, precise location unknown. *Robson's Commercial Directory* of 1839 lists Thomas Bennett, upholsterer, at St Giles' Street.

BENTON'S YARD
5 St Mary's Alley, became Bantam's Yard.

BER STREET
Ber Street runs from the junction of Timberhill and All Saints' Street to Bracondale. It's one of the earliest roads in Norwich and was known as Berstrete from the early 12th century. It's thought that the name originates from the Anglo-Saxon *berg*, meaning 'hill' or 'mound', as the street runs along a ridge. Some historians believe that it was once a Roman road, part of the Roman marching route from Caister St Edmunds to the coast. Before the street-widening schemes to accommodate the trams, Ber Street was the widest street in the city.

Locally, it was known as 'Blood-and-guts street', partly because there were many butchers and slaughterhouses on the street near the old cattle market. According to the 18th-century historian John Kirkpatrick, the trade had always been carried out there. The mayor's court rolls from the Elizabethan period said that Ber Street was the only place within the walls of the city where cattle could be killed, and it was known then as 'carnifices de Berstrete'.

In the late 19th century the Italian community moved in and there were many ice cream parlours and pubs. Horses were also put through their paces by 'running the gauntlet' to St John de Sepulchre horse trough and back.

The area was densely populated, with many yards and courts leading off the street; few remain following the slum clearances between the 1930s and the 1960s.

Streets and yards off Ber Street
West:
Baker's Arms Yard (9–11)*
Brooks Court (9–23)*
Avey's Yard (13)*

Jubilee Yard (21)*
Alden's Yard (23)*
Black Swan Yard (23–25)*
Crawfoot's Yard (27–29)*
Berry's Yard (43)*
Cogman's Court/Yard (49–51)*
Houghton's Yard (65–67)*
Brooke Place (formerly Till's Court, Ratcatcher's Yard and Brook's Yard) (71)
Chapel Loke (79–81 – leads to 56–58 Surrey Street)
Lock & Key Yard (89–91)
Newman's Yard (93–95)*
Pegg's Yard (95–101)*
Fiddy's Yard (101–103)*
Hewitt's Yard (103–113)*
Butcher's Yard/Alley (117–119)
Scott's Yard (119–121)
Jolly Butchers' Yard (123–125)
Bennett's Yard (133–135)*
Turrell's Yard (149)*
Fox & Hounds Yard (149–153)*
Little Fox & Hounds Yard (155–157)*
Grimmer's Yard (159–167)*
Wright's Yard (157–159)*
Foulgar's (or Foulger's) Yard (165–167)*
Finkelgate (169 – leads to junction of Queen's Road and Surrey Street)
Hayward's (or Heywood's) Yard (173)*
Gatehouse Yard (181)*
Jeckell's Yard (formerly Blacksmith's Yard) (179–185)*
Clarke's Yard (185)*

East:
Emms Court (4–6)
White Hart Yard (6–8)
Cannell's Court (10–12)
Mason's Yard (14–16)
Mason's Court (16–18)
Exhibition Court (20)*
Windmill Alley (26)*
Thorn Lane (28 – formerly led to King Street, now leads to Rouen Road)
Warminger Court (28–64)
Lamb Yard (28–30)*
Twiddy's Court (34–36)*
Flecked Bull Yard (38–40)*
Varnish Yard (46)*
Boarded Entry Yard (54–58)*
Royal Oak Yard (64–66)*
Horns Lane (68–70 – formerly led to King Street, is now a cul-de-sac)
George the Fourth Yard (76–78)*

St Michael at Thorn
Church, Ber Street, in
1908, picture courtesy of
Norfolk County Council
Library and Information
Service.

Butchers' Arms Yard (86–88)*
Greyhound Yard (102–104)*
Fitt's Yard (110–112)*
Park's Yard (114–116)*
Howes Buildings (120–122)*
Watson's Yard (formerly Knights Yard) (122–124)*
Mariner's Lane (124–126) (formerly led to King Street, is now a cul-de-sac)
Bayfield Yard (146–152)*
Ashbourne Street (formerly Russell Street) (146)*
Lily Terrace (formerly from Ashbourne Street) (130–156)
Paul's Yard (154–156)*
Field's Court or Yard (162)*
Livingstone Place (172–174)*
Foulger's Opening (176–178)

Exact location unknown:
Banes' Yard (west side)*
Bayes' Yard*
Burrages Yard*
Cocksedge's Yard*
Hodds' Yard*

Buildings on Ber Street

City Wall

Ber Street Gate was situated at the junction with Bracondale; its name lives on in the pub called Berstrete Gates. It was one of the first gates to be built, and the original gate had a portcullis. According to Blomefield, it was the most frequented gate of the city, as it led to the

Remains of St Bartholomew's Church. (Photograph by author)

castle. The gate was rebuilt in 1726 and faced in red brick. On 19 December 1770 there was a bad storm, and the City Wall between Brazen Door and Ber Street fell down, crushing a new house. The arch was pulled down in 1806 and the Watch Tower (located on the wall near St John's Church) collapsed in January 1807 'with a tremendous crash', along with around 40ft of wall, killing four cows. There is still a stretch of the City Wall running along the south end of the street.

Churches

St Bartholomew's Church, sometimes called St Bartholomew per Mountergate, was located on the south side of Skeygate (now Horns Lane). The church fell into ruin after 1549 and the parish was added to St John de Sepulchre in 1550. Part of the building survived until the 1930s; it was used as a tallow factory and a cattle shed.

St John's Church Timberhill, previously called St John ad Montem (as it's on the hill) or St John at the Castle Gate (as it was near to the castle gate), is one of the few churches in the city that doesn't have a tower, because the tower collapsed in 1784. The interior was repaired in 1874, and three years later the bell-turret and windows were also restored. Like that of St Michael at Thorn, the churchyard was used to bury people who died in the castle gaol. The churchyard had a new wall in 1882. According to Blomefield, the church was founded by Wodowin the Priest.

St John's Church, Timberhill. (Photograph by author)

St John de Sepulchre Church (St John the Baptist and of the Holy Sepulchre) was recorded in Domesday as St Sepulchre's Church. According to Blomefield, it was also known as St John at the Gates (as it was near to Ber Street gate). It had new lead in 1492 and was restored in 1866; it was used by the Russian Orthodox Church. In the reign of Henry III a recluse lived in the churchyard.

St Michael at Thorn Church was a pre-Conquest church which was also known as St Michael in Ber Street, St

Black's Hall. (Photograph by author)

St John's Church, Ber Street. (Photograph by author)

Michael ad Spinas (at the Thorns), St Michael super Montem and St Miles on the Hill. It was surrounded by a hedge of thorns at one point, hence the name. As with St John's Timberhill, the churchyard was used to bury people who died in the castle gaol, and the church gained the parish of St Martin in Balliva (i.e. the old castle church) in 1542. Burials there include that of William Samon in July 1612. He refused to plead when charged with a crime, so he suffered 'peine forte et dure' – he was stripped naked, pegged to the ground, a heavy weight was laid on him and then he was pressed to death. According to Blomefield, the guilds of St Austin and of St William were held there. The tower was blown down during a gale in November 1886, damaging the interior, and was rebuilt at a cost of several hundred pounds, but the church was destroyed by air raids in June 1942. Only the church tower remained; it was demolished in July 1952 and the area was converted into a car park. The church had a Norman doorway, which was moved to St Julian's when it was rebuilt.

There was also a Wesleyan chapel on the street, built in 1858 but later demolished.

Other buildings of note

Blomefield says there was a common well and pit in the street at one point.

Black's Hall, 156 Ber Street, was owed by William Blackamore in the reign of Edward III.

Events at Ber Street

On 29 October 1774 fire broke out in a house near the pit in Ber Street; according to the *Norwich Mercury*, some children had set fire to dried bean stalks under the stairs during their mum's absence. Just over two years later a fire on Christmas Day 1776 destroyed the house of Mr Ward, a butcher on Ber Street. Mrs Ward, her mother, two children, one grandchild and a maidservant were killed.

In January 1826 the Paving Act commissioners decided to macadamise (tarmac) Ber Street 'in order to afford relief work' for people in the workhouse.

On a more cheerful note, the Greyhound Gardens in Ber Street were known as the 'Rural Retreat', and featured gardens and a bowling green, as well as fireworks and performances by vocalists. Special performances during Assize Week in 1840 included Mons Plege, a tight rope walker from Batty's circus. Two years later, the acrobat and tightrope walker Alleni 'descended in a chariot of fire', but there was a serious accident when the rope broke and he fell 30 feet.

The area was badly bombed in World War Two. On 27 June 1942 an air raid flattened several buildings, including 1 Ber Street (then Hastings the Greengrocer's – now John Lewis) and the Church of St Michael at Thorn.

BERRY'S YARD

43 Ber Street. *White's Directory* of 1883 lists George J. Berry, baker, at 43 Ber Street. The yard was lost 1890–96.

BERRY'S YARD

Bull Close Road, precise location unknown.

BETHEL STREET

Bethel Street runs from St Peter's Street to the junction of 66a-68 St Giles' Street and Cleveland Road. The street was originally called Over or Upper Newport, as it led to

War damage in Bethel Street, picture courtesy of Norfolk County Council Library and Information Service.

Newport Gate (St Giles' Gate). According to Blomefield, the east part was the ropery, where the cord and rope makers lived. For a while it was known as Committee Street, after Committee House; after the Bethel Hospital was built, the street became Bedlam or Bethel Street.

Streets off Bethel Street

North:
Blazeby's Yard or Court (24–26)*
Jay's Court (30–32)*
Springall's or Sizeland's Court (42–44)*
St Giles' Terrace (58–60)
Rigby's Court (64–66 – runs to St Giles' Street)

South:
Lady's Lane (15–17)*
Austin's Court (21)*
St Peter's Street (25)
Little Bethel Court (formerly Bell's Court/Yard) (29–31)
Little Bethel Street (37–49 – runs to Chapel Field North)
Coach and Horses Yard (51–53)
Watts' Court (55 – runs to 10 Chapel Field North)
Marjorie Hinde Court (61a – runs to Chapel Field North)
Ninham's Court (formerly Master's Court) (63 – runs to 10–11 Chapel Field North)

Exact location unknown:
Long Walk*

Buildings on Bethel Street

The Athenaeum, at number 18, was an educational institution set up by J.J. Gurney; the building was demolished by 1938.

The Bethel Hospital was the earliest purpose-built asylum in the country, built by Mary Chapman at her own expense in 1713; her husband left money in his will to build 'a hospital for the habitation of poor lunatics, and not for natural born fools or idiots'. The emphasis was on cure, and patients had medical supervision and facilities for worship; they could play bowls, croquet, tennis and billiards. One of its famous inmates was Richard Cricknell, a boxer. After a fight in January 1840, where he sustained a blow to the head, he lost his reason and was admitted to Bethel Hospital; he died there in 1842. *White's Directory* of 1845 says that the hospital could accommodate 70 patients. Gas light was installed in 1848 and electricity before 1900. During World War Two the hospital was taken over by the American Red Cross, and the patients were evacuated to the country.

The Committee House was the scene of a riot in April 1648, known as the 'Great Blowe' (see page 30).

The city fire station transferred from Pottergate to a new

Bethel Hospital. (Photograph by author)

station in Bethel Street, opened in November 1934 by the Lord Mayor. In April 1933 part of Bethel Street, Jay's Court and Blazeby's Yard were knocked down to make way for the building. Lots of potholes and wells were discovered on the site; they had been used to store arms and ammunition during the civil war.

Behind 38–40 Bethel Street is a skating rink dating from 1875–76; the area has been used as a warehouse from 1995.

The Wheatsheaf inn at number 14 (closed in 1928) was once the chief centre for skittles in Norwich. It was demolished in 1936 during work on the site of the new fire station.

Skating Rink, Bethel Street. (Photograph by author)

People linked with Bethel Street

Mary Chapman was born in 1647; at the age of 35 she became the second wife of Reverend Samuel Chapman. Both had relatives who were mentally ill and the Chapmans were worried about their wellbeing, so when Samuel died leaving money to build a hospital, Mary built it. She lived at the hospital until her death in 1724.

Dr Edward Copeman, obstetrician and gynaecologist, lived in Bethel Street in the 1870s.

Nathanial Easthaugh, who lived at 43 Bethel Street, was the town crier from 1780 until his death in March 1810.

Knipe Gobbet, mayor in 1771, lived in Bethel Street until 1778. In June 1772 he gave a dinner which served two 'barons of beef', each weighing five stone. His son died in infancy from a smallpox inoculation.

Frederick William Harmer, mayor in 1887–88, was head of the clothing manufacturer F.W. Harmer & Co for 50 years; they had a factory in Bethel Street. Harmer was also a geologist and became a Fellow of the Geological Society.

Robert Hawkes, mayor in 1822, lived at 18 Bethel Street. He was a warehouseman who'd started as a shop boy.

Events at Bethel Street

One of the biggest events on Bethel Street was the 'Great Blowe' in 1648, when the city thought that its Royalist mayor was going to be taken to London. The crowd gathered in the market place and turned on the Puritan aldermen. They marched on Committee House, where the county arms and armour were stored together with 98 barrels of gunpowder. When a shot from inside the building killed a boy in the crowd, the crowd stormed the building. Gunpowder had been spilled through Committee House – and when it caught light 98 barrels of gunpowder went up. The explosion destroyed Committee House and blew out the windows of St Peter Mancroft Church, St Stephen's Church and many neighbouring houses; 40 people were killed and 120 were injured. Special parish rates were levied to meet the cost of repairing the churches. Following extensive investigations, on Christmas Day 1648 108 accused rioters were tried in the Guildhall. Twenty-six of them were fined £30, seven were imprisoned, two were whipped and eight were hanged in the castle ditches.

The Bethel Hospital was the scene of a tragedy in April 1813 when patient Jonathan Morley was scything the lawn, then stabbed James Bullard, the master of the hospital, in the stomach. In 1816 Morley was sent to the new Criminal Lunatic Asylum in St George's Fields, London.

53–57 Bethel Street were casualties of air raids in June 1942.

BETT'S COURT

14 Cross Lane. *Chase's Directory* of 1783 lists woolcomber Benjamin Betts nearby at 55 Gildengate (aka St George's Street). The yard was lost by 1830.

BETTS' YARD

31 Oak Street, behind the Staff of Life pub (listed at 31 Oak Street, later known as the Baker's Arms). The landlord was John Samuel Betts, a baker.

BIDLE'S YARD

Oak Street, precise location unknown. *White's Directory* of 1845 lists John Bidle, shopkeeper, at Oak Street.

BIGNOLD'S COURT/YARD

13–15 Surrey Street. This was lost by 1941 and became the bus station. It was named after the Bignold family, who set up Norwich Union.

BIRD'S COURT

6 Red Lion Street (roughly where Debenham's is now). *White's Directory* of 1883 lists game dealer Daniel Wilson at Red Lion Street; *Kelly's Directory* of 1935 lists Bird Brothers, bakers, round the corner at 6 Orford Place. The yard was lost by 1890.

BIRD IN HAND YARD

72–74 Barrack Street, took its name from the Bird in Hand pub, which is recorded at 53 Barrack Street (renumbered as 74 in 1900) from 1760; the Bird in Hand closed in 1908 and the yard was lost 1935–41.

BIRD IN HAND YARD

75–77 King Street, took its name from the Bird in Hand pub, which is recorded at 17 King Street from 1840; the Bird in Hand closed in 1898 and the yard became part of the Boulton and Paul site.

BISHOP'S BRIDGE ROAD

Runs from Bishop's Bridge to Barrack Street. Weeds Square is at number 7.

BISHOP'S COURT/YARD

60–62 Magdalen Street. *White's Directory* of 1883 lists Thomas Bishop, joiner, near there. The yard was lost by 1960.

BISHOPGATE

Bishopgate runs from St Martin at Palace Plain to Bishop's Bridge. It's one of the oldest streets in the city, formerly known as Holmstrete or 'water meadow'. It was called Bishopgate Street in the 17th century, after the city gates;

part of the street was once known as Tabernacle Street, after the Methodist Tabernacle (which was built near to the Adam and Eve in 1753) and part was known as Hospital Lane, after the Great Hospital. It has been known simply as Bishopgate from the middle of the 19th century.

Streets off Bishopgate

North:
Goodrum's Yard (7–9)*
Adam & Eve Yard (17)
St Helen's Square (19)
Hospital Yard
Granby Yard (23)*
Inkerman Cottages (23)
Cotman Fields (31)
Rose & Crown Yard (35)*
Balaclava Terrace/Yard (35)
Bull Yard (45–47)*
Green Dragon Yard (79)
Goldsworth's Buildings (79)

South:
Queen Elizabeth Close (opposite the Adam & Eve pub)
St Helen's Wharf (near the Adam & Eve)

Exact location unknown:
Long Yard

Buildings on Bishopgate

City Wall

Bishop's Gate was built as a fortified tower to the west of the bridge, with a folding door; it was set on fire by Kett during his rebellion in 1549. Because the opening was only 9ft wide, loads of hay used to get stuck, and there were plenty of complaints about it in 1790! It was the first of the city gates to be demolished, in 1791, at a cost of £170.

Churches

St Helen's Church was built in 1380 by Henry Despenser; the original church was demolished in the 13th century and the new one was built in the transept of St Giles' Hospital. The wooden roof has 252 panels, each containing an eagle; this was a tribute to Richard II and Anne of Bohemia, who visited in 1383. Anne was the daughter of Charles IV, the Holy Roman Emperor, whose symbol was an eagle. Legend has it that Anne was the first person to ride side-saddle in the city.

Other buildings of note

Bishop Bridge is the last remaining mediaeval bridge in the city, built by the bishops around 1340 and given to the city in 1393. It was the only entry to the city on the east until the 19th century.

St Helen's Church, Bishopgate. (Photograph by author)

The Great Hospital (references also as St Giles' Hospital, and as the Old Men's Hospital in Blomefield's time) was founded in 1249 by Walter de Suffield, the bishop of Norwich in 1245–57, for 30 'poor and decrepit chaplains'; it

Bishop's Bridge. (Photograph by author)

was also supposed to provide a daily hot meal for 13 poor people and for seven poor scholars of the Grammar School, and there was provision for four 'sisters' over the age of 50 to look after domestic issues. There is a swan pit in the ground, where cygnets were fattened for eating. *White's Directory* of 1845 says that in the gardens there was a fig tree that was over 200 years old, and a 40ft-high elder tree that had a girth of 8ft 6in.

The Great Hospital. (Photograph by author)

The Hermitage – this is one of the five original thatched houses left in the city.

The Hermitage. (Photograph by author)

The Magistrates' Court – this was built 1982–85, and during preliminary excavations the foundations of a stone Norman house were discovered; they include early latrines, and the site has been preserved in the basement of the court. The Crown Court, next door, was finished in 1988.

St Helen's house was built by the architect Thomas Ivory as his home; he lived there from 1756–79, and his son William moved there in 1779 after Thomas's death.

The Tabernacle was built in 1772 by Calvinistic Methodists, under the guidance of The Reverend James Wheatley. Three years later it was sold to the Countess of Huntingdon, who put the building in trust and appointed a minister in accordance with the Church of England's homilies. It was no longer used by the 1930s and was pulled down in 1953.

Events at Bishopgate

Although Bishopgate is one of the quietest parts of the city, its peace was shattered on 31 March 1973 when 74-year-old William Warner was battered to death with an iron bar at cottage number 6 in the Great Hospital. Nicholas Painter, aged 20, broke into the cottage; when Warner saw him and asked him what he was doing, Painter hit him on the head with a lead pipe. Painter was arrested and given a life sentence.

BLACK BOY'S YARD

127 Barrack Street, takes its name from the Black Boys pub, which is recorded at 94 Barrack Street from 1811. The Black Boys closed in 1867, although the yard was still there in 1935. The yard was lost 1935–41.

BLACK BOY YARD

32 Colegate, takes its name from the Black Boy pub, which is recorded at number 32 in 1760. It stands on the site of the Blackfriars Convent. According to *White's Directory* of 1845, Black Boy Yard held a school for 65 girls; the school was partly supported by subscriptions and the scholars paid a weekly fee of 2d each. The pub was damaged by enemy bombing in April 1942 and reopened in 1953. The Black Boy was renamed the Merchants of Colegate in 1980.

BLACK SWAN YARD

23–25 Ber Street, took its name from the Black Swan pub at 25 Ber street; the name changed to the Thorn Tavern in 1856, and the pub was damaged by enemy bombing in May 1942. It was renamed Wardy's Freehouse in 1996, and as Goldfingers in October 1998. The yard was lost 1935–41.

BLACKFRIARS STREET

Runs from Fishergate to St Saviour's Lane and St Paul's Opening. It was originally part of Peacock Street; in Georgian times it was called Rotten Row.

BLACKSMITH'S YARD

179–185 Ber Street, became Jeckell's Yard after 1883.

BLACKSMITH'S YARD

17–19 Fishergate, was referenced in *White's Directory* of 1883 but was lost 1912–25.

BLAKELEY'S YARD

Was located at 12–14 Pitt Street. The yard was lost 1935–41.

BLAZEBY'S BUILDINGS

Alternate name for Wilde's Yard, 1–2 Scoles Green. *White's Directory* of 1854 lists William Blazeby, whitesmith, at Scoles Green.

BLAZEBY'S YARD (sometimes referred to as BLAZEBY'S COURT)

Was located at 26 Bethel Street. It was knocked down in

April 1933 to make way for the new city fire station. *Harrod & Co's Directory* of 1877 lists James Blazeby, animal and portrait painter, and William Blazeby, photographer, at Bethel Street.

BLEACH YARD
4 Rising Sun Lane. The yard was lost by 1947.

BLOD'S COURT
South side of St Andrew's Street. The yard was referenced in *White's Directory* of 1845 and 1854 but lost by 1883. It may have been Blogg's Yard.

BLOGG'S YARD
South side of St Andrew's Street. *Pigot's Directory* of 1830 lists George Shreeve, brazier, at the yard; it also lists haberdasher William Blogg just around the corner in London Street.

BLOOMSBURY PLACE
63 Rose Lane.

BLOOMSBURY PLACE
67–71 Oak Street. *Kelly's Directory* of 1890 lists Francis S. Bloom, hair seating manufacturer. The yard was lost by 1900.

BLUE BOAR LANE
Former name for Bank Street.

BOARDED ENTRY YARD
54–58 Ber Street. The yard was lost 1935–41.

BOARDED ENTRY YARD
46 Pottergate. The yard was lost by 1925.

BOARDED HOUSE LANE
Was on the corner of Pig Lane and the Cattle Market. The Boarded House pub was listed at Castle Ditches from 1822; it was known as the Boarding House inn in 1856 and appears to have closed around 1861. The lane is referenced in 1845 and 1854 but lost by 1883.

BOAR'S HEAD YARD
2 Surrey Street, took its name from the Boar's Head at 2 Surrey Street. It was originally the private house of alderman Richard Browne in the 15th century, then became a pub called the Greyhound, listed from 1783. The pub was renamed the Boar's Head around 1843, after the family arms of a licensee, Norgate. The first Norwich music hall was held here in September 1854; it was known as 'The Shades', managed by Fred Phillips, and seated 200. The

Norfolk Chronicle reported that every evening there was a 'vocal and instrumental concert by parties of London professionals'; however, the venture wasn't successful. The Boar's Head was a thatched building which was seriously damaged by air raids in April 1943; it was demolished, then rebuilt further back from the original site so that St Stephen's Street could be widened. The Boar's Head reopened in 1952 and closed in 1974; the area forms part of the Norwich Union buildings.

People linked with Boar's Head Yard
Richard Browne, mayor in 1454, lived at the Boar's Head. He was a grocer and mercer and founded St Barbara's Chapel in the Guildhall.

BOATSWAINS CALL YARD
57 Botolph Street, took its name from the Boatswains Call pub, listed at 57 Botolph Street from 1806; the Boatswains Call was closed in 1907 and the building and yard were demolished in 1967. The yard was the scene of a riot in 1829, when discontented weavers broke into the house of manufacturer William Springhall, cut work from his looms, and shot at him with a pistol. He was badly injured, and the Corporation offered a £100 reward for the capture of his assailants – though the reward wasn't claimed.

BODDY'S YARD
155 Barrack Street. The yard was lost 1925–35.

BOLDES YARD
East side of Calvert Street. The yard was lost 1883–90.

BOLINGBROKE'S YARD
52 Calvert Street. *Robson's Commercial Directory* of 1839 lists Bolingbroke, Enfield & Co, bombazine manufacturers, just round the corner at Colegate. The firm won a medal for their poplins at the Great Exhibition in 1851 and again in 1862. The yard was lost 1883–90.

BORROW COURT
17 Cow Hill, is now modern flats named after George Borrow. The original house was built in 1812 and called King's Court, after its builder, Thomas King. Borrow's parents lived there from 1812. It became known as Borrow Court in 1897; in 1913 the Lord Mayor bought the house and presented it to the city to be used as a Borrow Museum, although sadly the museum was never opened.

BOSWELL'S YARD
Runs from 24 Magdalen Street. *Harrod & Co's Directory* of 1877 lists Boswell and Baxter, wine, spirit, porter, seed and hop merchants, at Magdalen Street.

BOTOLPH STREET

Botolph Street originally ran from 68–70 Magdalen Street (Stump Cross) to St Augustine's Street; following the Inner Ring Road development, Botolph Street is an extremely short road between St Crispin's Road and St Augustine's Street, and a footpath called Botolph Way leads to Anglia Square. The section between St Crispin's Road and Botolph Way was originally part of St George's Street; Cherry Lane (formerly on St George's Street) leads from Botolph Street to Upper Green Lane, and the rest of the yards are now lost. The street name was taken from the Church of St Buttolph the Abbot, which was demolished in 1538.

Streets off Botolph Street

East:
White Horse and Little White Horse Yards (13)*
Hart's Yard (19)*
Cossey's Yard (29–31a)*
Chapel Yard (31a–33)*
Globe Yard (37–41)*
Fountain Yard (formerly Tillett's Yard) (47–49)*
Boatswains Call Yard (57)*
Sultzer's (or Sutzer's) Court (61–63)*

West:
Cat & Fiddle Yard (8)*
Howlett's Court (14–16)*
Grimes' Yard (22–24)*
Hinde's Yard (possibly also known as Crape Factory Yard) (26–30)*
Calvert Street (40)
St George's Street (42)
Howard's Yard (42–44)*
Woolpack Yard (46)*
Hodd's Yard (46–48)*

Exact location unknown:
Bath House Court/Yard*
Cremer's Yard (south side)*
Princes Yard*

Buildings on Botolph Street

Churches
St Botolph's – sometimes known as St Buttolph the Abbot – was demolished in 1548; the White Horse pub was built on the site.

Other buildings of note
The Odeon Cinema was opened in 1938; it was demolished in 1971 and a new Odeon was built in Anglia Square.

People linked with Botolph Street

John Butte, 'thaxter' and mayor in 1462 and 1471, died in 1475 and was buried in the Church of St Botolph.

Events at Botolph Street

In 1701 the Old Globe tavern in Botolph Street saw a drama that ended in murder. Robert Watts, a weaver, was drinking in the pub when one of his friends bet that he could get Mrs Watts to give him her wedding ring. He did so; Watts was so jealous that he went straight back to his house, opposite the pub, and murdered his wife. He was hanged at his own door; legend says that the house was haunted, but it was pulled down in 1875.

There was a major fire in February 1932 at the Barfield & Richardson shoe factory, which gutted the factory and meant 300 people were laid off. The *Eastern Daily Press* reported 'flames 30 feet above the roof, a raging furnace below'.

The street was closed to traffic in May 1969 and then demolished for the Anglia Square development.

BOTOLPH WAY

Is a footpath following the old line of St Botolph's Street; it leads to Anglia Square.

BOULTON STREET

21 Rose Lane, led to the Rose Lane Iron Works (aka Boulton & Paul).

BRACEFIELD'S YARD

Cowgate, precise location unknown.

BRADFIELD YARD

134–136 Cowgate. The yard was lost 1935–41.

BRADY'S YARD

6–8 Redwell Street. *Robson's Commercial Directory* of 1839 lists G. Brady, oil and colour merchant, nearby at St Andrew's Hill. The yard was lost by 1900.

BRAY'S YARD

26–30 St George's Street. *Robson's Commercial Directory* of 1839 lists John Bray and son, tailors and drapers, at Bridge Street (aka St George's Street). The yard was lost 1935–41.

BREAM'S YARD

48–50 Oak Street; became Gay's Yard after 1883. The yard was lost by 1925.

BRENTON'S YARD

Barrack Street, precise location unknown.

Botolph Street in 1910, picture courtesy of Norfolk County Council Library and Information Service.

BREW YARD

Oak Street, may be linked with Little Brew Yard at 120 Oak Street.

BREWHOUSE YARD

Coslany Street, precise location unknown. *White's Directory* of 1845 lists Robert Dotheredge, brewer, at Coslany Street. The yard was referenced in *White's Directory* of 1845 and 1854 but lost by 1883. It may also have been part of the Anchor brewery site (now Anchor Quay).

BRICKWOOD'S BUILDINGS

World's End Lane, precise location unknown.

BRIDEWELL ALLEY

Bridewell Alley runs from 23–25 Bedford Street to 24 St Andrew's Street. It was originally called St Andrew's Lane, as it runs next to the churchyard; it became Bridewell Alley after the Bridewell, which in turn took its name from the London prison near St Bride's Well. St Andrew's Chancel Street (as it was known in 1783) runs along the back of the Bridewell and links the alley to St Andrew's Hill.

Buildings on Bridewell Alley

The Bridewell was originally the home of the Appleyard family, and has the biggest undercroft known in the city. It was built by Bartholomew Appleyard in 1370 and passed to his son William in 1404. The house changed hands a couple of times; it was known as Curson's Place, after Philip Curson who was the sheriff in 1477. The city bought it from Baron Sotherton in 1583 'for a Brydewell to keep and stay ydle persons to somme honest woorke and labor'. John Howard described the rooms in 1792: 'Four rooms, 21ft square, and 10 high, with fire places and two warehouses for wood'. The inmates had river water and pump water, and were allowed 2d of bread daily and firewood when they wanted it. Their employment was 'cutting logwood', and Howard said 'This employment is too laborious and severe, where most of the prisoners are women.' Historian Michael Gibbs says the prisoners had to work from 5am to 8pm, with a single 30-minute break for food and a 15-minute break for prayer. A fire in 1751 destroyed everything except the crypts and the flint wall, which measures 27ft by 79ft and was described by travel writer Celia Fiennes in 1698 as the 'finest piece of flintwork in England'. The Bridewell was rebuilt by Thomas Dove in 1786 and remained as a bridewell until the new gaol was built in 1828; then it became a tobacco factory and a shoe factory. In 1923 it was bought by Sir Henry Holmes, who gave it to the city. It's now used as a museum.

The Bridewell's flint wall. (Photograph by author)

People linked with Bridewell Alley

William Appleyard was the first mayor of Norwich under the 1403 charter; he was mayor six times and burgess in Parliament 10 times.

Robert Gardiner, mayor in 1490, 1499 and 1506, was a mercer; he lived at the Bridewell and financed much of the glazing and benches in St Andrew's Church, as well as giving the rood screen too.

John Rayley, mayor in 1649, is believed to have lived at the north end of Bridewell Alley

William Rogers, mayor in 1542, was a grocer who lived in Bridewell Alley, on the site of the house known as 18

Bridewell Alley. (Photograph by author)

Bedford Street. He died in 1533 and, according to historian Cozens-Hardy, his will left 'to 100 maidens each on their marriage one spoon of 1oz of good silver with the posy "Remember Rogers".'

Events at Bridewell Alley

A fire started on 22 October 1751 at a lumberer's in Bridewell Alley at one o'clock in the morning; the fire was so bad that the prisoners were released from the Bridewell. In October 1824 fire struck the alley again, this time at the premises of Mr Ling, upholsterer and cabinet maker. The shop was gutted and the Bridewell's prisoners were moved to the city gaol. Everything that could be saved from Ling's was stored in St Andrew's Church, and there was so much that the vicar was unable to hold a service there on the Sunday after the fire. In March 1902 John Lane (alias Whale) broke into Briggs' jewellers in Bridewell Alley and stole £1,000-worth of property, including 275 rings. He was brought to trial in January 1905 after he was caught trying to break into a jeweller's in Doncaster, and was sentenced to five years' penal servitude.

BRIDGE COURT

Fishergate, is a modern development which takes its name from Fye Bridge.

BRIDGE STREET

Former name of St George's Street.

BRIGG STREET

Brigg Street runs from 12–18 Rampant Horse Street to the top of the Haymarket. It takes its name from Augustine Briggs, mayor in 1670; it was originally called Brigg's Lane in 1783 and became Briggs Street by 1830. (the s was dropped by mistake!)

Streets off Brigg Street

Orford Place
Pilgrim's Court (exact location unknown)*
Toll's Court (ran to Orford Place)*

People linked with Brigg Street

Augustine Briggs was a royalist during the Civil War, when most of Norwich was Parliamentarian. He was a grocer and was also a major in the city militia; he became mayor in 1670. He lived on the west side of Briggs Lane and was described in 1981 as 'Alderman Briggs, an honest old cavalier and a very understanding man'. Sadly, the same couldn't be said for his son (also called Augustine), who was mayor in 1695; Dean Prideaux wrote that 'his disease is a perpetual thirst after brandy'.

Reverend William D'Oyley was a curate at Flordon and Stratton St Michael; he raised money for road improvements when he was nearly 70, by riding 12,000 miles on horseback. He raised £400 to improve a hilly road at Tasburgh and a bottleneck at Brigg Street but died before the money could be used.

BRIGG YARD

128–130 Cowgate. The yard was lost 1935–41.

BRISTOL TERRACE

89–99 Chapel Field Road, is now off Wessex Street.

BROAD STREET

St Andrew's, former name of St Andrew's Street.

BROAD STREET

St Giles', former name of St Giles' Street.

BROCK'S YARD

St George's Street, precise location unknown. *Robson's Commercial Directory* of 1839 lists Samuel Brock, baker, at Middle Street (aka St George's Street).

BROOKS COURT

9–23 Ber Street. *Robson's Commercial Directory* of 1839 lists John Brooks as the landlord of the Rose in Ber Street. *White's Directory* of 1845 also lists ironmonger John Brooks jnr at Ber Street. The court was lost 1925–25.

BROOKE PLACE

71 Ber Street, was known as Till's Court in 1883; it was also the site of Ratcatcher's Yard, which became known as Brook's Yard from the end of the 19th century.

BROWN'S BUILDINGS

St Faith's Lane.

BROWNE'S COURT

Was located at 41a St Stephen's Street; it was known as Pipemakers' Yard in 1830 and Mansfield Yard in 1883. *Pigot's Directory* of 1830 lists Joseph Browne, pipemaker, at Wellington Court, St Stephen's Street. The court was lost during air raids in World War Two.

BROWNE'S YARD/COURT

Runs from St Benedict's Street to Pottergate (precise location unknown). *Kelly's Directory* of 1912 lists Henry George Brown as the landlord of the Ten Bells pub on St Benedict's Street. The yard was lost by 1964.

BROWNE'S YARD

Is listed at both Lower Westwick Street and the north side of

Ten Bell Lane. *Kelly's Directory* of 1912 lists Henry George Brown as the landlord of the Ten Bells pub on St Benedict's. The Alefounders pub was located off Browne's Yard (listed at 75–95 Westwick Street); *Kelly's Directory* of 1912 lists Albert Brown (sic, no e), shopkeeper, at number 95. The yard was lost by 1964.

BROWNE'S YARD
All Saints' Green, precise location unknown.

BRUNDELL'S COURT/YARD
Redwell Street, precise location unknown. The yard was referenced in *White's Directory* of 1845 and 1854 but lost by 1883.

BUCK YARD and **LITTLE BUCK YARD**
139–141 Oak Street, took their name from the Buck pub, which is recorded at 139 Oak Street from 1760. The pub was also known as the Little Buck from 1852–79 and occasionally as the Stag. It was completely destroyed by enemy bombing in April 1942 and the yard was lost with it.

BUCK'S YARD
35–37 Oak Street. The yard was lost by 1964.

BUFFCOAT LANE
Ran from Golden Ball Street and was the southern half of the present Cattle Market Street. It took its name from the Buff Coat pub, which is recorded as the Sun & Buffcoat in 1763. The Buff Coat, located at 21 Cattle Market Street, was closed in 1961 and demolished in 1964. There was a street called Pump Street off Buffcoat Lane.

BULL CLOSE
Bull Close runs from 43–49 Cowgate to 66 Bull Close Road. It takes it name from the Bull pub, which is recorded at 40 Bull Close from 1822 and closed in 1970. The yards have been replaced by modern developments.

Streets off Bull Close
North:
White Entry Yard (15–17)*
Pipe Burners' Row (29)*
Pipe Burners' Yard (31)

South:
Balls' Yard (after 2)*
Plasterers' Arms Yard*
Gerrard's Yard*
Steward's Yard*
Jarrett's Yard (8–10)*
Howard's Yard (14)*

Annison's Yard (18)*
Fryer's Yard (formerly Friar's Yard) (22–24)*
Colman's Yard (30)*
Bull Row (38–40)

BULL CLOSE ROAD
Bull Close Road runs from 163 Magdalen Street to Silver Street. It takes its name from the Black Bull pub, which is recorded at 5–7 Magdalen Street from 1760; it was known as the Bull by 1845 and closed by 1932. See also the Bull at Bull Close Road. Bull Close Road was also where cattle were led out to Magdalen Gates where they could graze.

Streets off Bull Close Road
North:
Spencer Street (formerly Wodehouse Street) and Silver Street (just before number 55)
Steward Street (103–105)
Stewardson's Yard*

South:
Bull Close (64–66)
Leopard Court (98)
Charlton Road (134 – runs to Cowgate)

Exact location unknown:
Berry's Yard*

BULL LANE
Originally ran from 21 All Saints' Green (through the bus station) to 69–71 St Stephen's Street but now stops at the bus station; the All Saints Green end is very near the site of the Brazen Doors. It took its name from the Bull pub, which is recorded at 43 St Stephen's Street from 1760. The Bull was closed in 1948 and demolished when St Stephen's Street was widened.

BULL ROW
38 Bull Close.

BULL YARD
Former name for Bull's Head Yard, Ber Street.

BULL YARD OR SQUARE
45–47 Bishopgate, took its name from the Black Bull pub, which is recorded at Bishopsgate in 1806 and closed some time after 1830. The square was lost some time after 1975.

BULLARD'S YARD
50–52 St Stephen's Street, was also known as Wade's Yard. *Robson's Commercial Directory* of 1839 lists Samuel Bullard, fruiterer, at St Stephen's Street. The yard was lost by 1960.

BULL'S HEAD YARD

137 Ber Street, took its name from the Bull's Head pub, which is recorded at 135 Ber Street; it was known as the Blue Last in the late 1700s, renamed the Bull's Head in 1811, renamed The Dart in 1938 and became the Horse and Dray from 1977 to the present.

BURLEIGH STREET

27–29 Mariner's Lane, formerly William Street. It was lost during the 1960s when Rouen Road was built.

BURRAGES YARD

Ber Street, precise location unknown. *Pigot's Directory* of 1830 lists William Anthony Burrage as having an academy in Ber Street.

BURRELL'S YARD

Runs from 49–51 Colegate to 162 St George's Street; it was also listed as Guild Yard in *White's Directory* of 1883. *White's Directory* of 1854 lists Jonathan Burrell, hair seating manufacturer, at Colegate. The yard was lost 1935–41.

BURRELL'S YARD

41 Magdalen Street, former name for Loose's yard. *Peck's Directory* of 1802 lists James Burrell, boot and shoemaker, at 24 Magdalen Street. *Robson's Commercial Directory* of 1839 lists James Burrell's Toy and Shoe Warehouse at Magdalen Street.

BURRELL'S YARD

Peacock Street, precise location unknown.

BUSHEL YARD

27–29 St Augustine's Street, took its name from the Bushel pub, which is recorded at 27 St Augustine's Street from 1760. It was closed in 1928 and the site became a chemist's shop. The yard was lost by 1960.

BUTCHER'S YARD/ALLEY

117–119 Ber Street. *Kelly's Directory* of 1890 lists John Motts, butcher, at 117 Ber Street.

BUTCHER'S ALLEY

Runs from 59 Surrey Street to 59 Ber Street. *Kelly's Directory* of 1912 lists George Butcher, picture frame maker, at 71a Ber Street.

BUTCHERS' ARMS YARD

86–88 Ber Street, took its name from the Butchers' Arms pub, which is recorded at 88 Ber Street from 1806. The Butchers' Arms was closed in 1931 and the yard was lost near then.

BUTCHER'S COURT/YARD

9 Theatre Street. *White's Directory* of 1883 lists Robert Edward Butcher at the address. The yard was lost by 1964.

BUTCHER'S YARD OR SQUARE

3 St Martin's Lane. *Pigot's Directory* of 1830 lists Clare Parker, bricklayer, at the yard; the name of the yard itself may have come from someone's occupation rather than surname. The yard was lost 1890–96.

BUTCHER'S YARD

Was located at 41–45 Barrack Street from 1883 and was briefly known as Butchery Yard in 1890. *Kelly's Directory* of 1900 lists Mrs Adelaide Edwards, pork butcher, at 43 Barrack Street. The yard was lost 1925–64.

BUTCHERY

42–43 Market Place.

BUTCHER'S YARD

117 Ber Street. *Kelly's Directory* of 1900 lists Charles Paxton, butcher, at 117 Ber Street.

BUTLER'S YARD

Lower Westwick Street, between 86 and 90. *White's Directory* of 1845 lists Henry Butler, tailor, at Lower Westwick Street. The yard was lost by 1890.

CALVERT COURT

Calvert Street, is a new development near St Crispin's Road, which takes its name from the street.

CALVERT STREET

Calvert Street runs from 29 Colegate, originally to 40 Botolph Street but now to St Crispin's Road. The name may have come from John Calvert, who was sheriff in 1741; he may have built a house there. According to Kirkpatrick, the street was originally called Doughty's Hospital Street. It was known as Snailgate by 1783 (though the derivation is unclear), and as Calvert Street by 1830.

Streets off Calvert Street

West:
Octagon Court
Balderston Court (9)
Pope's Buildings (9)
School Yard (11)*
Runnymede/Golden Dog Lane (35)
Calvert Court
Baldwin's Yard (49–53)*
Stannard Place
St Crispin's Road

Interior courtyard of Doughty's Hospital, Calvert Street, picture courtesy of Norfolk County Council Library and Information Service.

East:
Lowe's Yard (2–10)
Peter's Court (formerly Hall's Yard) (12–14)
Cross Lane (22–26 – runs to St George's Street)
Sexton's Yard or Court (28–38)*
King's Head Lane (42–44 – runs to St George's Street)*
Bolingbroke's Yard (52)*
Boldes Yard*
Singer Court (new)
St Crispin's Road
Two Brewers' Yard (52–54)*
Green's Lane (62–64 – originally ran to St George's Street)
Anchor (or Crown & Anchor) Yard (98–102 – running to 107 St George's Street)*

Buildings on Calvert Street
Churches
In 1810 a Methodist church was built on the street; it closed in 1966 and was demolished to make way for the ring road.

Other buildings of note
Doughty's Hospital was founded by William Doughty in 1687, when he left £6,000 in his will (more than £750,000 in today's money) for a building and endowments to house a master, 24 poor, aged men and eight women.

People linked with Calvert Street
Herbert Frazer, Lord Mayor in 1936–37, was born here. He was awarded the CBE in 1966.

Robert Partridge was mayor in 1784 and lived at 1 Calvert Street during that year. In 1816 he founded the Michaelmas day feast of roast goose, plum pudding and a penny loaf for the inmates of the Great Hospital in Bishopgate. He died the following year, aged 70, and was buried in the cathedral.

Events on Calvert Street
In February 1832 Thomas Foyson, who owned a vinegar works on Calvert Street, fell into a vat of vinegar and was drowned before he could be rescued.

The street was badly bombed in August and September 1942, and there was a bad fire in June 1975 at 1 Calvert Street, just before the building was being restored.

CAMPLING'S YARD OR SQUARE
20–22 St Saviour's Lane. *Hunt's Directory* of 1850 lists Jacob Campling, beer retailer, nearby at Magdalen Street. The yard was lost by 1964.

CANNELL'S COURT
10–12 Ber Street. *Harrod & Co's Directory* of 1877 lists George S. Cannell, shoemaker, and Isaac W. Cannell, draper, at Ber Street. The yard was lost during World War Two.

CANNELL'S COURT
Former name of Freeman's Court, 29–31 St Giles' Street. *Pigot's Directory* of 1830 lists Nunn Cannell, baker, at St Giles' Street. The court's name changed after 1883.

CAVENDISH COURT
West side of Recorder Road.

CARDINAL'S CAP YARD and LITTLE CARDINAL'S CAP YARD
84–86 St Benedict's Street, took their names from the Cardinal's Cap pub, which is recorded at 86 St Benedict's Street from 1760. It was also known as the Cardinal's Hat and the Coroner's Cap. The building was damaged during air raids in April 1942, and the pub was closed by 1963. According to pub historian Walter Wicks, the Cardinal's Cap sign was probably put up in honour of Cardinal Wolsey, who visited Norwich in 1517 and 1520.

CARPENTERS' ARMS YARD
33 Thorn Lane, took its name from the Carpenters' Arms pub, which is recorded at 33 Thorn Lane (the corner of Thorn Lane and Garden Street) from 1830. It was damaged during air raids in April 1942 and closed in 1963.

CARTER'S YARD
11 All Saints Green, *Pigot's Directory* of 1830 lists John Carter, dyer, at All Saints Green. Lost 1912–25.

CARTWRIGHT'S COURT
15–17 Rampant Horse Street. *Harrod & Co's Directory* of 1877 lists William Cartwright, gunmaker, at Rampant Horse Street. The court was lost 1941–47.

CARTWRIGHT'S YARD
1–3 Rosemary Lane. *Harrod & Co's Directory* of 1877 lists Henry Cartwright as a shopkeeper in Rosemary Lane and as the licensee of the Rosemary Tavern. The yard was lost 1925–35.

CASE & STEWARD YARD
7 Duke Street. *Kelly's Directory* of 1912 lists corn merchants Case & Steward near number 7. The yard was lost by 1964.

CASTLE DITCHES
Former name for Castle Meadow. In 1774 the castle ditches were 'a common receptacle for rubbish'. According to *White's Directory* of 1890, the hill was planted with trees in the early 1780s but they were damaged by 'the idle and ill-disposed', so the hill was divided into garden plots in 1784 and leased to private occupiers.

In June 1827 the castle ditches were the scene of a riot. Weavers from Wymondham who had damaged £1,000-worth of looms and silk were taken to Norwich Gaol. The Norwich weavers barricaded the Golden Ball Street entrance to Castle Meadow and also the bridge, so the people testifying against the weavers wouldn't be able to give their statements. They also threw stones at the military who accompanied the testifiers – so in the end the Lancers came from the Barracks and 'charged the mob at full gallop' to disperse them.

In April 1835 23-year-old bank clerk Johnstone Wardell was charged with embezzling £1,431 18s 7d (over £100,000 in today's money) from the Bank of England. The jury acquitted him because he said he'd been knocked down and robbed of the money on Castle Ditches; however, a few months later he confessed his guilt and returned all the money.

On a happier note, Castle Meadow was also where menageries were exhibited during the fairs. These included Bagshaw's Menagerie; Miss C. Morgan's Menagerie; Drake's Menagerie, in 1823, which included a performing elephant, a boa constrictor and a live sea serpent measuring 'more than 300 feet in length'; Polito's Menagerie; Shore's Menagerie; Wombwell's Menagerie, billed in 1824 as 'the greatest variety of living animals ever collected together since the days of Noah', and Atkins' Menagerie, which in 1832 was the first to boast a lion tamer with an iron cage in which the keeper put the lions through their performances. In 1836 the 85ft-long skeleton of a giant whale (which had been caught at Plymouth in 1831) was exhibited; it was advertised as 'the Prince of Whales at home'. In 1838 Wombwell's Menagerie included three elephants; the biggest one needed a cart which had six roller wheels to support it, and 18 horses to draw it! Though the *Norfolk Chronicle* has a truly disgusting report from the fair in December 1863: 'a man and woman, said to be Kaffirs, actually fed upon live rats, in the presence of continually succeeding audiences'. When the Mayor banned it, they ate raw flesh instead!

CASTLE GREEN
Sits above the Castle Mall shopping development, built in 1992–93 by developers Estates and General Investment.

CASTLE HILL
Runs from above Bell Avenue to Castle Bridge.

CASTLE MEADOW
Runs from Red Lion Street to the junction of Bank Plain, Prince of Wales Road and Market Avenue. It was originally the middle ditch of the castle bailey and used to be known as the Castle Ditches; local historian Geoffrey Goreham says

that in the 18th century the Castle Ditches led to the open yard of the Bell. Castle Meadow stopped at the Bell until the bottom of Orford Hill was cut through for the trams in 1900, linking it to Red Lion Street. The street was widened in 1926–27, when part of the castle mound was cut back.

Streets off Castle Meadow
York Alley (2–4)
Arcade Street (6–7)
Davey Place (7–9)
Opie Street (25–27)

Other streets whose exact locations could not be placed include:
Harrison's Yard*
Holkham Street*
Paragon Buildings*

Buildings on Castle Meadow
The castle keep is a Norman building measuring 95ft by 90ft by 70ft. The Domesday Book says that 98 properties were destroyed to make way for the earthwork – and it was a very, very visible reminder of the Norman Conquest. In 1200 the castle fee stretched as far as London Street and King Street; Castle Meadow, Farmer's Avenue and Cattle Market Street run along the edge of the original boundaries. Archaeologist Brian Ayers says the castle was invested in 1075 and 1217. Then it became the official residence of the Sheriff of Norfolk, and it was used as a prison from 1340.

Prisoners tried to escape from the gaol – though they didn't succeed. In May 1772 Edmund Plumb tried to escape from the castle with John Bacon and William Merriston. They sawed off their irons and broke out of their cells, but were found hidden in the roof of the privy in the gaol yard and re-apprehended. Plumb was executed on 19 September that year. In February 1830 John and William Brooks, who were on trial for highway robbery, tried to escape by making their blankets into ropes and lowering themselves from Bigod's Tower. The rope broke and William fell 70ft; he broke his left thigh, pelvis and left arm as well as all the ribs on his left side. He recovered and, although crippled, was sentenced to transportation for life.

Rather more sadly, John and Edmund Hunt died in a fire in February 1773; John, the old man, was ill and the keeper had put him in St Nicholas Chapel where his son could look after him more comfortably. However, that night the castle bell rang and the keeper saw smoke; some straw had caught fire and the smoke suffocated the Hunts. In February 1876 there was an outbreak of smallpox among the prisoners; of the 12 cases, two were serious but nobody died.

The castle was refaced in Bath stone in 1834–39 by Anthony Salvin, and the prison buildings (now part of the museum) were designed by Sir John Soane 1783–93. In September 1803 a telegraph was erected on top of the castle to allow the city to communicate with Strumpshaw Mill, Filby Church and Great Yarmouth.

When the new prison was opened at Plumstead Road in July 1887, the prisoners were transferred there and the castle was handed over to the Mayor. The City & County of Norwich converted the castle to a museum, at a cost of £4,000. The museum was opened on 23 October 1894 by the Duke and Duchess of York (later George V and Queen Mary). The museum underwent a £12 million refurbishment in 2001 – showcasing the original Norman pillars for the first time, as well as giving much more interactive exhibits. But some things never change: the polar bear is still there, just as he was when the museum first opened.

Norwich Castle. (Photograph by author)

People linked with Castle Meadow

William Foster, attorney, lived in Castle Meadow; he founded many charities and died at his home in 1810.

William Stevenson, a vet, lived in Castle Meadow; he died there in 1819 at the age of 53, and his obituary said 'He… stood alone and unrivalled in comparative anatomy and pathology'.

Events at Castle Meadow

Public hangings took place in the castle ditches – usually on a Saturday, and they were seen as public entertainment. A report in the *Norwich Mercury* from April 1774 discussed the hanging of two housebreakers: 27-year-old Henry Jacques and 17-year-old James Jex (also known as 'Bonny Lock'). They spent the night before their execution 'in an abandoned manner', singing and scoffing – to the disgust of the *Mercury* – and during the execution a woman near the gallows had her pocket cut and lost 14 shillings. Trains were laid on from London to see the execution of James Blomfield Rush in April 1849 for the murder of the

Recorder of Norwich, Isaac Jermy – though the 'swell mob' (or London pickpockets) was stopped on the train at Attleborough and sent back to Norwich.

The spectacle could be gory. John Pycraft had murdered his baby son with arsenic, and when he was hanged in August 1819 it took seven or eight minutes after the trapdoor fell for him to die. In April 1854 21-year-old William Thompson was hanged for the murder of Lorenzi Beha; the *Norfolk Chronicle* reported that 'the criminal's struggles continued five minutes' and lambasted the audience when 'more scenes of drunkenness and immorality were exhibited than had been seen for a long time previously in Norwich'. The last public execution in Norwich was in August 1867, when 22-year-old Hubbard Lingley was hanged for the murder of his uncle, Benjamin Black. The execution was held on a Monday instead of the usual market day, at 8am, to prevent the crowds forming.

The one hanging that the crowd definitely wouldn't have wanted to see was that of wife-murderer Robert Goodale in November 1885: something went wrong, so when the trapdoor dropped Goodale's head was severed from his body.

CASTLE STREET

Castle Street runs from Royal Arcade Street to 22–28 London Street and takes its name from the castle.

Streets off Castle Street

Old Post Office Court (6–8 – runs to the Market Place)
Davey Place (8–10)
Rose Yard (led to 10 Back of the Inns)*

Events on Castle Street

Castle Street saw a major bankruptcy in the 19th century – that of Sir Roger Kerrison, who was mayor in 1778 and 1802. Kerrison was also the Receiver-General for taxes, but when he died in 1808 his bank in Castle Street was in debt, and he owed well over £580,000. When the government couldn't recover the taxes Kerrison had collected, it made the firm bankrupt. It caused a major scandal in the city, and the crowd of people who came to 'prove their debts' at the King's Head was so large that many of them didn't get a chance to add their names to the creditors' list. Eventually, the 3,600 creditors received 16s and 4d in the pound.

There was a major fire in the street on 9 March 1854, when the *Norwich Mercury* building caught fire. The roof fell in, and the compositors' room – along with most of the cases of type – was destroyed.

CAT & FIDDLE YARD (sometimes known as OLD CAT & FIDDLE YARD)

Runs from 8 Botolph Street to Magdalen Street. The yard

was lost in the mid to late 1960s for the Anglia Square development. (See Cat & Fiddle Yard, Magdalen Street.)

CAT & FIDDLE YARD

Runs from Magdalen Street to 8 Botolph Street, and took its name from the Cat & Fiddle pub, which is recorded in Magdalen Street from 1760. The pub was known as the Old Cat & Fiddle from 1811 and was closed in 1868. It then became the Edinburgh Castle, which closed in 1914. Cat & Fiddle Yard was demolished in 1967.

CATHEDRAL STREET

Was originally a long street split into two, known as Cathedral Street North and Cathedral Street South. By 1912 Cathedral Street North was renamed Cathedral Street, running from 727–724 Prince of Wales Road to 8–10 St Faith's Lane. Cathedral Street South became St Vedast Street.

CATHEDRAL STREET NORTH

Former name of Cathedral Street.

CATHEDRAL STREET SOUTH

Former name of St Vedast Street.

CATHERINE WHEEL OPENING

Runs from 32–34 Magpie Road to 61–63 St Augustine's Street. It took its name from the Catherine Wheel pub, which is recorded at 61 St Augustine's Street from 1742. The original building was thatched; it was rebuilt in the early 1800s and is still open today.

CATHERINE WHEEL YARD

61–63 St Augustine's Street – see Catherine Wheel Opening.

CATTERMOUL'S LANE

London Street, precise location unknown. *Chase's Directory* of 1783 lists Thomas Cattermoul, wine and brandy merchant, just round the corner at 12 Redwell Street. The lane was lost by 1883.

CATTERMOUL'S YARD

79–81 and 14–16 Pitt Street. *Pigot's Directory* of 1830 lists Everett Cattermoul, bricklayer, near the yard. The yard at 79–81 was formerly known as Mitchell's Yard and was lost by 1941; the yard on the other side of the street was lost by 1947.

CATTLE MARKET STREET

Cattle Market Street runs from the junction of Golden Ball Street and Farmers Avenue to Rose Lane. It was originally part of the castle ditches but became the cattle market in

1740 when the southern part of the castle ditches were levelled. The northern part of the street may have been known as Common Pump Street and the southern side may have been known as Buffcoat Lane; *White's Directory* of 1890 says that these two streets were cleared in the 1880s to enlarge the cattle market. The cattle market was moved to Harford Road in July 1960.

Streets off Cattle Market Street

Osborne Square (4)
Golden Ball Street (17)
Rising Sun Lane (18)*
Rouen Road
Globe Lane (23 – led to Scoles Green)*
St Martin at Bale Court (28)
King Street (39)
Boarded House Lane*

Buildings on Cattle Market Street
Churches

St Martin at Balliva's Church once stood on the right-hand side of Golden Ball Lane, near the castle gate. It was also known as St Martin at the Castle Gate, St Martin Supermontem, St Martin Berstreet (sic), St Martin's Priory or St Martins at the Bale. The name of 'in balliva' comes because it was sited in the castle bailiwick or area of jurisdiction; there was a priory in the area until the Whitefriars Churches were united. People who died in the castle were buried here until 1562, when the church's functions were transferred to St Michael at Thorn and the church was demolished.

Other buildings of note

Crystal House was built in 1863 as a showroom for engineers Holmes & Sons; it was taken over by Panks Engineers in 1902, and they used it from 1906–83. A similar building once existed in Davey Place.

Crystal House, Cattle Market Street. (Photograph by author)

Events at Cattle Market Street

There was an extensive fire on the street on 14 August 1873 at the engineering works of Holmes & Sons. Three troops of the Dragoon Guards and Norwich Rifle Volunteers were needed to help the fire brigade control the blaze, and the damage ran to £10,000 (over £½ million in today's money).

After the cattle market moved to Harford Bridges, the area became a car park; the Easter fair used to be held there (and I can remember going to the fair as a small child, as well as practising parking a car there on a quiet Sunday afternoon in the mid-1980s). The area was developed as the Castle Mall shopping centre in the 1990s.

CELLAR HOUSE YARD

On King Street, took its name from the Cellar House pub, which is recorded at 249 King Street from 1830. The building was demolished in 1935 when the road was widened and was rebuilt as the Kingsway at 249 King Street. The Kingsway was closed in 2001 and demolished in 2005, and the area is being redeveloped as flats.

CHAMBERLIN COURT

Off Guildhall Hill, was named after Henry Chamberlin & son's department store, located there in the 19th century.

THE CHANTRY

Runs from 10 Theatre Street. It took its name from the Chantry Chapel of the College of St Mary. Several buildings (including a Victorian Gothic house, the vicarage of St Peter Mancroft and a row of Georgian houses) were demolished in 1964 when Theatre Street was widened.

CHANTRY COURT

Theatre Street.

CHANTRY ROAD

Runs between Malthouse Road and 15–16 Chapel Field East. It took its name from the Chantry Chapel of the College of St Mary.

CHANTRY YARD

St Miles's Church Alley Yard.

CHAPEL FIELD EAST

Chapel Field East runs from Bethel Street to the junction of Theatre Street, Little Bethel Street and Chapel Field North. It was previously known as Chapel Field Road and was named after the chapel built by John le Brun before 1250.

Streets off Chapel Field East
Chantry Road (16)

CHAPEL FIELD NORTH

Chapel Field North runs from the junction of Theatre Street, Little Bethel Street and Chapel Field East to St Giles' roundabout.

Streets off Chapel Field North
Watts Court (11–12 – runs to 55 Bethel Street)
Marjorie Hinde Court (runs to 61a Bethel Street)
Ninham's Court (10–11 – runs to 63 Bethel Street)
Hales Court (runs to Cleveland Road)

CHAPEL FIELD ROAD

Chapel Field Road runs from the St Giles' roundabout to the St Stephen's roundabout. It takes its name from the chapel built by John le Brun before 1250. According to pub historian Walter Wicks, Chapel Field Road was formerly called Rising Sun Road, after the Rising Sun pub on the corner of Vauxhall Street. There were a few changes to one side of the road when the inner ring road was built; the Nestlé chocolate factory (formerly Caley's) has been redeveloped as the shopping mall and opened in Autumn 2005.

Streets off Chapel Field Road
Vauxhall Street (19–21)
Rising Sun Row (29–31)*
Middle Row (33–5)*
Rose Terrace (35–39)*
Eldon Row (35–41)*
Walpole Gardens (formerly Walpole Street) (45–47)
Coach and Horses Avenue
Union Street (53)*
The Crescent (53)
Bristol Terrace (89–99 – now off Wessex Street)*
St Stephen's Square (99–101)*
Crooke's Place (99–101)
Chapel Field North (after 6)
Chapel Field East (after 58)

Buildings on Chapel Field Road
City Wall
A tower from the City Wall was used in the 19th century as part of the Drill Hall – see below.

Churches
A Congregationalist church was opened on Chapel Field Road in September 1858, but the last service was in December 1966 due to declining attendances and difficulty of access. The building was demolished in 1972.

Other buildings of note
Chapelfield Gardens was used as an 'exercise ground' for the

Chapelfield Gardens. (Photograph courtesy of Norwich City Council)

city's militia in 1578 – as well as archery, it included 'shooting with hand guns and arquebusks'. It was fenced in 1707, and Thomas Churchman (see St Giles' Street) laid out the elms in 1746–49. Unofficially, it became a park in 1852; in August 1867 parts of old City Wall were removed and a railing was erected, and it was reopened to the public. It was closed again in 1879 and laid out as a park by the city Corporation (mayor Harry Bullard planted the first of the new trees there in November), and it opened to the public in November 1880 with the new wrought-iron pavilion in the middle, made by local firm Barnards and Bishop.

The Drill Hall, used by the Volunteer and Territorial Units of Norwich, was built in 1866 by J.S. Benest using part of a tower from the City Walls and opened by the Prince of Wales in the same year. The Prince of Wales returned in April 1881 to open the National Fisheries Exhibition – which saw 70,000 visitors over the course of a month. The hall was demolished in 1963.

The Pagoda in the Park was designed by Jekyll and made by local iron founders Barnard, Bishop and Barnard. It was first erected at Philadelphia Centennial Exhibition in 1876, and the city bought it in 1880 and placed it in Chapelfield Gardens. It was damaged by air raids in World War Two and demolished in 1949.

There was a reservoir in Chapelfield Gardens, measuring 88 yards x 50 yards, owned by Norwich Waterworks Co. In October 1768 there was an almighty bang when the reservoir burst – a 'sand gall' or vein of sand couldn't support the 50,000 barrels of water and collapsed. Within three hours, the newspaper reported that the 'bason [sic] [was] left empty', and there were holes in the reservoir between 6 and 20 feet wide! The reservoir was rebuilt (and was the perfect skating rink for city residents in the winter), and was finally removed in 1865.

The Norfolk and Norwich Magdalen (or Female Home) was established at York Villa on Chapel Field Road in 1826. According to *White's Directory* of 1890, the object of the home was 'to afford an asylum for females who, having deviated from the path of virtue, may be desirous of being returned to their station in society, by religious instruction of moral and religious habits'; it had room for 12 people and was 'generally very full'.

People linked with Chapel Field Road

A.J. Caley originally had a chemist's shop in London Street and made mineral waters. They were so popular that he ended up buying larger premises in Bedford Street, and in 1880 the business expanded again as he took over the glove cloth factory of George Allen in Chapel Field Road. Because he wanted to keep his workers employed over the winter months, he started making cocoa in 1883 and then eating chocolate from 1886. Caley's Marching Chocolate was part of the rations for soldiers in World War One

Sir John Harrison Yallop, a goldsmith and mayor in 1815 and 1831, lived at 4 Chapel Field North. His firm was an agent for government lottery tickets. All unsold numbers had to be returned; when he was left with one unsold ticket, he spoke to his wife about it and bought a lottery ticket for the first time – and won a big prize!

Events on Chapel Field Road

According to the *Norwich Mercury*, in Christmas 1772 Mr Hoyle, the Surveyor of the Customs, seized 'a considerable quantity' of smuggled foreign brandy near Chapel Field. One of the city's strangest wagers took place in Chapel Field Gardens in March 1815 – a race between Thomas Jenner and William Palmer. According to the newspaper, they were 'two men with two wooden legs each'! It's recorded that Jenner won the £1 bet. On 15 May 1926 there was a fire, when the tank set in Chapel Field Gardens as a war memento caught fire. It was used as a petrol store and contained 20 cans of petrol; luckily because the inside of the tank was enclosed and there wasn't air to feed the fire, the fire was easily put out – and the only damage was to the seat of the tank.

CHAPEL LOKE

Runs between 79–81 Ber Street and 56–58 Surrey Street; it took its name from the Methodist Chapel built there in the 1790s. It was known as Chapel Lane in 1845 and Chapel Look in 1854, and was Chapel Loke by 1883. The Surrey Chapel was founded by Robert Govett, a curate at St Stephen's Church; in 1845 he believed that the New Testament teaches baptism by immersion, and built the Ebenezer Chapel in 1854. In the 1980s the building was crumbling and moved to its current location in 1985.

CHAPEL YARD

31a–33 Botolph Street, took its name from the Primitive Methodist Chapel at 43 Botolph Street. The yard was lost by 1960.

CHAPEL YARD

39 Cowgate, took its name from the Wesleyan Chapel at Cowgate.

CHARING CROSS

Charing Cross runs from the junction of Duke Street at St Andrew's Street to the junction of St Benedict's Street and Westwick Street. The stress was originally called Tonsoria as it was the area where the shearers lived. It was known as Shering Cross by the 1300s, after the stone cross that was once sited there but was removed in 1732. In the 18th century, when it was fashionable to copy London street names, it became Charing Cross. Part of Charing Cross was demolished in 1970 when the street was widened.

Streets off Charing Cross

North:
Charing Cross Court
Lord Camden Yard (15–17)*
Gooch's Yard (17–19)*
Long Lane (23–25)
Nash's Yard (at the junction with Westwick Street)*

Exact location unknown:
Fuller's Old Lane*
Golden Cross Yard*
Nailor's Lane*

Buildings on Charing Cross

Strangers' Hall was built in 1320, and the undercroft dating from that house is still there. The house was rebuilt a hundred years later by merchant William Barley, who was also the Sheriff of Norwich. Several Norwich mayors have lived there, including Thomas Caus, Francis Cock, Sir Joseph Paine, Nicholas Sotherton and Thomas Sotherton. Nicholas Sotherton added the crown post roof. During the 15th century, trade was bad and Sotherton decided that the weavers from the Netherlands might be able to teach the city weavers new techniques. The Protestant weavers were being persecuted by the Spanish at the time, so Sotherton arranged for 30 families to join the city. These weavers were known locally as the 'strangers', and because they used Sotherton's house as a staging post the house became known as Strangers' Hall. Francis Cock had the street front remodelled in 1621. Roman Catholic priests lived there

Strangers' Hall. (Photograph by author)

from 1797–1880 and let part of the building out; tenants included the Italian sculptor Mazzotti in 1819. In 1899 Leonard Bolingbroke restored it and gave it to the city in 1922. It's currently used as a museum.

People linked with Charing Cross
Thomas Bawburgh, a mercer who was mayor in 1530, lived in the house once sited at 16 Charing Cross.

Thomas Caus, a mercer who was mayor in 1495 and 1503 and burgess twice, lived in Stranger's Hall. He left money in his will to repair Ber Street gates and for 'fying' (i.e. cleaning) of the river of Norwich 'when the comens goo ther aboute to doo it'.

Francis Cock(e) was a grocer and mayor in 1627. He bought Stranger's Hall from Sir Lestrange Mordaunt in 1612, and added a room in the garden, a large oak bay window and part of the Jacobean staircase.

John Marsham, a grocer who was mayor in 1518, lived in a house on the corner of St John Maddermarket and Charing Cross, formerly known as 'Ralf Segrym's house'. He had to go to London in 1511 to represent the city in their contest with the prior and convent of London, and again in 1516 to settle it.

Sir Joseph Paine, a hosier who was mayor in 1660, lived in Stranger's Hall. He gave Charles II a voluntary gift of £1,000 (around £92,000 in today's money).

Nicholas Sotherton, a grocer who was mayor in 1539, lived in Stranger's Hall. Like Caus, he left money in his will for 'fyeng' (sic) of the river.

Thomas Sotherton, Nicholas's grandson, was mayor in 1605; he also lived in Stranger's Hall.

Events at Charing Cross
William Cork, an artisan, was merrily singing in a pub in October 1835; the song was written about the death of General Wolfe. Cork sang the last words, 'and I to death must yield' – and promptly fell down dead.

CHARING CROSS COURT
On the north side of Charing Cross, may have taken its name from the Charing Cross pub, which is recorded at Charing Cross from 1745 and was closed by 1867.

CHARLES JAMES COURT
Is a modern development on the north side of Fishergate.

CHARLTON ROAD
Runs from Bull Close Road to Cowgate. It was named after Reverend Thomas Charlton, who introduced Methodism to Norwich in 1821 after walking from King's Lynn on a mission; he was known as one of the 'ranter' preachers (i.e. a Primitive Methodist') and dedicated his life to helping the poor.

CHATHAM STREET (CHATHAM PLACE in *White's Directory* of 1845)
Originally ran from 62–64 Sussex Street to Jenkin's Lane; now it ends just before Pitt Street.

Streets off Chatham Street
Quaker's Lane (runs to St Crispin's Road)
Gildencroft (runs to St Augustine's Street)

CHEQUERS' YARD
13–15 Coslany Street, took its name from the Chequers pub, which is recorded at 13 Coslany Street from 1802. The Chequers was renamed the Brewers Arms by 1851 and was closed in 1907, and the yard was lost by 1941.

CHEQUERS PASSAGE
St George's Street. The yard was referenced in *White's Directory* of 1845 and 1854 but lost by 1883.

CHERRY LANE
Originally ran from 35–43 Pitt Street to 138–140 St George's Street, but now leads from Botolph Street to Upper Green Lane. The street took its name from the Cherry Tree pub, which is recorded at 43 Pitt Street from 1879 (but was listed at 51 Gildengate, aka St George's Street, from 1801). It was renamed the Golden Sovereign in 1975 and closed in 1988. It was once known as St Tooley's Lane (or Tooley Street) after St Olave's Church, which stood there until 1546.

CHERRY TREE YARD
160–162 St George's Street, takes its name from the Cherry Tree pub in Pitt Street, which backs on to it. It was known as Little Cherry Tree Yard in 1883. Its address is listed as 140 St George's Street before 1927.

CHESTER PLACE
Foulger's Opening (Ber Street).

CHESNUTT'S COURT
See Chestnut Court, St Giles' Street.

CHESTNUT COURT
7–8 Cow Hill.

CHESTNUT COURT (also called CHESNUTT'S COURT)
15 St Giles' Street. *Pigot's Directory* of 1830 lists Jonathan Chesnutt, hairdresser; the court was known as Schumach Court in 1830 but Chestnut Court by 1854.

CHESTNUT PLACE
25–27 Palace Street. The yard was lost 1935–41.

CHICKERELL'S YARD
Colegate – former name of Chickering's Yard.

CHICKERING'S YARD
South side of Colegate, precise location unknown; it was also known as Chickerell's Yard. It may have taken its name from Thomas Chickering, a brewer, who was mayor in 1676 and who lived at Colegate.

CHIDDICK'S COURT
33–37 Palace Street. *Kelly's Directory* of 1890 lists Eliza Chiddick, plumber. The yard was known as Love's Yard in 1883 and was lost by 1925.

CHITTOCK'S COURT
5 Rising Sun Lane. *White's Directory* of 1854 lists Mr James Chittock, resident of Chittock's Yard at Rising Sun Lane.

CHRONICLE OFFICE COURT
8 Market Place, took its name from one of the local newspapers in the 18th and 19th centuries, the *Norfolk Chronicle*.

CHURCH ALLEY
Listed as Church Walk in 1883 and as St Michael At Plea's Alley in 1905. Runs from 10 Redwell Street to Prince's Street.

CHURCH STREET
Was formerly Gun Lane, now William Booth Street. It was known as Church Street as it runs opposite St Stephen's Church. It includes Page's Court, precise location unknown but probably nearer the Haymarket end.

CHURCH WALK/ALLEY
10 Redwell Street.

CINDER OVENS YARD or **ROW**
266 King Street, was named after the Cinder Ovens pub on the opposite side of the road, which is recorded at 257 King Street from 1882. The pub closed in 1893. According to pub historian Walter Wicks, the pub took its name from the ovens at the back, which were built into one of the old boom towers and used for the manufacture of coke. The yard became known as 'Row' by 1935 but appears to be lost before 1960.

CITY OF NORWICH YARD
5 Westlegate, was named after the City of Norwich pub, which is recorded at 5 Westlegate from 1760. In February 1825 the floor collapsed during a Ranters' (or Primitive Methodists') meeting when 120 people were squeezed into the room; 25 of them were taken to the Norfolk and Norwich Hospital with injuries, and one man had to have his leg amputated. The pub was renamed the Ipswich Arms in 1866 and was damaged in air raids in April 1942. The pub closed in 1974 and the yard has been lost.

CLABBURN'S COURT
79 Pitt Street. *Harrod & Co's Directory* of 1877 lists James W. Clabburn, painter, plumber and gas fitter, at Pitt Street; and also Clabburn, sons, and Crisp, manufacturers of dress fabrics. The latter won a gold medal at the London Exhibition in 1862 for their fillover shawls. The yard was lost 1925–35.

CLABBURN'S YARD
150 Magdalen Street, former name for Whiting's Court. *Peck's Directory* of 1802 lists John Clabburn, confectioner, at 11 Fye Bridge Street. The yard was lost by 1964.

CLARK'S YARD
St Benedict's Street, exact location unknown. *Pigot's Directory* of 1830 lists William Clark, jeweller, at St Benedict's Street; *Robson's Directory* of 1839 lists Robert Clark, watchmaker and jeweller.

CLARKE'S YARD
185 Ber Street. *White's Directory* of 1854 lists three members of the Clarke family (all shoemakers) at Ber Street: David, Thomas and William. The yard was lost 1925–35.

CLEMENT COURT
2–3 Redwell Street. Frances Burges published the first edition of the *Norwich Post* – the first provincial English newspaper – here on 1 September 1701.

CLEVELAND ROAD
Runs from the south side of St Giles' Street to the Grapes Hill roundabout and was built in the 1960s. It was named after Dr Arthur J. Cleveland, who was Lord Mayor in 1942–43. He was born in Brighton but settled in Norwich in 1902; he was a radiologist at the Norfolk and Norwich Hospital, and became a consultant physician and neurologist. Hales Court runs from here to Chapel Field North.

THE CLOSE
The Close runs from St Faith's Lane to Bishopgate. In Saxon times, the area was common grazing lands; it also covered part of the original Tombland, which was on the site of the crossroads of the two main roads of Conesford, thought to be the earliest settlement in Norwich. According to Blomefield, the area was called Cow-Holm (meaning 'the marsh where cows fed'); he felt that Conesford was

originally called Couesford or Cowesford, i.e. the ford the cows travelled over en route to the marsh.

Streets off The Close
Almary Green
Holland Court

Buildings on The Close
Churches

The Cathedral was founded in 1096 by Bishop Herbert de Losinga and finished in 1145, built using stone from Caen in Normandy, France. The cathedral measures 461ft long and 27ft wide; the spire, at 315ft, is the second-highest in England. It was consecrated to the Holy and Undivided trinity in the 12th century and had a community of Benedictine monks. Bishop Thomas Percy rebuilt the clerestory in 1362 and the cloister was completed by 1450. The cathedral contains around 1,200 bosses on the vaulting, telling Biblical stories. It also contains the Bishop's Throne, which is believed to have been the original throne from the earlier see at Thetford. Although the Cathedral suffered some losses during the Civil War, quick thinking saved some treasures – for example, the Despenser reredos of St Luke's Chapel was turned upside down and used as a table. It's thought that it was painted by Thomas de Okell (who may also have painted the Wilton Diptych) and the picture contains the arms of Bishop Henry Despenser.

Norwich Cathedral. (Photograph by author)

St Mary in the Marsh was founded by de Losinga in the lower close of the cathedral. Its parish was added to St Peter Permountergate in 1564 and the building was destroyed, although one wall remains in the site of numbers 10 and 11 Lower Close. According to Blomefield, the dean stripped the church of lead, worth £160, sold it – and didn't account for it!

St Matthew the Apostle's Church was originally situated in the close, near Bishopgate, from around 1286. It never recovered from the effects of the Black Death; the church was in ruins by 1368, the last rector died in 1377 and the parish was transferred to St Martin's. The church was then demolished.

Other buildings of note

Alnwick Gate (see St Martin at Palace Plain).

Cow Tower is the oldest brick building in Norwich and was rebuilt in 1390. It was a former toll house, a prison for the ecclesiastical court (described in *White's Directory* of 1845 as 'the Dungeon Tower in St Giles' Hospital Meadow'), a lock-keeper's house and part of the city defences (though it was never actually part of the City Walls). The tower is 50ft high, and the walls are 6ft thick in places; it was fired upon twice during Kett's Rebellion.

Erpingham Gate (see Tombland).

Ethelbert Gate (see Tombland).

Norwich School was founded in 1316 as a chapel and converted to a school by Edward VI in 1547–53; former pupils include the dramatist Robert Greene, the playwright John Bale, Admiral Horatio Nelson, Sir Edward Coke, Lord Chief Justice for Edward I (who sent Raleigh to the axe) and writer George Borrow. In Nelson's time the school was called the Royal Grammar School; it had 45 pupils and two teachers, and the school workday ran from 7.30am to 5pm with a two-hour break for lunch at 12.

Pull's Ferry is the site of the 15th-century Watergate (the fourth gate to the cathedral). Previously, a canal ran from

Pull's Ferry. (Photograph by author)

the river into the Close and was used to transport the Caen stone for building the castle and the cathedral. The canal was filled in around 1780. John Sandlin, a chorister, was the first ferry keeper. The ferry was known as 'Sandlin's Ferry' or 'Sandling's Ferry' until 1841, when the name was changed to 'Pull's Ferry' to commemorate John Pull, the keeper of the ferry until 1841. The last ferryman was Cecil Mollett, who took over from his father; the ferry finished in 1943. The area was restored by Cecil Upcher in 1947–48.

People linked with the Close

Edith Cavell was a nurse who was executed in World War One for helping soldiers through enemy lines in Belgium. Her grave is in Life's Green, and the bronze monument to her on Tombland is by J.G. Gordon Munn, 1918.

Edith Cavell's monument. (Photograph by author)

Herbert de Losinga was born in Suffolk in around 1054 and was educated at the Benedictine Abbey of Fécamp in Normandy; he became prior there and was Bishop of Thetford in 1091. It is said that he committed the sin of simony – that he paid for his bishopric, and also for his father to be made Abbot of Winchester. He resigned, but the Pope reappointed him. He moved to Norwich in 1094 and allegedly began building the cathedral in penance for his simony; interestingly, the ground plan of the cathedral resembled that of Fécamp. He demolished the Saxon

Church of St Michael's at Tombland to make room for the cathedral and laid the foundation stone in 1096; the cathedral was consecrated in September 1101. He died in July 1119 and was buried by the high altar. Although his tomb was demolished during the Civil War, a stone tablet in the cathedral commemorates him as 'a man imbued with every sort of learning, of incomparable eloquence, handsome in person, and of bright countenance, so that those who knew him not might guess he was a bishop only from looking at him'.

Matthew Nall, an attorney and scrivener, was mayor in 1709; he lived in the Close.

Osbert Parsley, chorister in the cathedral in 1535–85, has a monument in the cathedral. During his career he sang in both Latin and English (depending on which monarch was on the throne). His setting of the *Magnificat* was sung when Elizabeth I visited the cathedral in 1578.

Events at the Close

In 1272 there was a three-day riot between the citizens and the monks in the Close over tithing rights and the rights to the Trinity fair in Tombland. The prior brought in some armed men from Yarmouth (Norwich's traditional rival at the time) and they killed and wounded several people and looted property, as well as allegedly burning down some houses. The citizens complained to the king – but they also took matters into their own hands and burned down the Ethelbert Gate. In the fracas that followed, some of the wooden buildings in the Close also burned down. Henry III, although ill, came to the city himself to calm things down.

He clearly saw blame on both sides as he put both the city and the priory under separate wardens. Thirty citizens were hanged, and their bodies either drawn and quartered or burned. Henry III died a few weeks later, and Edward I ordered an investigation; the jury decided that the prior was guilty of murder and robbery and the fires were mainly accidents. The Pope retaliated by excommunicating the whole city! The row was finally settled in 1275, when the citizens had to pay the prior 500 marks for six years (a mark was 2/3 of a pound – so this was a total of 3,000 marks, or today's equivalent of over a million pounds), give the priory a gold pyx weighing 10lbs and make new gates for the priory. In return, the Pope gave the city a General Absolution in 1276.

There was a major fire at the cathedral in June 1801, when 45ft of lead on the roof was destroyed and £500-worth of damage was caused. The fire was blamed on the 'carelessness of plumbers' who were working on the roof.

COACH AND HORSES AVENUE
Chapel Field Road.

COACH AND HORSES AVENUE-COLEGATE

COACH AND HORSES YARD

51–53 Bethel Street, was named after the Coach and Horses pub, which is recorded at 51 Bethel Street from 1760.

COBB'S YARD

Former name for Russell's Yard, 145–147 Ber Street. *Hunt's Directory* of 1850 lists John Cobb, furniture broker, at Ber Street. The yard was lost by 1960.

COBB'S YARD

54–56 Magdalen Street. *Kelly's Directory* of 1900 lists Leggett Augustus Myhill Cobb, butcher, at 56 Magdalen Street. The yard was lost by 1964.

COBURG STREET

Coburg Street runs from 72–74 St Stephen's Street to Chapel Field East. According to Sandred and Lingström, the name commemorates the house of Saxe-Coburg-Gotha: that is, the Royal Family name following the marriage of Queen Victoria and Prince Albert, which George V changed to 'Windsor' during World War One. The street was closed to the public in 1954.

Streets off Coburg Street

Malthouse Lane (formerly St Stephen's Back Street) (22–24).
Starling Place (24–26).

Buildings on Coburg Street

Sections of the City Wall are still visible along Coburg Street. At the time of writing in early 2005, the Nestlé Shopping Development is being constructed there. During excavations, the largest Roman remains in the city were found there.

COCK YARD

80–82 St Giles' Street opposite the church tower. It was named after the Cock pub, which is recorded at next door (and also as 7–8 Upper St Giles) from 1760. The Cock was closed in 1929.

COCK & PIE (OR PYE) YARD

3–5 Quayside, was named after the Cock and Magpie pub, which is recorded at 8 Quayside from 1760 (as the Magpie). The Cock and Magpie was closed in 1878,

COCK HOUSE YARD (also known as COCK & HOUSE YARD)

Was on the corner of Muspole Street and Duke Street. It was named after the Cock & House pub, which was recorded at Muspole Street in 1760 as the Cock & Dove and by 1861 as the Cock Houses. It closed in 1861 and the yard was lost.

COCKELL'S OR COGGLE'S YARD

West side of Rosemary Lane. *Pigot's Directory* of 1830 lists William Coggle, shopkeeper and 'dealer in sundries', at Rosemary Lane. The yard was lost by 1890.

COCKEY LANE

Former name for Abbey Lane, King Street.

COCKEY LANE

Former name for Back of the Inns.

COCKEY LANE

Former name for London Street.

COCKSEDGE'S YARD

Ber Street, precise location unknown. *White's Directory* of 1845 lists Mrs Martha Cocksedge as a resident of Ber Street.

COE'S OR COX'S YARD

19–21 St Benedict's Street (formerly Upper Westwick Street). *Peck's Directory* of 1802 lists John Coe, broker, at 9 Upper Westwick Street. The yard was lost by 1925.

COGMAN'S COURT/YARD

49–51 Ber Street. *Peck's Directory* of 1802 lists Benjamin Cogman, baker, at 19 Ber Street; *Harrod & Co's Directory* of 1877 and *Kelly's Directory* of 1912 lists Miss Sarah Cogman, shopkeeper, at Ber Street. The yard was lost 1935–41.

COLEBY PLACE

Lower Westwick Street, precise location unknown. *Harrod & Co's Directory* of 1877 lists Coleby and Durrell, harness and shoe curriers, at Westwick Street.

COLEGATE

Colegate runs from 2 Magdalen Street to the junction of Coslany Street and Oak Street. It may take its name from the surname Cole; there is evidence for the name in the city from 1220, and Tomas de Lingcole may have lived in the area (see St Mary's Plain). Many of the city's mayors have lived in Colegate. It was known as Colegate Street from 1783–1830 – but, because 'gate' means 'street', the second half of the name was dropped.

Streets off Colegate

North:
Old Meeting House Alley or Yard (17)
Calvert Street (29)
St George's Street (29–31)
Muspole Street (47)
Burrell's Yard (formerly Guild Yard) (49–51)*
Woolpack Yard (51)

Hook's (formerly Crook's) Yard (53)*
Duke Street (57)
Queen Ann's Yard (59)
St Miles Alley (59)
Oak Street (formerly Coslany Street)

South:
St Clement's Alley (just after church – runs to Fye Bridge Street)
Shave's (formerly Shaw's) Yard or Court (16)
Friar's Quay
Corrick's Yard (16)*
Nightingale's Yard (24–26)*
Black Boy Yard (32)
St George's Street
Water Lane (36)
Moon & Stars Yard (54)*
Duke Street (54–60)
Barnard's Yard (formerly Barnes Foundry Yard) (60 – leads to 30–32 Coslany Street)
Grapes' Yard (70)*

Exact location unknown:
Chickerell's Yard (became Chickering's Yard), south side

Buildings on Colegate
Churches
The first Blackfriars church in the city was built in 1226; they were given the Church of John the Baptist as their chapel. The site was later built upon and used for the Old Meeting House (see Old Meeting House Alley).

The Octagon Chapel, sometimes known as 'the Devil's Cucumber Frame', was designed by Thomas Ivory and built as the result of a competition. The first stone was laid on 25 February 1754. John Wesley called it 'the most elegant Meeting House in Europe' but also wondered 'how it could be thought the old coarse gospel would find admission

Octagon Chapel. (Photograph by author)

here'. It was used by many dissenting families in the 18th century – particularly the Martineaus, Aldersons, Norgates, Taylors and Bolingbrokes.

St Clement the Martyr's Church near Fye Bridge is thought to date from around 1040. *White's Directory* of 1845 refers to a Leper's Tomb there, and the legend that the leper was allowed to be buried here in return for leaving all his lands to the church. The church was declared redundant in 1976 and placed in the care of Norwich Historic Churches Trust. It has been used as a centre for prayer and meditation since 1978.

St Clement's Church, Colegate. (Photograph by author)

St George's Church was formerly known as St George in Coslany and St George of Muspool – according to Blomefield, from a large pond that was near it and 'is now stopped up'. The tower was built in 1459 and building was

St George's Church, Colegate. (Photograph by author)

completed in 1513; John Crome was buried here and the church also contains an unusual terracotta tomb of Robert Jannys. There is a Victorian drinking fountain on the churchyard wall. The church was almost derelict in 1949 and was restored by John Chaplin.

The parish of St John the Baptist Colegate was added to St George's Colegate in the 13th century. The building was used by the Blackfriars as their chapel, but it burned down in 1449.

St Michael (or Miles) Coslany was famous for its flushwork (flint). It dates from before 1428, although it was rebuilt extensively from 1500–12. It was declared redundant in 1976 and placed in the care of Norwich Historic Churches Trust. It was a martial arts centre and sports hall in the early 1990s and became Inspire Science Centre in 1995.

St Michael Coslany. (Photograph by author)

Detail of flushwork at St Michael Coslany. (Photograph by author)

Other buildings of note

Bacon's House at 31 Colegate was built by Henry Bacon in the mid-15th century; his initials and merchant's mark are in the spandrels of the main doorway. The building was enlarged until it became a courtyard house by the 17th century. It has been a pawnbroker's, the People's College (used by J.J. Gurney in 1850) and a shoe works – which involved large-scale reconstruction in 1878 – a tobacco factory, a café and a theatre. It was partly rebuilt after a bad fire in 1925 and renovated again in 1978.

Bacon's House, Colegate. (Photograph by author)

The Norvic Shoe Factory was built for Howlett & White by Edward Boardman in 1876. It was converted to factory units in the 1980s, then to Merchants' Court shopping arcade in 1984.

People linked with Colegate

Henry Bacon, a worsted merchant, was mayor in 1557 and 1566. He entertained the Earl of Warwick during Kett's Rebellion in 1549. During his mayoralty he altered the city's seal, replacing a representation of the Trinity with the city arms.

Timothy Balderston, a weaver, was mayor in 1736 and 1761; he was buried in Monument in St George's Colegate.

John Black, a worsted weaver, was mayor in 1729 and was also the captain (later the colonel) of the Norwich

Artillery Company. He lived on the corner of Colegate and Magdalen Street. His son, also called John Black, was mayor in 1729 and 1744.

Reverend William Bridge was the rector of St Peter Hungate and vicar of Tombland, but he was thrown out of the church in 1636 for preaching puritanism at St George's Tombland. He became a pastor in Rotterdam for a while, and in 1641 he returned to Norwich and established the Old Meeting House in Colegate.

Thomas Chickering, a brewer who was mayor in 1676, is buried in St Clement's. He played a prominent part in the Great Blowe of 1648 (see Bethel Street).

George Cocke, mayor in 1613, lived in Bacon's House.

William Hankes, a merchant, was mayor in 1816. Instead of giving a lavish mayoral dinner in St Andrew's Hall, he gave the Corporation members a cold buffet in the Guildhall, and spent the rest of the money he would have spent on the dinner on his own parish poor.

Jeremiah Ives Harvey, mayor in 1783, lived at 18 Colegate. His father Thomas was the mayor in 1748.

Robert Harvey, a wool merchant, was mayor in 1738 and lived at 20 Colegate. The castle ditches were levelled during his year of office. According to Cozens-Hardy, he was known as 'Snuffy Bob' because he used to stand by the iron gates at 18–20 Colegate taking snuff; he also dressed eccentrically.

Thomas Harvey, a merchant, was mayor in 1748; he lived at 18 Colegate.

John Herring, mayor in 1799, lived at 4 Colegate. He introduced a scheme to employ workhouse children in spinning wool; in later years he declined a knighthood.

Jeremiah Ives, mayor in 1769 and 1795, lived at 1 Colegate, opposite St Clement's Church. The house was later used as St Clement's rectory. His father – also Jeremiah Ives – was mayor in 1733. Jeremiah junior was known as 'Alderman Ives' to distinguish him from his cousin Jeremiah Ives (who was also mayor in 1756 – and known as 'Justice Ives').

Robert Jannys, a grocer, lived in a house on Colegate known as the 'Two Rammes'. He was mayor in 1517 and 1524; he has a terracotta tomb in St George's Colegate.

William Norwich, mayor in 1461, founded a chapel to the Belled Virgin Mary at St George's Colegate.

Matthew Parker – the original 'Nosey Parker' – was christened at St Clement the Martyr's Church in 1504. He was educated at Corpus Christi college, Cambridge, and was vice-chancellor there. He was also the chaplain to Anne Boleyn, who on the eve of her execution placed her daughter Elizabeth in his care; she made him her first Archbishop of Canterbury in 1559.

William Wiggett, an attorney, was mayor in 1742; he lived in Bacon's House.

Events at Colegate

Colegate has suffered very badly from fires. In 1449 a fire destroyed the Dominican Friars' House and St John's Church; the site was used for the Old Meeting House. On 4 June 1507 a fire started on Colegate in the house of a French surgeon called Peter Johnson. The fire burned for two days from Colegate to Coslany, and burned St Michael's Church completely. The 20th century has seen some spectacular fires, too: on 23 December 1909 Jewson's mills were burned out, and it was thought that at one point the whole area to Wensum Street would go up. Lots of spectators ended up with burns to their hands because of the sparks.

In April 1924 Jewson's was hit again when the mills and box-making department on the corner of Colegate and Calvert Street were gutted by fire. According to the *Eastern Daily Press*, the fire was 'so bright that the cathedral spire stood out sharply', and fireman Mr Hardiment fell from the roof and hurt his back. Just over 18 months later, in December 1925, the warehouse toe puff makers Flextoe was guttered – though it could have been a lot worse, as their premises contained extremely flammable celluloid in 10-gallon drums.

COLEMAN'S OR COLMAN'S YARD

30 Bull Close. *White's Directory* of 1883 lists Frederick Coleman, shopkeeper. The yard was lost 1935–41.

COLMAN'S COURT

Formerly Baker's Yard, 57–59 Pottergate, takes its name from the Colman family, who had the mustard and starch works at Carrow (King Street) and were incredibly influential in 19th-century Norwich.

COLLEGE COURT

21–23 Palace Street, contained the Lancastrian School; it may have also been known as Lancastrian School Yard. The school opened in April 1811 for 420 boys, in accordance with the system of Joseph Lancaster. Lancaster was a Quaker schoolmaster who developed the monitorial system. This meant that the schoolmaster or mistress taught the senior pupils, who then (at the age of about 10) taught those lessons to groups of younger children. Lancaster claimed that by this method he could superintend up to 1,000 children at a cost of 5–6 shillings per head per year. However, the school figures were disappointing: in the first year 537 enrolled, 160 left, 70 were discharged for non-attendance and 7 died. The yard was lost 1935–41.

COMMERCE YARD/COURT

30 Thorn Lane, was named after the Sons of Commerce pub, which is recorded at 30 Thorn Lane from 1856; the pub closed in April 1940 and the yard was lost by 1947.

COMMON PUMP STREET

See Pump Street (Buffcoat Lane).

COMPASS STREET

39–41 Mariner's Lane, was named after the Compasses pub, which is recorded at 4 Upper King Street from 1760. The pub is listed as having a sand floor even after 1945; it was closed in 1984 and became an estate agent's office. The street originally ran to Argyle Street.

COOK'S COURT/YARD

Near 27 Pottergate. *Chase's Directory* of 1783 lists James Brittan, pastry cook, next door at St Gregory's Churchyard (later Alley).

COOK'S LANE

King Street, exact location unknown – referenced in *Chase's Directory* of 1783. *Pigot's Directory* of 1830 lists Reverend Cook at King Street. It may also have been known as Cook's Yard in 1830, after Robert Cook, whitesmith. The lane appears to have been lost by 1883.

COOPER'S YARD

Barn Road. *White's Directory* of 1883 lists William Cooper, furniture dealer.

COPEMAN STREET

Runs from 108 Pottergate, on the site of the former Wellington Square. It was named after Edward Copeman, who was the physician of the Norfolk and Norwich Hospital from 1851 and co-founded the Jenny Lind Infirmary for Sick Children. He was also a magistrate and the author of several works including *A Treatise on Apoplexy*, *Records of Obstetric Practice*, *Illustrations of Puerperal Fever* and *Cerebral Diseases of Infancy*.

CORNCUTTERS CLOSE

A modern development that runs from Friar's Quay.

CORRICK'S YARD

16 Colegate, *Harrod & Co's Directory* of 1877 lists Benjamin Corrick, cabinet maker and upholsterer, nearby at Calvert Street. The yard was lost by 1896.

COSLANY SQUARE

Runs between the end of Coslany Street and 26 Westwick Street; it dates from 1982–87 when Coslany Street was widened and the factories were converted to flats.

COSLANY STREET

Coslany Street runs from 26 Westwick Street to the beginning of Oak Street – in fact, part of Oak Street was actually known as Coslany Street until 1890. The street takes its name from the city district of Coslany and means 'an island among river marshes'; the name was established by 1850. According to Pevsner, the area was a maze of small courts and alleys in the late 19th century (though that seems to be more the Oak Street end).

Streets off Coslany Street

West:
Coslany Square
Robert Gybson Way
Gent's Yard or Upper Yard (formerly Abbs Court) (1–5)*
Dyers' Yard
Chequers' Yard (13–15)*
Waggon & Horses Yard (17–19)*

East:
Anchor Quay
Red Lion Yard (26)*
Barnard's Yard (30–32, leads to 60 Colegate)

Exact location unknown:
Brewhouse Yard*
Cotton Court*
Sadd's Yard*

Buildings on Coslany Street

Anchor brewery is now a housing development, Anchor Quay.

Barnard, Bishop & Barnard Ironworks from 1851 was demolished and replaced by new housing in the 1970s and 1980s (Barnard's Yard). The kerbs of the streets around Barnard's iron foundry were actually made of iron! Barnard's made the Pagoda in the Park (see Chapelfield Gardens) and the gates that were placed at the entrance of the Queen's home at Sandringham in November 1864. In November 1860 they made something really unusual – an iron lighthouse, for the Brazilian government. The lighthouse was made in sections and had 144 iron plates; it was 17ft in diameter, 46ft tall, and the lantern was 16ft high. It was temporarily put up by the riverside next to St George's Bridge and provided quite a spectacle!

Coslany Bridge, also called St Miles Bridge, is the oldest cast-iron bridge in Norwich; it was designed by James Frost, and is dated 1804. According to early 20th-century historian Walter Rye, there's a legend that there was once a dragon's head on St Miles Bridge with the inscription 'When dragon drinks Heigham sinks'. Rye interprets this as meaning 'when the water got so high as to run through the dragon's mouth, Heigham was sure to be flooded.'

People linked with Coslany Street

Gregory Clerk, a mercer, was mayor in 1505 and 1514. His

house became Dial Yard (address now Oak Street). The building was pulled down during slum clearances in 1937.

Events at Coslany Street

There was a severe fire in August 1878 at Bagshaw's paper mills in Coslany Street, which was under control within two hours but took a lot longer to put out and caused several thousand pounds of damage to the engine room and paper loft. Cottages nearby had melted glass and blistered doors. And the cause? The *Norfolk Chronicle* said that 'the origin of the fire is involved in mystery'.

Coslany Street saw a lot of slum clearance in the 1930s and was badly hit during air raids in World War Two.

COSSEY'S COURT

118–120 St George's Street, *White's Directory* of 1883 lists Mrs Sarah A. Cossey near there. The yard was lost 1935–41.

COSSEY'S YARD

29–31a Botolph Street; *Pigot's Directory* of 1830 lists John Cossey, house agent, at Botolph Street. The yard was lost in the mid to late 1960s for the Anglia Square development.

COTMAN FIELDS

31 Bishopgate, is a 1960s housing development on Bishopgate, named after the artist John Sell Cotman (see St Martin at Palace Plain).

COTT'S YARD

19–21 Pottergate. *Harrod & Co's Directory* of 1860 lists Thomas Cott, pawnbroker, silversmith and jeweller, at Pottergate. The yard became known as Emm's Yard between 1912 and 1925.

COTTON COURT

Coslany Street, exact location unknown. *Pigot's Directory* of 1830 lists Marshall & Peacock, 'Archill Manufacturers', at Cotton Court. The yard was lost by 1839.

COW HILL

Cow Hill runs from 73–75 St Giles' Street to 92–94 Pottergate. It was named after the Red Cow pub, which is recorded at 14 Cow Hill from 1760. The pub closed in 1908. The street was cobbled until 1925.

Streets off Cow Hill

South:
Willow Lane
Borrow Court (17)

North:
King's Yard (2)

Chestnut Court (7–8)
Watling's Court (formerly Watling's Yard) (12)
Cow Yard and Little Cow Yard (14–16)

People linked with Cow Hill

George Borrow (see Willow Lane)

Josiah Buttifant was the secretary of the Provident Building and Land Society at St Andrew's Plain; he lived at Cow Hill and in 1874 featured in a huge fraud case. On 18 June 1874 there was a meeting of the Norfolk and Norwich Provident Building Society at the Bell Hotel in Timberhill, after it was discovered that Buttifant had left claiming he was 'on holiday' but had 'committed defalcations' of £5,000. His clerk, William Frederick Fish, was taken into custody on 6 July for defrauding the society members of £10,000 (around £568,000 in today's money). Buttifant was arrested 'at Valentia' (sic) on 7 August by Detective Williamson of Norwich Police – Williamson's telegram took a week to reach Norwich! Buttifant was tried in Norwich on charges of forgery and embezzlement. In the end, Fish was charged with stealing £39 2s and aiding and abetting Buttifant's embezzlement; he got 16 months' imprisonment with hard labour. Buttifant got 14 years' penal servitude.

COW YARD

14–16 Cow Hill, takes its name from the Red Cow pub (see Cow Hill). According to *Chase's Directory* of 1783, the freemasons lodge met at the Red Cow on the first and third Tuesday of the month from 1754.

COWGATE

Cowgate runs from 99–101 Magdalen Street to Whitefriars Bridge. The part leading to Magdalen Street was once known as All Saints Street. Cowgate was known as Cowholme in Saxon times, as cattle were kept on it. As with Pottergate and Colegate, Cowgate had the appendix 'street' in the late 18th and early 19th centuries – and lost it for the same reason! Cowgate is one of the streets that has suffered a lot from renumbering; the numbers below are as they were in 1900.

Streets off Cowgate

East:
Little Bull Close (35)
Chapel Yard (39)
Bull Close (43–49)
Yarn Mews (formerly Finch's Yard) (53–55)
Harpley's Yard (63)*
Charlton Road (67–69)
Phoenix Yard (71)*
Beckham's Yard (91)*
Barrack Street (95 – Cowgate no longer reaches that far)

Priory Yard or Playground (109–111)*
Factory Yard (141)*

West:
Charlton Road (runs to Bull Close Road)
Severn's Court or Yard (16–18)*
Peacock Street (20–22)
Willis Street (80–96 – now off Peacock Street)
Barrack Street (96–98 – Cowgate no longer reaches that far)
Bennett's Yard (98–104)*
Ship Yard (106–108)*
Pestell's or Pestle's Yard (110–112)*
General Windham Yard (122–124)*
Brigg Yard (128–130)*
Bradfield Yard (134–136)*
Pump Yard (after 146)*
Fishergate (152 – Cowgate no longer reaches that far)

Exact location unknown:
Appleton's Yard*
Barley Corn Yard*
Bracefield's Yard*
Fox's Yard*
Magdalen Place*
Queen's Head Yard*
St Paul's Square (now runs off Willis Street – the remainder is under St Crispin's Road)*

Buildings on Cowgate
Churches
St James Pockthorpe Church (see Barrack Street).

St Paul's Church – according to Blomefield, the Church and Hospital of St Paul was founded on Cows' croft. It was consecrated to St Paul the Apostle, and, according to Kirkpatrick, it was the first hospital in Norwich. It was known as Norman's Spital after a monk who was master of the hospital for strangers, vagrants and the sick. The building was used as the city bridewell from 1571 to 1573. It was gutted during an air raid in June 1942 and was demolished in 1952. The site lies underneath the inner ring road.

Other buildings of note
Fastolff House, 104–108 Cowgate, was the town house of Sir John Fastolff (who owned Caister Castle and was probably the basis for Shakespeare's Falstaff). It became the Ship inn in the 19th century but was demolished in 1936 during the slum clearances.

Norman's Charity School was built in 1839; the money for the buildings came from John Norman of Catton, who left money in his will in 1729 to set up a trust. The original idea was to build a hospital and school in Catton, but the

St James' Yarn Mill. (Photograph by author)

money was mismanaged, and *White's Directory* of 1845 says that the treasurers lost £890 in 1777, so there wasn't enough money to build the hospital and school.

St James' Yarn Mill was built in 1839. There was a major fire there in June 1846, and over a thousand people were laid off as a result.

Events at Cowgate
There were wide slum clearances in 1936; then Cowgate was cut in half by the inner ring road.

COWLING'S YARD
68–70 Westwick Street. *Kelly's Directory* of 1900 lists Marie Elise Cowling, baker, at number 68; *White's Directory* of 1883 lists Joseph Cowling, grocer, at Westwick Street. The yard was lost by 1960.

CRAPE FACTORY YARD
Botolph Street, may have been an alternate name for Hinde's Yard, 26–30 Botolph Street.

CRAWFOOT'S YARD
27–29 Ber Street. *Harrod & Co's Directory* of 1877 and *White's Directory* of 1883 lists Mrs Sarah Crowfoot, furniture broker. The yard was lost 1935–41.

CREMER'S YARD
South side of Botolph Street, exact location unknown. *Harrod & Co's Directory* of 1860 lists Robert Cremer, surgeon, nearby at Magdalen Street.

THE CRESCENT
53 Chapel Field Road, took its name from the shape of the road.

CRICK'S BUILDINGS
Fishergate, exact location unknown. They're referenced in *White's Directory* of 1854 but lost by 1883.

CROOK'S YARD
Colegate – see Hook's Yard.

CROOKE'S PLACE
99–101 Chapel Field Road. Schoolroom Yard ran off it – the school was then known as Crook's Place School, but is now known as Bignold First. *White's Directory* of 1845 lists resident Mrs Crook at Chapel Field Road; however, the road was probably named after John Crook, a Manchester silk merchant who levelled the clay pits nearby and built houses on them.

CROSS KEYS YARD
110–112 Magdalen Street, was named after the Cross Keys pub, which is recorded at 112 Magdalen Street from 1760. The pub closed in 1906 and the yard was lost by 1964.

CROSS LANE
Runs from 57–59 St George's Street to 22 Calvert Street. According to Sandred and Lingström, there was a stone cross at the Calvert Street junction, which was demolished in the 17th century but replaced in the 18th century and was known as 'Cow Cross'. The Little Portion Mission House at number 5 was the Rifleman Ale House before 1963 – painter John Crome's local (see St George's Street for John Crome). Bett's Court is listed at 14 Cross Lane.

The Rifleman, Cross Lane – John Crome's local. (Photograph by author)

CROSS STREET
40–42 Sussex Street, former name for The Lathes.

CROTCH'S YARD
42 Barrack Street. *Robson's Commercial Directory* of 1839 lists William Crotch, beer retailer, at Barrack Street. The yard became known as Stewardson's Yard by 1900.

CROW'S YARD (or **CROWE'S COURT**)
20–22 St Benedict's Street – former name for Gaffer's Yard.

Pigot's Directory of 1830 lists Mary Crowe, painter and coal merchant, at St Benedict's Street. The yard was known as Gaffer's Yard by 1890.

CROWN & ANCHOR YARD
Alternate name for Anchor Yard, Calvert Street.

CROWN & ANGEL YARD
41–43 St Stephen's Street, was named after the Crown & Angel pub, which is recorded at 41 St Stephen's Street from 1789; the pub and yard were demolished during an air raid in June 1942.

CROWN COURT YARD
20–22 Elm Hill was named after the Crown pub, which is recorded at 29 Elm Hill from 1760. The pub was closed in 1927. Augustine Steward (see Tombland) lived at 20 Elm Hill at the time of his death.

CROWN ROAD
Ran from Agricultural Hall Plain/Prince of Wales Road to Rose Avenue but is now a cul-de-sac. It took its name from the Crown Bank (see Agricultural Hall Plain).

CROWN YARD
71–73 St Benedict's Street (also known as 32 Upper Westwick Street in 1802), was named after the Crown pub, which is recorded at 71 St Benedict's Street from 1760. The pub was severely damaged during an air raid in April 1942 and was closed; the yard was lost at the same time.

CRUSOE STREET
Ran from 18–20 St Julian Street to Garden Street.

CURTIS BUILDINGS
Middle Square, 18 Thorn Lane. *White's Directory* of 1854 lists G. Curtis, bricklayer, nearby at Rising Sun Lane. The buildings were lost by 1947.

THE CUT
103–105 Barrack Street.

CUTELER ROWE
Former name for London Street.

DABSON'S COURT/YARD
Magdalen Street, exact location unknown.

DAMOCLES COURT
Runs from the south side of Pottergate, and was built on the site of Wellington Square, which was destroyed during air raids in World War Two.

DARK ENTRY YARD

43–51 Pitt Street. The yard was lost by 1925.

DAVEY PLACE

Runs from 19–20 Market Place to 7–9 Castle Meadow and bisects Castle Street. The section leading down from Castle Meadow is known as Davey Steps. It takes its name from Jonathan Davey, the grocer and alderman who built it in 1812; it was the first pedestrianised street cut into the city since mediaeval times. Davey announced, 'Gentlemen, I mean to put a hole in the King's Head' – at a time when Norwich was still jittery after the French Revolution and Davey was a prominent Jacobin. He was placed under armed guard for a week; then everyone realised it was Davey's odd sense of humour when the King's Head pub (formerly at 8 Castle Street) came up for sale and he bought it and knocked a hole in it so he could build his new street. The King's Head was rebuilt at 10 Davey Place but closed in 1981. The 18th-century diarist Parson Woodforde used to stay at the original King's Head in Castle Street; boxing matches were held there, and the Irish boxer O'Brien was noted as 'outstanding' in 1797: he was 8ft 4in tall!

One unusual exhibition in the city took place at the Great Room in Davey Place in July 1817: Haddock's exhibition of automata.

Davey Place with the castle in the background. (Photograph by author)

DAVISON'S COURT

South side of Rising Sun Lane, exact location unknown. *White's Directory* of 1854 lists baker Matthew Davison nearby at Thorn Lane.

DAWSON'S YARD

Near 7 Golden Ball Street. *Harrod & Co's Directory* of 1860 lists George William Dawson, cabinet and ecclesiastical carver in wood and stone, at Golden Ball Street. The yard was lost by 1900.

DAY'S COURT/YARD

St Peter's Street, exact location unknown. *Robson's Commercial Directory* of 1839 lists P. Day, agent to British Fire Office, at Upper Market Street (aka St Peter's Street).

DAY'S YARD

St Stephen's Street; *Peck's Directory* of 1802 lists William Day's Eating House at 16 St Stephen's Street. The yard was referenced in *White's Directory* of 1845 and 1854 but was lost by 1883.

DE CAUX'S COURT OR YARD

Wensum Street, probably near number 4. *Chase's Directory* of 1783 lists William de Caux, cabinet maker, at 4 Cook Street (aka Wensum Street), and *Pigot's Directory* of 1830 lists De Caux, son and Pratt, grocer and tea dealers, at Wensum Street. The court was lost by 1854.

DE HAGUE'S COURT

10 Elm Hill. *Peck's Directory* of 1802 lists Elisha de Hague, Attorney, at 5 Elm Hill. De Hague was also the town clerk of Norwich from 1792 until 1826, as well as being the Norwich postmaster for a quarter of a century; his father, also Elisha de Hague, held the post of town clerk from 1774 until his death in 1792. The yard was lost by 1890.

DIAL YARD/COURT

5 Oak Street (Coslany Street before 1890). This was formerly the house of Gregory Clerk (see Coslany Street); it was known as Dial Court in 1845 and Dial Yard by 1854. It was pulled down during the slum clearances of 1937.

DELPH'S YARD

31–39 St Augustine's Street. *Harrod & Co's Directory* of 1877 lists William Delph, painter and plumber, at St Augustine's Street. The yard was lost 1960–64.

DIAL YARD

113–117 Barrack Street, was named after the Dial pub, which is recorded at 117 Barrack Street from 1839–84. The yard was lost by 1941–47.

DISTILLERY YARD

25–27 Oak Street (Coslany Street before 1890). The yard was lost 1935–41.

DOG YARD

104–106 Oak Street, possibly named after the Dog pub, which is recorded at St Paul's Plain from 1760 and closed in 1879.

DOLPHIN YARD

54–56 Oak Street, was named after the Dolphin pub, which was recorded at 26 Coslany Street (later Oak Street) in 1760; the pub closed in 1887 and the yard was lost with it.

DOVE STREET

Dove Street runs from 6 Market Place to 2 Pottergate; until the 19th century it was the only exit from the market place. According to Blomefield, it was originally called Holtor Lane (or 'ditch tower lane') after a tower built by the Jews in the 11th century. It became Dove Lane in the late 17th century, taking its name from the sign of an inn; the Dove pub was listed at Dove Street in 1830 and 1845 and became the Edinburgh Arms.

Events at Dove Street

On 7 February 1860 there was a fire at pastry cook W. Aberdein's. It wasn't that serious, but Cubitt's ironmongery was next door – and it had over 400lbs of gunpowder stored there! The *Norfolk Chronicle* reported that the gunpowder was removed safely in wet blankets.

There was a much more serious fire there on 1 August 1898, which started at Daniel Hurn the ropemaker's and spread to Chamberlin's department store. The fire also gutted the library and its 60,000 volumes, and the Edinburgh Arms collapsed three days later. The library reopened on 2 August 1899, at a cost of £1,719.

People linked with Dove Street

The printer Anthony de Solempne (or de Solen) was the first printer in Norwich; he moved here from Brabant with his wife and two children and opened his printing shop in 1567 at the sign of the White Dove. He produced his first book in 1570; many of his books were about clocks and perpetual calendars. Thomas Brooke was one of the ringleaders of a group which planned to throw the 'Strangers' out of Norwich (see Stranger's Hall in Charing Cross). Brooke was sentenced to be hung, drawn and quartered, and wrote a testament before he died; ironically, it was printed by de Solempne – one of the 'Strangers' Brooke had sought to expel!

DOVE YARD

62–64 Barrack Street; may have taken its name from the Dove pub, which is recorded at 43 Barrack Street from 1830 and closed in 1907. The yard was lost 1935–41.

DOWSON'S YARD

King Street, exact location unknown. *Robson's Commercial Directory* of 1839 lists B. W. Dowson and sons, corn and coal merchants, at King Street.

DRAKE'S COURT

126–130 St George's Street. *White's Directory* of 1845 lists resident Mrs Charlotte Drake at Gildengate Street (aka St George's Street). The yard was lost 1935–41.

DRAY'S YARD

116 King Street, is part of King's Quarter, a new development on the site of the old Morgan's Brewery. The name is linked with brewing – a dray is a type of horse-drawn vehicle used to transport beer.

DRUM YARD

64–66 Westwick Street, took its name from the Drum pub, listed at 64 Westwick Street from 1760; it was a beerhouse from 1867 and closed in 1936.

DUCK LANE

110 St Benedict's Street, former name of Wellington Lane. The area between here and Neale's Square was replaced by modern housing.

DUKE OF WELLINGTON YARD

13 Bedford Street, took its name from the Duke of Wellington pub, which became the Bedford Arms by 1865 and closed in 1975.

DUKE OF WELLINGTON YARD

42–44 St Stephen's Street, was named after the Marquis of Wellington pub (later the Duke of Wellington), listed at 42 St Stephen's Street from 1822. The pub closed in 1908 and the yard was lost by 1912.

DUKE STREET

Duke Street originally ran from 1 Charing Cross to St Mary's Plain and the junction with Pitt Street; now it runs to the St Crispin's Road roundabout. It was built in 1822 when the Duke's Palace Bridge was built. It was named after the Duke of Norfolk's Palace, which used to be located on the corner of Duke Street and St Andrew's Street.

Streets off Duke Street
East:
Museum Court*
Duke's Palace Yard (5)* – now the site of the car park)

Case & Steward Yard (7)*
Colegate (23–5)
Muspole Street (after 69)
Cock House Yard (on the corner of Muspole Street)*

West:
Thorns' Yard*
Mary Chapman Court
Colegate
St Mary's Plain (also known as Southgate Street or Soutergate Street)
St Mary's Alley

Buildings on Duke Street
Churches
St Mary's Baptist Church was built in 1951–52 by Stanley Wearing, on the site of lecture rooms which were destroyed in air raids during World War Two.

Other buildings of note
The Duke of Norfolk's Palace was the home of the Duke of Norfolk from 1561–1711 and was one of the largest town houses in England. It was rebuilt in 1602 by Henry, Duke of Norfolk. Sir Thomas Browne described festivities there in Christmas 1664: 'They had dancing every night and gave entertainments to all that would come. He built up a room on purpose to dance in... a banquet was given every night after dancing, and three coaches were employed to fetche ladies every afternoon.' Charles II entertained people at the palace in 1671, but Thomas Baskerville, writing in 1681, was less impressed: 'We rowed under 5 or 6 bridges, and then landed at the new-built house not yet finished within, but seated in a dung-hole place, though it had cost the Duke already 30 thousand pounds on building... for it hath but little room for gardens and is pent upon all sides both on this and the other side of the river, with tradesmen's and dyers houses.' In 1708 there was a huge row between Henry's grandson, Thomas, and the mayor, Thomas Havers. Thomas wanted his company of comedians to enter the city with trumpets and banners. Havers refused permission, so Thomas pulled down the palace and left the city in a huff.

According to Blomefield, it then became a workhouse; there was also a play house, bowling alley and tennis court there. In 1764 Charles Howard built a Roman Catholic chapel on the site; by 1794 it was used as the Norwich Subscription Library, and in July 1806 the estate (with the exception of the library and the house next to it) was sold for £5,055. In 1839 it became the Norfolk and Norwich Museum. In 1894, when the museum moved to the castle, the site was used as offices for Corporation of the Guardians of the Poor. The buildings were demolished in the late 1960s when St Andrew's Street was widened.

Duke's Palace Bridge: the foundation stone was laid on 28 August 1821, and the bridge opened in 1822; foot passengers had to pay a toll of half a penny. The City bought the bridge for £4,000 in 1855 and scrapped the toll. In May 1972 the road was closed and widened to feed into the inner ring road. A new bridge was put in, and the old cast-iron bridge was used in the Castle Mall development, supporting the roof to the entrance of the car park by the Shire Hall.

St Andrew's Workhouse was approximately where Howard House is now on St Andrew's Street/Duke Street.

Events at Duke Street
August 1829 saw a case linked with the workhouse, when John Stratford was hanged as the 'dumpling poisoner' – he had had an affair with Jane Briggs, whose husband was in the workhouse suffering from 'cancer of the face', and could only drink 'thick milk' (presumably milk thickened with flour). Jane didn't want her husband to suffer so Stratford sent a parcel of flour to Briggs, laced with arsenic – except the flour was taken by John Burgess, husband of the workhouse nurse, to make dumplings. Burgess died, and Stratford was arraigned for murder – particularly when Jane testified that he'd tried to make her abort his child.

John Stratford's deathmask. (Photograph by author)

On 25 September 1866 the boiler at Stark & Co's dye and chemical works exploded. Three men (Taylor, Breeze and Clarke) died on the spot, and three others died later of their injuries. Nearly 10 years later, on 1 February 1876, there was a large fire at Riches & Watts, agricultural engineers, causing £3–4,000 of damage.

DUKE'S PALACE YARD
5 Duke Street, was named after the Duke's Palace pub, recorded at 7 Duke Street from 1783; a resident in 1783 was Fran Gostling, distiller, rectifier, brandy and vinegar merchant. In the early 1800s Polito's Wild Beasts were exhibited at the pub. The pub was demolished in the 1960s and the site was used for a multi-storey car park in 1968 – which was itself demolished in August 2002 and rebuilt for opening in late 2005.

DUN COW YARD
149–151 Barrack Street. See Red Cow Yard.

DUNK'S COURT

18 Muspole Street. The yard was lost by 1890.

DUTTON'S COURT

18–20 Elm Hill

DYERS' YARD

Runs from the west side of Coslany Street. It takes its name from the Jolly Dyers' pub, which was listed at Coslany Street before 1844; the pub was demolished by 1933.

EAGLE YARD AND LITTLE EAGLE YARD

100–112 Westwick Street, was named after the Eagle pub, which is recorded at 100 Lower Westwick Street from 1850 and closed in 1893.

EAGLE OPENING

31–35 Sussex Street, takes its name from the Eagle pub, which is recorded at 35 Sussex Street from 1830. The pub was damaged during air raids in April 1942 but was rebuilt.

EASTBOURNE PLACE

87 Prince of Wales Road, is a short street running between Prince of Wales Road and 67 Rose Lane.

EBENEZER PLACE (previously **EBENEZER TERRACE**)

Runs from 43–45 Sussex Street, originally it led to 166–176 Oak Street, and was known in the Oak Street location as Osborne's Buildings from 1883–1912. See also Osborne's Yard.

EDWARD STREET

Runs from Esdelle Street to Magdalen Street.

Streets off Edward Street

The street has included:

Upper Green Lane (leads to St Crispin's Road)

Beckham Place

EIGHT RINGERS' YARD

12–14 Oak Street (Coslany Street before 1890), was named after the Eight Ringers pub, which is recorded at 14 Oak Street from 1760 and closed in 1913. Scholar's Court is a newish development on the site.

ELDON ROW

35–41 Chapel Field Road. The yard was lost by 1960, firstly for a car sales outlet then for the office block of Norvic House.

ELEPHANT YARD

58–60 Magdalen Street, was named after the Elephant pub, which is recorded at 60 Magdalen Street from 1783 and closed in 1931. The yard was also lost.

ELEPHANT & CASTLE YARD

110–112 King Street, was named after the Elephant & Castle pub, which is recorded at 102 King Street from 1840; it was damaged during air raids in April 1942 and closed shortly afterwards; the yard was lost as well.

ELM HILL

Elm Hill runs from 2–6 Prince's Street to 10–12 Wensum Street. The street takes its name from the elm, which is located at the corner of Waggon and Horses Lane; it was known as Elm Hill Street in 1783, but became just Elm Hill by 1830. There was a common pump by the elm in 1883.

Elm Hill. (Photograph courtesy of Norwich City Council)

Streets off Elm Hill

South:

Leache's Court (near 9)*

Waggon and Horses Lane (formerly Elm Hill Lane) (19 – leads to Wensum Street)

Norris Gardens (formerly Norris Court/Yard) (35–37)

Wright's Court (43–45)

St Simon's Court (runs to Waggon and Horses Lane), by the church*

North:

The Monastery (formerly Monastery Yard and Goss Yard) (8)

De Hague's Court (10)*

Dutton's Court (18–20)

Crown Court Yard (20–22)

Towler's Court (24–26)

Roache's Court (30–34 – runs to Wensum Street)

Exact location unknown:

Houghton's Yard*

Buildings on Elm Hill

Churches

St Simon & St Jude's Church is named in the Domesday book; according to Blomefield, it was the bishop's church before the see of Norwich was settled here. The church was rebuilt in the 15th century and closed in 1892, in ruins. It was renovated in 1913 and used as a Sunday School; after falling into ruins yet again in the 1920s, it was repaired in 1940, then used as the local headquarters for the Boy Scouts Association from 1952.

St Simon & St Jude's Church. (Photograph by author)

Other buildings of note

The Briton's Arms dates from the early 14th century and is the only building in Elm Hill that survived the 1507 fire intact – it's one of the five original thatched houses left in the city. It was known as Le Godes House at one point, and

has also been Surgeon's House; it was then used for weaving, cordwaining and saddlemaking, and was used as a béguinage (a place where women live as nuns but don't take formal vows). In 1760 it was a pub, originally called the King's Arms, but renamed The Briton's Arms in 1804. It was closed in 1941 and restored in 1953.

The Briton's Arms, Elm Hill. (Photograph by author)

Pettus House, at 41–43 Elm Hill, was the home of the Pettus family. The house was rebuilt by Augustine Steward after the 1507 fire.

The Strangers Club, at 22–26 Elm Hill, was known as

Pettus House, Elm Hill. (Photograph by author)

Paston Place. (Photograph by author)

Back of Paston Place. (Photograph by author)

Paston Place in the 15th century. As with Pettus House, it was rebuilt by Augustine Steward after the 1507 fire.

People linked with Elm Hill

Peter Barlow, mathematician, was born in St Simon's parish in October 1776. He became professor of mathematics at the Royal Military Academy in Woolwich in 1801, and in 1814 he published Barlow's Tables; these give the factors, squares, cubes, square and cube roots, reciprocals and hyperbolic logarithms of the numbers from 1 to 10,000. He also invented the Barlow Lens – an achromatic lens used for telescopes – was elected a Fellow of the Royal Society in 1823 and received the Copley Medal in 1825 for his discoveries in magnetism.

Francis Columbine, a merchant and grocer who was mayor in 1776, lived at 28 Elm Hill.

The Friars de Sacco lived at 6 Elm Hill. They were a small penitential order who dressed in sackcloth. When the smaller orders were dissolved by the Pope in 1307, the land was granted to the Black Friars on the condition they looked after the remaining Sack Friar, who was elderly and almost blind.

William Gostlin, a royalist merchant, was mayor in 1642. He was imprisoned because of his political views in 1643; he lived at 28 Elm Hill. The Paston family lived at 22–24 Elm Hill; John and Margaret wrote a series of letters in the 15th century, which give incredible insight into her life and responsibilities as a wife, mother and looking after the estate during her husband's absence. Margaret was also the first recorded English recipient of a Valentine letter.

The Pettus family – which included several city sheriffs and mayors – lived at 41–43 Elm Hill. These include Thomas Pettus, mayor in 1590; Sir John Pettus, a merchant who was mayor in 1608, built a conduit to the spring by Bishop Bridge and was knighted by Elizabeth I; and Thomas Pettus, who was mayor in 1614.

Samuel Rainbird, carpenter, lived at 'Church Street St Simon' (presumably Elm Hill). In February 1854 he patented a new invention: 'an apparatus for grappling and raising sunken vessels and other submerged bodies'.

Thomas Whall, a grocer who was mayor in 1567, lived in Elm Hill opposite the Church of St Simon and St Jude.

Events at Elm Hill

The whole street was almost destroyed by fire in 1507, with the exception of the Briton's Arms – one of the five remaining original thatched houses of the city. Elm Hill was a slum in the 1930s and was allegedly saved from clearance by one vote.

ELM HILL LANE

See Waggon & Horses Lane.

ELY'S OR ELEY'S YARD

23–27 Pitt Street. *White's Directory* of 1845 lists Robert Ely, shopkeeper (grocer), at Pitt Street. The yard was lost 1935–41.

EMM'S COURT

4–6 Ber Street. *White's Directory* of 1883 lists William Emms, hay and straw dealer, at Ber Street.

EMMS' YARD (formerly COTT'S YARD)

19–21 Pottergate, *Kelly's Directory* of 1912 lists William J. Emms on Pottergate – as a house furnisher at number 19 and as a draper at number 21. The yard became the Stranger's Court development some time after 1974.

ENGLISH'S YARD

Lower Westwick Street, exact location unknown. *Peck's Directory* of 1802 lists Joseph English, woolcomber, nearby at 14 St Margaret's Churchyard. It also lists James English, writing master, at 87 Upper Westwick Street.

ESDELLE STREET

Runs from 51–53 St Augustine's Street to 62 Magpie Road.

ESPERANTO WAY

Was formerly known as Lady Lane. The name was introduced in 1962 after the library was built, but didn't find favour with Norwich residents.

EXCHANGE STREET

Exchange Street runs from the north side of the Market Place (number 10–11, at the junction between London Street and Guildhall Hill) to 12–14 St Andrew's Street; it takes its name from the corn exchange, built in 1828. The section between the Market Place and Lobster Lane was built in 1828 and opened to the public in August that year; the old buildings at the north end of new road were removed in April 1829 and the lower section of the street, between Lobster Lane and St Andrew's Street, was opened on 21 May 1832. The lower section of the street was known as Museum Street and then Post Office Street.

Streets off Exchange Street

East:
Bedford Street (23–25)
Parsonage Square (35–37)

West:
Lobster Lane (22–24)

Buildings on Exchange Street

The corn exchange was built in 1828, which *Pigot's Directory* of 1830 describes as 96ft long and 85ft wide, and 'the interior forms one of the largest rooms of the kingdom'. On the east side of the corn exchange was an exhibition room for the Norfolk and Suffolk Institution for Promoting the Fine Arts. It was opened to the public in October 1828 but was demolished in 1860. A new Corn Exchange was built on the same site in 1861 at a cost of £17,000; the first brick was laid on 1 May and it opened for business on 9 November. Internally it was 126ft long, 81ft wide and 66ft up to the apex of the roof, which *White's Directory* of 1890 says was 'mainly made of glass'. The second corn exchange was demolished in 1964.

The post office opened for business on 25 June 1832.

Events at Exchange Street

In January 1829 there was a fire at Trivett & Cozens ironmonger's; the report says that the '*Norfolk Chronicle* office narrowly escaped destruction'. Much more destructive was the explosion on 16 October 1963 at Tony's Place, a new snack bar at 20 Exchange Street, at 3am. It wrecked the snack bar and also damaged Thorns' ironmonger's and Sutton's Piano Showrooms. On 11 June 1973 there was another fire, this time at Jarrold's in the basement of their office equipment department. It took firemen four hours to control the blaze, but the 30 employees were safe. Storm has also damaged the street; on 9 July 1853 there was a severe thunderstorm, and the main sewer in London Street burst and its contents inundated the local business premises. All the houses at the bottom of Exchange Street were flooded and their cellars had to be pumped out by fire engines.

On a lighter note, Exchange Street has also been a place of entertainment. In July 1831 Paganini performed for two nights at the Corn Exchange; the *Norfolk Chronicle* called him 'the fascinating, but by no means fair-dealing, foreigner'. In December 1841 there was an exhibition of a new system of skating called 'Tachypos', which was invented by J. Ayton of Norwich. The *Norfolk Chronicle* recorded it as a 'kind of skait [sic] each running on two iron wheels about six inches in diameter, and fastens onto the foot in a similar way to the common skait, with protection to the legs up to the knees'. Rather less successful was the 'glove fight' at the Corn Hall on 19 May 1879 – it wasn't legal, so the police were called. The boxers had to keep the peace for six months and find a surety of £50 each, and the people who set it up (including the sub-editor of the *Sporting Life* in London) were bound over at £20 each to keep the peace for six months.

A rather bizarre event happened in March 1896 when John Fields, a hansom cab diver, was summoned before the Guildhall. He'd driven his horse and cab straight at the Salvation Army procession, at a speed of about 12mph. Fields was found guilty of dangerous driving and fined 10 shillings, plus 25 shillings costs.

EXCISE OFFICE YARD

Pottergate, exact location unknown. The Excise Office was listed at Pottergate from 1830, when Francis Parker was the Chief Excise Collector.

EXHIBITION COURT

20 Ber Street, was named after the Exhibition Tavern, which is recorded at 20 Ber Street by 1865; it closed in 1908 and the yard was lost by 1912.

FACTORY YARD

141 Cowgate, took its name from the St James's Yarn Factory and also the Yarn Factory Tavern, which is recorded

Corn Exchange, Exchange Street, in 1964, picture courtesy of Norfolk County Council Library and Information Service.

at 152 Cowgate from 1867. The pub was damaged during an air raid in September 1942 and closed in 1950; the yard was also lost.

FACTORY YARD

St Stephen's Street, exact location unknown. *Pigot's Directory* of 1830 lists John Bullimore, blacksmith, at the yard. The yard appears to have been lost by 1839.

FAIRMAN'S YARD

99–101 Barrack Street. *Robson's Commercial Directory* of 1839 lists William Fairman, beer retailer. The yard was lost by 1935–41.

FAIR FLORA YARD

Westwick Street, exact location unknown, was named after the Fair Flora pub, which is recorded at Westwick Street from 1760 (as St Lawrence Low Steps in 1830) and closed in 1869.

FARMER'S AVENUE

Runs from the junction of Golden Ball Street and the Cattle Market to Orford Street. Castle Hill runs off it. It took its name from the Jolly Farmers' inn, which is recorded at 5 Farmers Avenue (formerly the Castle Ditches) from 1760. The pub was burned out during an air raid in 1942 and was rebuilt but closed in 1962. Adrian Parmenter, a grocer who was mayor in 1641, opened the first Norwich office of the Excise in 1643 at 1 Farmer's Avenue – a move which didn't make him popular, particularly with the butchers in the city. During the Civil War he was a parliamentarian, and his house was attacked by rioters in 1648 (see Bethel Street – The Great Blowe). Parmenter died in 1663 after being bitten by a mad fox.

FARNELL'S YARD/COURT

St John Street (Maddermarket), stood between the church and the chapel. *White's Directory* of 1845 lists resident Thomas Farnell, gentleman, at St John Maddermarket and also J.T. Farnell, who had an academy at St John Maddermarket.

FELLMONGERS' YARD (or FELLMONGERS' ARMS YARD)

90 Oak Street, was named after the Fellmongers Arms pub, which is recorded at 90 Oak Street from 1822. It was renamed the Railway Arms in 1930 and destroyed during an air raid in 1942, but the business continued being run from a garage at the back until the pub was rebuilt. It was one of the first pubs in the city to get a licence for entertaining on Sundays. It closed in 1967 and was demolished as part of a road widening scheme.

FERRY YARD

243–247 King Street. *White's Directory* of 1883 lists Mark Widdows, boat builder, near there. The yard was lost by 1941; at the time of writing, early 2005, the area is being redeveloped into flats.

FIDDY'S YARD

101–103 Ber Street. *Harrod & Co's Directory* of 1877 lists Robert Hicks Fiddy, grocer, at Ber Street.

FIELD'S COURT OR YARD

162 Ber Street, was built 1912–25. The court was lost 1941–47.

FILBEY'S YARD

Westwick Street, exact location unknown. *White's Directory* of 1845 lists John Filbey, Woolstapler, at Lower Westwick Street.

FINCH'S YARD

53–55 Cowgate – now Yarn Mews.

FINKELGATE

Runs from 169 Ber Street to Queen's Road. It was formerly known as Finket Street. Sandred and Lingström list several possible derivations for the name – a Scandinavian personal name, from the mediaeval 'fenkel' meaning 'corner or bend', from 'fennel', which may have been sold there, or from 'finkle' (meaning 'cuddle or pet') meaning that it was a lovers' lane. The last one is a possibility because Ber Street has been the city's red light district.

Streets off Finkelgate
Woodhouse Yard (5–7)*
Alderson's Street (7–9) (see Alderson Place)

FINKET STREET

Former name for Finkelgate.

FISHER'S COURT

63–65 Magdalen Street. *Harrod & Co's Directory* of 1877 lists James Fisher, rope maker, and William Fisher, carpenter, at Magdalen Street. The yard was lost by 1947.

FISHER'S LANE

Fisher's Lane originally ran from 39–41 St Giles' Street to 48–50 Pottergate and is a continuation of St Laurence's Lane. It was originally called Smalegate or Small Lane (from 1285) because it was narrow – and the St Giles' end is now a footpath. It was known as Sloper's Lane in the 14th century; according to Kirkpatrick, Richard le Slopere had a house here in 1286; Sandred and Lingström say that a sloper was a maker of 'slops' (or outer clothes), and that Fisher's Lane probably took its name from someone who owned a house in the street. However, herrings were apparently fished there until the 16th century, so the street name may have the same kind of derivation as Fishergate. It was also the area where the Norwich Board of Guardians gave money to the poor and destitute – the last step before the workhouse.

Streets off Fisher's Lane:
Jay's Court*
Bear and Staff Yard*
Shibley's Court (1–3)*
Pump Lane or Yard (9–10)*
Wright's Court*
Roache's Court (after 10)*

FISHER'S YARD
Fishergate, exact location unknown. *Harrod & Co's Directory* of 1856 lists William Fisher, carpenter, nearby at Magdalen Street. The yard was lost by 1883.

FISHERGATE
Fishergate runs from 5 Fye Bridge Street to 152 Cowgate. It was formerly known as Fishgate Street (as with Pottergate and Colegate, the 'street' was dropped in the 19th century) and has been referenced as Fishergate or Fishgate since 1285. According to Sandred and Lingström, this was the area where the city's fishermen were concentrated – hence the name (i.e. street of fishermen). The fish were apparently landed at St Edmund's Quay (opposite the present Quayside). Fishergate, along with Quayside, is being redeveloped at the time of writing (May 2005).

Streets off Fishergate
North:
Mint Yard (3–5)*
French's Yard (7)*
Charles James Court
Barnard's Yard (13–15)*
Blacksmith's Yard (17–19)*
Thoroughfare Yard or Road (27 – runs to Magdalen Street)
Rampant Horse Yard (31–33)*
Thompson's Yard (39)
Tiger Yard (43–47)*
Blackfriars Street (formerly Peacock Street) (47–49 – runs to St Paul's Opening)
Staff of Life Yard (53)*
Fleece Yard (63–67)*

South:
Bridge Court (modern)
Soup Office Yard (6)*

Long Yard (4–16)*
Soman's Yard (16–20)*
Jolly Sawyers Yard (26–28)*
Hansard Lane (formerly Water Lane) (42)
Saw Mill Yard*

Exact location unknown:
ABC Yard*
Baker's Yard*
Crick's Buildings*
Fisher's Yard*

Buildings on Fishergate
Churches
St Edmund's Church dates from 1423; *White's Directory* of 1845 says that there used to be a relic of St Edmund the King and Martyr's shirt kept there in a crystal box. The church was restored in 1882, when *White's Directory* of 1890 says that part of its churchyard was 'thrown out into the street for widening of the thoroughfare'. The church has been redundant since the 1980s and is in the care of the Norwich Historic Churches Trust.

St Edmund's Church, Fishergate. (Photograph by author)

Other buildings of note
Boys' and Girls' Hospital Schools – Thomas Anguish left a house and estate here to be used for teaching very young and poor children. The house was set up in 1618 and the school was refounded in 1621 by a charter of Charles I. The endowment income was used to help boys with apprenticeships rather than elementary school after 1885, and the schoolhouse was demolished in the 1930s so the road could be widened.

Events at Fishergate
Fishergate has seen more than its share of fires. On 5 January 1858 Orfeur's timber yard burned down; the following night Andrews & French's soap factory was

Sexton boot factory fire,
Fishergate, 1913, picture courtesy
of Norfolk County Council
Library and Information Service.

burned down (and the two fires, together with another in the area, caused over £6,000 of damage). Porter's Sawmills was also the victim of fires – on 27 July 1900 it was gutted, along with Soman's Shoe factory and ABC Wharf. It was rebuilt, but on 13 November 1904 it was gutted again: it's thought that a bearing overheated on the Saturday, was overlooked, and the fire smouldered until the Sunday. Extensive damage was caused in just 45 minutes. Sexton's shoe factory was the site of a spectacular fire on 16 January 1913, when it was completely destroyed; the headline in the *Eastern Daily Press* was 'an acre of flame'. £100,000-worth of damage (over £6 million of today's money) was caused, and 1,000 people were put out of work.

FISHGATE (STREET)
Former name for Fishergate.

FISHMARKET
44 Market Place.

FITT'S YARD
110–112 Ber Street. The Fitt family were butchers at number 112, there for a long time – William Fitt is listed in 1883, Susan Fitt in 1896 and Noah Darby Fitt in 1912. The yard was lost by 1925.

FLECKED BULL YARD
38–40 Ber Street, was named after the Flecked Bull pub, which is recorded at 38 Ber Street from 1870 (known as the Flickered Bull from the late 1700s). It closed in 1877. The yard was known as George's Yard in 1883, named after Robert George, draper, at number 38, but had reverted to its old name by 1900. The yard was lost 1935–41.

FLEECE YARD
63–67 Fishergate, was named after the Fleece pub, which is recorded at 12 Tombland from 1764. It was renamed the Duke's Tavern in 1856 and closed in 1908. The yard was lost by 1925.

FLINT HOUSE YARD
13 St Andrew's Hill, was named after the Flint House Tavern, which is recorded at 13 St Andrew's Hill from 1875 (was the Shoulder of Mutton from 1760–1870 and the Flint Tavern from 1872–75). It was closed in 1906 – according to the *Norfolk Chronicle*, because it was used by 'women of ill fame and convicted thieves'.

FLOWER POT YARD
127 Oak Street, was named after the Flower Pot pub, which is recorded at 127 Oak Street from 1830. It closed in 1907.

Buildings at Flower Pot Yard
The Great Hall dates from around 1480. In the 16th century it was owned by worsted weavers. It has long weavers' windows on the first floor (which caused John Tompson, the owner in the early 18th century, to be in the highest band for paying window tax) as well as an oriel window. The hall was nearly cleared away during the slum clearances in the 1930s – local historian George Plunkett says that Flower Pot Yard was condemned as 'the worst slum in Norwich' – but Major Glendenning took it over in January 1931 to restore it. The area was badly bombed in 1942 and the court around the house was destroyed. The house was restored in 1954.

The Great Hall, Flower Pot Yard (Oak Street). (Photograph by author)

FLOWER'S COURT
13 Wensum Street. *Hunt's Directory* of 1850 lists Jonathan Flower, linen draper, at Wensum Street.

FORD'S YARD
North side of Ten Bell Lane between 6 and 14. The yard was lost by 1890.

FOSTER'S YARD
River Lane, exact location unknown.

FOULGAR'S (or FOULGER'S) YARD
165–167 Ber Street. *White's Directory* of 1883 lists Horatio

Foulger, joiner and owner of a 'general shop', there. The yard was lost 1935–41.

FOULGER'S OPENING
176–178 Ber Street – see Foulgar's Yard, Ber Street. Chester Place is listed as running off Foulger's Opening.

FOUNDRY COURT
Runs from Prince of Wales Road to the west side of Recorder Road and is an early 21st-century development. It takes its name from the foundry that once stood opposite, by the bridge.

FOUNDRY YARD
South side of Thorn Lane. The yard was lost by 1925.

FOUNTAIN YARD
47–49 Botolph Street, was named after the Fountain pub, which is recorded at Botolph Street in 1830 and 1845. It was known as Tillett's Yard in 1883. The yard was lost in the mid to late 1960s for the Anglia Square development.

FOUNTAIN YARD
85–87 St Benedict's Street, was named after the Fountain pub, which is recorded at 89 St Benedict's Street from 1760. The pub was destroyed during an air raid in April 1942 and closed.

FOX & GOOSE YARD
46 St Martin's Lane, took its name from the Fox & Goose pub.

FOX & HOUNDS YARD
149–153 Ber Street, was named after the Fox & Hounds pub, which is recorded at 153 Ber Street from 1763. Little Fox & Hounds Yard was next door at 155–157 Ber Street. The pub closed in 1967 and the yard was lost.

FOX'S COURT
Runs from 76 St Giles' Street to Chapelfield. *Robson's Commercial Directory* of 1839 lists Isaac Fox as the landlord of the Queen's Head, which is listed at 90 St Giles' Street from 1760 and closed in 1982.

FOX'S YARD
Cowgate, exact location unknown. *Robson's Commercial Directory* of 1839 lists William Fox, baker, at Cowgate Street.

FOY'S or FOYSON'S YARD
4 Rose Lane. *White's Directory* of 1883 and *Kelly's Directory* of 1912 list Robert Burrage Foyson, joiner, builder and carpenter, at 4 Rose Lane. The yard was lost by 1964.

FRANKLIN'S COURT
North side of All Saints' Green. There by 1883, lost by 1890.

FREEMAN'S BUILDINGS
17 Thorn Lane. *Kelly's Directory* of 1912 lists John Freeman, cabinet maker. The buildings were lost by 1960.

FREEMAN'S COURT
29–31 St Giles' Street, was known as Cannell's Court in 1883. *Harrod & Co's Directory* of 1877 lists James Freeman, baker, at 15 St Giles' Street.

FREMOULT'S YARD
St George's Street, exact location unknown. *Chase's Directory* of 1783 lists Samuel Fremoult, beer brewer, at St George's Bridge Street, as well as Samuel Fremoult jnr, attorney at law. Fremoult jnr was the clerk to the Corporation of Guardians of the Poor in 1783.

FREESTONE YARD
St Benedict's Street, exact location unknown.

FRENCH'S YARD
7 Fishergate. *Chase's Directory* of 1783 lists John French, soap boiler, at 7 Fishgate (aka Fishergate). The business (as Andrews & French) was burned down in 1858 (see Fishergate).

FRIAR'S LANE
King Street, exact location unknown. It may have been near Greyfriars, named after the friary there, or near St Ann's Lane, named after the priory there. The yard was listed in *White's Directory* of 1854 but does not appear after then.

FRIAR'S QUAY
Is a modern development that runs from the south side of Colegate; Corncutters Close runs from it.

FRIAR'S YARD
Former name of Fryer's Yard, Bull Close.

FROMANTEEL'S COURT
13 Chapelfield Lane (aka Theatre Street). *Chase's Directory* of 1783 lists Daniel Fromanteel jnr, merchant, at 13 Chapelfield Lane; Revd Daniel Fromanteel is listed at the same court. The court was lost by 1830.

FRYER'S YARD
22–24 Bull Close, was formerly known as Friar's Yard. The yard was lost 1935–41.

FUGGLE'S YARD
102 King Street, is part of King's Quarter, a new

4

development on the site of the old Morgan's Brewery. The name is linked with brewing – fuggle is a variety of hop.

FULLER'S HOLE
Oak Street, was the name given to the location around Coslany Gate. It took its name from Henry Fuller, mayor in 1544, who had a house there. *Pigot's Directory* of 1830 lists William Ellis, maltster, there. It appears to have been lost by 1883.

FULLER'S OLD LANE
Charing Cross, exact location unknown. *Pigot's Directory* of 1830 lists William Barnes, whitesmith, there; the yard was lost by 1839.

FYE BRIDGE STREET
Fye Bridge Street runs from the end of Wensum Street to the beginning of Magdalen Street (i.e. between the bridge and St Clement's Church). According to Sandred and Lingström, the name of Fye Bridge Street originally applied to the whole of Wensum Street and Magdalen Street as well. The street takes its name from Fye Bridge, which has been mentioned in the city records as 'Fibrigge' as far back as 1153.

Streets off Fye Bridge Street
East:
Fishergate (5–7)
Jack of Newbury Yard (17–19)
Peak's Court*

West:
Mollett's Yard (also known as Mollett's Staith
St Clement's Alley

Buildings on Fye Bridge Street
Fye Bridge is thought to be the oldest location for a bridge in the city. In 1570 the stone bridge was washed away in a flood. It was rebuilt in 1573 and repaired in 1756. It was replaced by a cast-iron bridge in 1829, built to the design of Francis Stone. During a draining scheme in 1896, archaeologists discovered wooden piles and Saxon pottery around the bridge. With the increase in traffic in the early 20th century, a wider bridge was needed; the current bridge was built in 1932 and opened in July 1933. Fye Bridge was also the site of the city's 'cucking stool' or ducking school. The last person recorded as ducked there was Margaret Grove, a 'common scold', who was sentenced in 1597 to be carried there 'with a basin rung before her' and ducked three times.

King of Hearts, 11–15 Fye Bridge Street, was originally a house in the 16th century but was split into shops in the 18th-century. The house was restored in 1990 by John Sennitt.

GAFFER'S YARD
20–22 St Benedict's Street, was formerly Gaffer's Court and Crow's Yard.

GAOL (or GOAL) HILL
Runs along the side of the Guildhall next to the market place, from St Peter's Street to Gentleman's Walk. It took its name from when the Guildhall was used as a prison. Livingstone's Court and Terrace ran off it in the mid-1800s.

GARDEN BACK LANE
27–31 Thorn Lane, ran along the back of Garden Street. See Garden Street for the derivation of the name.

GARDEN PLACE
155–157 Magdalen Street, was also the site of the Red Lion Yard.

GARDEN STREET
Runs from 31–33 Thorn Lane, originally to 18–20 Horns Lane, but is now a cul-de-sac. It took its name from the hillside between Ber Street and King Street, which consisted of gardens until the 19th century. Crusoe Street ran from here to St Julian Street. It was lost during the 1960s as part of the slum clearances.

GATEHOUSE YARD
181 Ber Street. The yard was lost 1935–41.

GAY'S YARD
48–50 Oak Street, was listed as Bream's Yard before 1883. The yard was lost by 1925.

GAYS' YARD
St Benedict's Street, exact location unknown.

GENERAL WINDHAM YARD
122–124 Cowgate, was named after the General Windham pub, which is recorded at 122 Cowgate from 1858. It closed in 1908, and the yard was lost by 1941.

GENT'S YARD OR UPPER YARD
Formerly Abbs' Court. 1–5 Coslany Street. *White's Directory* of 1845 lists George Gent, Fishmonger, at Coslany Street. The yard was lost by 1925.

GENTLEMAN'S WALK
Gentleman's Walk, which runs along the east side of the Market Place, took its name from the fact that gentlemen

Gentleman's Walk.
(Photograph courtesy of
Norwich City Council)

walked and talked there on market day. It was originally known as Nether Rowe.

Streets off Gentleman's Walk
Bear Yard (near 13)

Events at Gentleman's Walk
On 8 November 1886 fishmonger Arthur Riches stabbed his wife Matilda to death on Gentleman's Walk 'in full view of passers by'. She'd left him two weeks before, and, when he saw her wearing earrings he thought another man had bought her, he pulled out a knife and stabbed her in the throat. She got away but he attacked her again and said 'I will hang for you'. He was tried, found guilty and sentenced to death, though the sentence was later commuted to penal servitude for life because he had been 'greatly provoked' – even his father-in-law had told him not to bother with Matilda. Riches was sent to Parkhurst Prison on the Isle of Wight and died there in April 1898.

On 29 January 1904 there was another tragedy on the walk when Mrs Charlotte Thompson of Coburg Street was killed opposite the Maypole Dairy Company. A large van going along the pathway knocked a lamp-post down, which hit Charlotte on the back of the neck. She died, leaving four kids. The distraught driver said he'd tried to get out of the way of a tram and his wheels skidded, sending him into the lamp post.

On a happier note for pedestrians, traffic was finally banned from Gentleman's Walk at the end of the 1980s.

GEORGE THE FOURTH YARD
76–78 Ber Street, was named after the George IV pub, which is recorded at 72 Ber Street from 1830. The pub was damaged during an air raid in April 1942, was closed in 1962 and was demolished for road widening. The yard was lost at the same time.

GEORGE YARD
92 Barrack Street, was named after the George pub, which is recorded at 90 Barrack Street from 1760. The pub was known as the George and Dragon in 1822 and closed in 1869. In the late 1800s the yard was briefly known as Griffin yard (clearly from the dragon!). The yard was lost 1935–41.

GEORGE YARD
64 St Stephen's Street, was named after the George inn, which is recorded at 66 St Stephen's Street from 1763. The yard may have been known as the King George Yard at one point. The pub closed in 1907. The yard was lost 1960–64.

GERRARD'S YARD
West side of Bull Close, exact location unknown. The yard was lost 1883–90.

GIBSON'S COURT
69 Pitt Street. *Kelly's Directory* of 1900 lists Mrs Elizabeth Gibson, china and glass dealer, at Pitt Street. The yard was lost 1925–64.

GILBERT'S YARD
48–52 Pitt Street. *White's Directory* of 1845 lists Elizabeth Gilbert, milliner, at Pitt Street. The yard was lost by 1947.

GILDENCROFT LANE AND ROW
Run from St Augustine's Church Row to Chatham Street; the name came from 'guild brethren's croft'. According to

Sandred and Lingström, Gildencroft was originally an open space between Jenkins Lane and the City Wall.

GILDENGATE
Former name for St George's Street.

GILLINGS' YARD
131–133 Magdalen Street, was originally known Gillings' Yard, became Jennings' Yard by 1883, then switched back to Gillings' Yard in 1890. *Pigot's Directory* of 1830 lists Edmund Gillings, gardener and seedsman, at Magdalen Street.

GLADSTONE PLACE
43–45 Mariner's Lane.

GLOBE LANE
Ran from 21 Cattle Market Street to Scoles Green until the 1960s. It was named after the Globe pub, which is recorded at 17 Globe Lane from 1822. The pub was originally called the Globe and Seven Stars and was built on the site of the Hell Cellar pub. It was closed in 1905 when it was reported as being the 'haunt of prostitutes and thieves'. The lane itself was lost between 1965–70 when Rouen Road was built.

GLOBE YARD
37–41 Botolph Street, was named after the Globe pub, which is recorded at 37 Botolph Street from around 1700. It was known as the Old Globe from 1836–54 and closed in 1908. The yard was lost in the mid to late 1960s for the Anglia Square development.

GLOBE YARD
After 15 Scoles Green, took its name from the Globe pub (see Globe Lane).

GLOUCESTER PLACE
St Catherine's Plain, exact location unknown.

GOAT YARD
96–102 Oak Street. *Robson's Commercial Directory* of 1839 lists William Goat, shopkeeper, at Coslany Street (aka Oak Street before 1890). The yard was lost 1935–41.

GOLDEN BALL STREET
Golden Ball Street runs from the junction of Ber Street and All Saints Green to the junction of Cattle Market Street and Farmers Avenue. The street takes its name from the Golden Ball pub, which is recorded at the Castle Ditches in 1783; the address eventually changed to 18 Golden Ball St (on the corner of Cattle Market Street and Rising Sun Lane) in 1845. The pub closed in 1961.

Streets off Golden Ball Street
On the east side, the street has included:
Manning's Yard (3–5)*
Dawson's Yard (near 7)*
Woolpack Yard and Thoroughfare (9)
Rising Sun Lane (21)*

On the west side, the street has included:
Grout's Thoroughfare (before 14)

Other streets whose exact locations could not be placed include:
Lamb's Court*
Buffcoat Lane*

People linked with Golden Ball Street
John Angell, mayor in 1830, lived at Golden Ball Street.

GOLDEN CAN YARD
15 St Andrew's Street, was named after the Golden Can pub, which is recorded at 15 St Andrew's Street from 1806 and closed in 1890, when the building and yard were demolished.

GOLDEN CROSS YARD
Charing Cross, exact location unknown, ran to St Gregory's Lower Church Alley. The yard was named after the Golden Cross pub, which is recorded at Charing Cross from 1830; the pub closed in 1873 and the yard was lost.

GOLDEN DOG LANE
Runs from 35 Calvert Street to 32–34 Magdalen Street. It was named after the Golden Dog pub, which is recorded at

Golden Dog Lane. (Photograph by author)

34 Magdalen Street from 1850 (although the pub was believed to date from the 17th century, and there are references to Golden Dog Lane as far back as 1626). It was known as Brent Lane in the 16th century, after the Church of St Mary the Brent, which stood at the corner of Golden Dog Lane and Magdalen Street. Grace Jarrold Court runs off the street.

GOLDEN LION YARD
15 St John Maddermarket, was named after the Golden Lion pub, which is recorded at 15 St John Street (or Maddermarket) from 1789. The pub was damaged during an air raid in August 1942 and closed in 1965; the yard was also lost.

GOLDSWORTH'S BUILDINGS
79 Bishopgate, is the site of the Red Lion pub (see also Green Dragon Yard). *White's Directory* of 1883 lists Edmund Goldsworth, builder, at Bishopgate.

GOOCH'S YARD
17–19 Charing Cross. *Pigot's Directory* of 1830 lists Noah Gooch, shopkeeper, in Charing Cross. The yard was lost during street widening in the 1970s.

GOODMAN'S YARD
Former name for Barwell's Court, 10 St Stephen's Street. *Robson's Commercial Directory* of 1839 lists George Goodman, beer retailer, at St Stephen's Back Street.

GOODRUM'S YARD
9–13 Bishopgate. *Pigot's Directory* of 1830 lists John Goodrum, shopkeeper, nearby at St Martin at Palace Plain. The yard was lost 1935–41.

GOSS YARD
8 Elm Hill, former name for The Monastery. It took its name from the 18th-century dyer Matthew Goss, who in 1797 presented the city with the Mayor's gold chain for the city regalia. *Chase's Directory* of 1783 lists John Goss, also a dyer, at 3 Elm Hill.

GOWING'S PASSAGE
St Stephen's Street, exact location unknown. *Robson's Commercial Directory* of 1839 lists Mr Gowing, surgeon, at St Stephen's Street. The yard was lost by 1883.

GRACE JARROLD COURT
Runs from Golden Dog Lane.

GRAHAM'S COURT
9–11 St Peter's Street, was also known as Bennett's Court.

Peck's Directory of 1802 lists George Graham, glover, at 10 Upper Market (later St Peter's Street).

GRANBY YARD
23 Bishopgate, was named after the Marquis of Granby pub, which is recorded at 23 Bishopsgate from 1806. At 50sq ft, the Marquis of Granby was one of the smallest pubs in Norwich! The pub was closed in 1966 and demolished; the yard was also lost then.

GRAPES HILL
Runs from Grapes Hill to Chapelfield Road. Lincoln's Yard ran off it at number 19. Grapes Hill was originally known as St Giles Hill but took its modern name from The Grapes Hotel, which is recorded at St Giles' Gate from 1830. The Grapes Hotel was destroyed by fire in 1942; it was rebuilt and became known as Sideeky's from 1985–87 and as the Last Resort in 1988–89. It closed in 1989. Grapes Hill is now part of the inner ring road; most of the houses were demolished in the 1960s, and the new inner ring road opened in 1971.

The pre-Raphaelite painter Frederick Sandys was born at 19 St Giles Hill in 1829; he was educated at St John Maddermarket school, Norwich School and the Norwich School of Design.

GRAPES' YARD
70 Colegate, was named after the Grapes pub, which is recorded at number 72 Colegate from 1830. The pub closed in 1908 and the yard was lost.

GRAY'S YARD
St Benedict's Street, exact location unknown. *White's Directory* of 1845 lists Mary Ann Gray, pork butcher, at St Benedict's Street.

GREAT WHITE LION YARD
104–106 St Benedict's Street, was named after the White Lion pub, which is recorded at 106 St Benedict's Street from 1760. The pub was damaged during an air raid in April 1942; it reopened in 1945 but closed by 1959 and the yard was lost with it.

GREAT YARD
World's End Lane, exact location unknown. It appears to be lost some time between 1854–83, so it may have been in the area where the gas works were built in 1858.

GREEN DRAGON YARD
79 Bishopgate, was named after the Green Dragon pub, which is recorded at 79 Bishopgate from 1760. It was rebuilt in 1874 and changed its name to the Red Lion. The Red

Lion was damaged during an air raid in April 1942 but still exists today.

GREEN MAN YARD

131 King Street, was named after the Green Man pub, which is recorded at 131 King Street from 1760. The pub was closed in 1921 and demolished in 1937, along with its yard.

GREEN YARD

96–98 Barrack Street, may have taken its name from the George pub (as the George & Dragon) at 90 Barrack Street, or from the Green Lion at 26 Cowgate from 1760–1807 (in those days, Cowgate ran to Barrack Street). The yard was lost 1935–41.

GREEN (OR GREEN'S) LANE

62–64 Calvert Street to 89–91 St George's Street. William Crotch, the organist, was born here in 1775. His father Michael was a carpenter and self-taught musician, but Crotch was a prodigy – he was able to play 'God Save the King' at the age of two, and added the bass accompaniment two days later! Crotch played the cathedral organ at the age of two and a half, and played before George III at the age of three – half the age that Mozart was when he played for the king. Crotch had perfect pitch and studied at Cambridge from the age of 11. He was appointed the Professor of Music at St John's College at the age of 22; his first duty was to assess his own doctorate (which, of course, he passed). He taught for 50 years at Oxford and was also the first principal of the Royal Academy of Music in 1822, though apparently he was a very difficult character, very dogmatic and narrow, perhaps as a result of his early fame. He's remembered now for composing the Westminster chimes for Big Ben, based on a figure from Handel's *Messiah*, and his *Palestine* is one of the few surviving oratorios by an English composer.

GREEN'S COURT OR YARD

8–10 St Benedict's Street. *Harrod & Co's Directory* of 1877 lists Elizabeth and Ann Green, drapers and hosiers, and Robert Green, basket maker, at St Benedict's Street. The yard was lost 1890–96. There was another Green's Yard on the street at 40–42 (see Grigg's Yard).

GREENLAND FISHERY

141 King Street. *Chase's Directory* of 1783 lists T. Tompson, (sic) corn and coal merchant, there, but the yard was gone by 1830.

GREENLAND FISHERY YARD

30–32 Oak Street (Coslany Street before 1890), was named after the Greenland Fishery pub, which is recorded at 30 Oak Street from 1760. The pub closed in 1918 and the yard was lost with it.

GREYFRIARS

Runs from 25–27 King Street to 4 Rose Lane; at the Rose Lane end it's known as Greyfriars' Road. It was known as Greyfriars' Priory from 1830–54 and took its name from the Grey Friars who came to the city in 1226 and built a church at the site of 44 Prince of Wales Road.

GREYHOUND YARD

102–104 Ber Street, was named after the Greyhound pub, which is recorded at 102 Ber Street from 1830. The pub had a bowling green and a garden and was closed by 1871. In November 1846 the first recorded canary show in Norwich was here, with 300 specimens exhibited. The yard was lost before 1960, when King's metal merchants had a building on the site.

GRIFFIN'S COURT

114 Barrack Street, was named after the Griffin pub, which is recorded at 86 Barrack Street from 1760. The pub was closed in 1930 and the yard was lost by 1925.

GRIFFIN LANE

Just before the end of St Benedict's Street. It was also known as Griffin's Yard or Court at the end of the 19th century. The lane was lost during air raids in World War Two.

GRIFFIN YARD OR LANE

1 Upper King Street, was named after the Griffin pub, which is recorded at 1 Upper King Street from 1760. The pub was closed in 1898 and demolished. The yard and lane have not been referenced since 1830.

GRIGG'S YARD

40–42 St Benedict's Street. *Pigot's Directory* of 1830 lists Elizabeth Griggs, straw hat maker, and William Grigg, tailor, at St Benedict's Street. The yard became known as Green's Yard by 1935 and was lost 1960–64.

GRIMES' YARD

22–24 Botolph Street. *White's Directory* of 1854 lists Thomas Grimes, baker, at Botolph Street. The yard was lost 1947–60.

GRIMMER'S COURT

6–8 St Andrew's Street. *White's Directory* of 1883 lists Samuel Grimmer & Co, wine and spirit merchants, near here. The yard was lost some time after 1975.

GRIMMER'S YARD

159–167 Ber Street. *White's Directory* of 1854 lists William Grimmer, gentleman, at Ber Street. The yard was lost 1890–96.

GROUT'S COURT

Timberhill, exact location unknown; it was probably in or near Grout's Thoroughfare.

GROUT'S THOROUGHFARE or PASSAGE

Runs from 14 Golden Ball Street to 24–26 Timberhill. It may be named after George Grout, who was unable to become sheriff in 1828 because he wasn't a freeman. There was a school there in 1845.

GUILD YARD

Former name for Burrell's Yard, Colegate. There was a pub called the Guild on Colegate some time before 1811. The yard was lost 1935–41.

GUILDHALL HILL

Guildhall Hill runs along the north edge of the market place, between the junction of St Giles' Street and St Peter's Street and the junction of Gentleman's Walk with Exchange Street and London Street. It takes its name from the guildhall.

Streets off Guildhall Hill
See Market Place.

Buildings on Guildhall Hill
According to Blomefield, the city gaol used to be the Lamb inn; this was later the site of Chamberlin's Court. The Lamb was bought by St George's Company in Henry VII's time and used as their guildhall. The gaol was used as the city gaol until August 1826, when the prisoners were moved to the new gaol at St Giles' Gates.

The guildhall was built 1407–13 by masons John and Thomas Marwe, with superintendents John Danyel and Robert Brayser. The original site had the Toll Booth, a small thatched building where the market tolls were collected. In 1407 the city had a warrant to press all carpenters, carters and workmen to built the new guildhall; the constable could make them work from 5am to 8pm. The windows were glazed in 1453; in 1512 part of the roof fell in, and Augustine Steward reconstructed it in 1534–37 at a cost of £208. The cellars were used as a prison until 1597; the prison moved to the Lamb from 1597 until 1826, then to the new city gaol at St Giles' Gates until 1881 (St John's Roman Catholic Cathedral was built on the site). One of the guildhall prison's most famous inhabitants was Thomas Bilney (see page 82). In 1635 the guildhall was almost demolished when saltpetre diggers went down too far; in

Guildhall. (Photograph courtesy of Norwich City Council)

1660, the cellar became a cloth hall. The clock turret was added in 1850, a gift from mayor Henry Woodcock. More renovations came in 1857 when the doorway from the house of a Tudor Goldsmith, John Bassingham, was taken from 57–59 London Street and placed in the south-west corner of the guildhall. Civic affairs were dealt with at the guildhall until 1938, when City Hall was opened.

Guildhall vaults. (Photograph courtesy of Norwich City Council)

People linked with Guildhall Hill

Thomas Bilney, the first Protestant martyr, was ordained as a priest in 1519. He was arrested in London in 1527 for preaching against idolatry; in 1531 he came to Norwich and gave a copy of Tyndale's English translation of the New Testament to an anchoress at the Dominican friary. He was arrested for heresy and kept in the guildhall; according to John Foxe, the night before his execution, Bilney held his hand in the flame of a candle to try his courage before death. He was burnt at the stake in the Lollard's Pit on 19 August 1531.

Events at Guildhall Hill

Several people tried to escape from the city gaol – and some of them succeeded! On 3 March 1770 the *Norwich Mercury* reports that Mary Clements (alias Oakes) broke out of the city gaol. Somehow, she managed to procure some clothes

that were rather better than her usual dress; she stuffed her old clothes with straw and persuaded the turnkey that she was a visitor. Being duped by her fine clothes, he actually let her out! A more desperate attempt was made in November 1808 when 35-year-old Mary Hudson made a hole through the wall – even though it was 2ft thick! She hid the bricks beneath her bed and the loose rubbish in her pillow, then crawled out into the street, taking her six-month-old baby with her. There is no record of her being recaptured.

Rather more sadly, on September 1858 Mountjoy the Pedestrian – who had brought pleasure to thousands with his 'walking feats' at the city pleasure gardens – tried to strangle himself with his pocket handkerchief when he was put in the guildhall gaol. The problem? He'd been doing a lot of pedestrian feats. However, he'd left his wife and family 'chargeable on the the fund of the St Pancras Union'. They were rather less than impressed with his behaviour – seeking fame above supporting his family – and put him in gaol.

GUN LANE

Former name of William Booth Street. It was known as Gun Lane until the 19th century, and then took its name from the Gun pub, which was listed at the corner of the lane and Gaol Hill from the 17th century. The *Norwich Mercury* reported in April 1774 that Mrs Smith's house on Gun Lane had been broken into and her linen and clothes stolen.

GUN WHARF

52–58 St George's Street.

GUNHOUSE YARD – see Gun Lane.

GUNN'S COURT

82a–84 St Giles' Street. *Kelly's Directory* of 1912 lists Thomas Edward Gunn, naturalist, at 84 St Giles' Street.

GURNEY'S COURT

31 Magdalen Street, was named after the Gurney family. Elizabeth Fry (née Gurney) was born there in 1780; she became a Quaker minister and campaigned for better conditions for female prisoners and those being transported. Writer Harriet Martineau was also born there in 1802 (although her family moved across the street to number 24 shortly afterwards). She was born without the senses of taste and smell and was deaf by the age of 18 – meaning that she couldn't become a teacher. She began to write in secret for a Unitarian publication called the *Monthly Repository*, and wrote her first book, *Illustrations of Political Economy*. She moved to London in 1832, spent some time in America, and returned to London where she became the first female journalist to join a large London

daily newspaper, the *Daily News*, in 1852. Maria Weston Chapman, who edited Martineau's *Autobiography*, said that Harriet's library of 2–3,000 books was 'probably the best women's library extant' and covered subjects such as art, biography, education, geography, history, political economy and theology as well as general literature.

GYNNE'S YARD

Red Lion Lane (aka Red Lion Street). *Chase's Directory* of 1783 lists George Gynne jnr, 'upholder', at 17 Red Lion Lane. The yard was lost by 1830.

HACON'S YARD

92 Magdalen Street. *Pigot's Directory* of 1830 lists James Hacon, glover and breeches maker, at Magdalen Street. *Chase's Directory* of 1783 lists Charles Hacon, schoolmaster, at 91 Magdalen Street. The yard was lost by 1970.

HALES' COURT

Runs between Cleveland Road, 72–74 St Giles' Street and Chapel Field North. *White's Directory* of 1845 lists Mrs Barbara Hales as a resident nearby at 55 St Giles' Street.

HALF MOON COURT

38–39 Market Place, was named after the Half Moon pub, which is recorded at 38 Market Place from 1761 and closed in 1923.

HALF MOON YARD

239 King Street, was named after the Half Moon pub, which is recorded at 240 King Street from 1760 and closed in 1886. The yard was lost by 1965; at the time of writing, early 2005, the area is being redeveloped into flats.

HALF MOON YARD

Back of the Inns (Castle Ditches), was named after the Half Moon pub, which is recorded at the Castle Ditches from 1760 and became the Cattle Market inn in 1876.

HALL'S YARD

12–14 Calvert Street. *Pigot's Directory* of 1830 lists William Hall, pawnbroker, nearby at St George's Street. The yard is now known as Peter's Court.

HALL'S YARD

Possibly also known as Holl's Yard, 127 Oak Street, takes its name from the Great Hall next door in Flower Pot Yard. The yard was lost during air raids in World War Two.

HAMPSHIRE HOG YARD

St Swithin's Alley, was named after the Hampshire Hog pub, listed at St Swithin's Alley from 1822. The pub – a cottage since the pub closed in 1912 – is one of the five original thatched houses left in the city after the fires of 1507. The Hampshire Hog was the last inn in the city where the game of logats was played – similar to bowls, but small poles were used instead of balls. John 'Licker' Pratt, the landlord, beat Jem Mace (the landlord of the Swan inn at Swan Lane) in a two-hour bare-knuckle fight at Drayton.

The Hampshire Hog. (Photograph by author)

HANNANT'S or HANNENT'S YARD

24–26 St Benedict's Street. *White's Directory* of 1833 lists Robert G. Hannent, butcher, in St Benedict's Street.

HANSARD LANE

Formerly Water Lane, 42 Fishergate, was named after printer Luke Hansard, who was born in Norwich in 1752. Hansard worked for Stephen White at the sign of the Bible & Crown in Magdalen Street and learned typesetting, layout, presswork and engraving. He went to London and became a master printer; by 1810 he had his own business and printed the *Journals of the House of Commons*. When he died he was worth £80,000 – not bad for a printer who'd gone to London with only a guinea! The Stationery Office took over his business in 1889, and the name Hansard was officially used for Parliamentary reports from 1943.

HARE'S YARD

Rosemary Lane, exact location unknown. The yard was lost by 1925.

HARPER'S YARD

King Street, exact location unknown.

HARPLEY'S YARD

Sometimes listed as Hartley's Yard, 63 Cowgate. *White's Directory* of 1854 lists Thomas Harpley, hairdresser, at Cowgate. The yard was lost 1935–41.

HARRISON'S COURT

St Giles' Street, exact location unknown. *Robson's*

Commercial Directory of 1839 lists T.T. Harrison, saddler, at St Giles' Street.

HARRISON'S YARD

Castle Meadow, exact location unknown. *Harrod & Co's Directory* of 1877 lists Mrs Jane Harris at the County Arms inn in Castle Meadow. The yard is referenced in 1845 and 1854 but was lost by 1883.

HART'S YARD

19 Botolph Street. *Peck's Directory* of 1802 lists Philip Hart, carpenter, at 1 Botolph Street. The yard was lost in the mid to late 1960s for the Anglia Square development.

HARTLEY'S YARD

135–137 Magdalen Street, was formerly White Lion Yard.

HARVEY'S YARD

21 Peacock Street. *White's Directory* of 1883 lists Samuel Harvey as a resident there. The yard was lost 1935–41.

HAWKES' YARD

79–81 Oak Street. *Pigot's Directory* of 1830 lists Robert Hawkes, fellmonger (i.e. a dealer in sheepskins, who separated the wool from the pelt), near here. The yard was lost 1935–41.

HAY HILL

Haymarket, took its name from the hay once sold here.

HAYES' COURT

Former name for May's Court, 83–85 St Giles' Street.

HAYMARKET

The Haymarket runs from Brigg Street to the junction of White Lion Street and 31 Gentleman's Walk. The name came from the site of the hay market. According to Blomefield, the New Synagogue and Schools of the Jews were based around here; the entrance from Haymarket was through Star Yard. In 1286 Edward I banished the Jews; the synagogue was destroyed and the area burned down.

Streets off the Haymarket

East:
Lamb Yard
Star Yard (8–9)*
Orford Place (formerly Little Orford Street) and Brigg Street (after 11)
William Booth Street (formerly Gun Lane, then Church Street) (18)*

West:
Weaver's Lane (runs to Pudding Lane)
Hay Hill
St Peter's Street (20)

Exact location unknown:
Museum Court

Buildings on the Haymarket

Curat's House – this was the mansion of former sheriff John Curat; it was damaged by fire in 1962, then restored.

The Picture House – according to cinema historian Stephen Peart, this cinema opened in 1911 in the building of the former London and Provincial Bank. It was enlarged in 1921 and 10 years later the first cinema organ in the city was installed there. It changed its name to the Gaumont in 1955 and closed in 1959. The building was demolished and became Peter Robinson (now Top Shop).

Norfolk and Norwich Museum moved here from St Andrew's Street in 1825; it moved again in 1894 to the castle.

There used to be a pub called the White Horse at 20 Old Haymarket; it was always used by the hangman, Mr Calcraft. The White Horse was closed in 1897 and was demolished.

People linked with the Haymarket

Sir Thomas Browne was a physician, philosopher and antiquarian; his first book was *Religio Medici*. He settled in Norwich at the age of 32, lived in Upper King Street from 1643–49, then moved to a house on the corner of Orford Place and the Haymarket where he stayed until his death in 1682. He also leased a meadow just off The Close, and the diarist Evelyn said Browne's garden was 'a cabinet of rarities'. Browne was knighted by Charles II at St Andrew's Hall in September 1671. He died on his 77th birthday and was buried in St Peter Mancroft. While another grave was being prepared in September 1840, his coffin was damaged; the newspaper reported that his skeleton was 'in good preservation and the hair of the beard very profuse', and added that 'the brain was considerable in quantity, but changed to a state of adipocere resembling ointment of a dark brown hue'. The sexton removed Browne's skull and sold it to a doctor, who gave it to the Norfolk and Norwich Hospital; it wasn't re-interred until 1922. Browne's monument on Hay Hill was by Henry Pegram in 1905.

John Buckle, mayor in 1793, was an ironmonger, tobacconist and colourman; his business was at 6 Haymarket, under the sign of the Golden Pipe.

John Croshold, mayor in 1724, lived in Curat House. He was forced to deal with a riot against the South Sea Bubble in December 1720, and William Massey reported that 'Mr

Statue of Sir Thomas Browne. (Photograph by author)

Crosshold was in danger of being stab'd by a virago in discharge of his offices'.

John Curat was the city sheriff during the reign of Henry VIII.

Events at the Haymarket

In 1825 the Norwich Museum opened at a house on the Haymarket.

When the tram tracks were brought into the Haymarket in 1899, the Norfolk & Norwich Savings Bank (built in 1844) was demolished, to avoid a sharp corner for the trams. Sir Thomas Browne's house was demolished at the same time.

In 1972 the city turned the gardens and lawns on the Haymarket into concrete seats with a 'water feature'; the water has long since gone, although Browne's statue is still there.

HAYWARD'S (or HEYWOOD'S) YARD

173 Ber Street. *Robson's Commercial Directory* of 1839 lists C. Hayward, tinman, at Ber Street. The yard was lost 1935–41.

HEALE'S BUILDING

59 Rose Lane. The buildings were lost by 1964.

HEATH ROAD

57–61 Magpie Road.

HELGATE COURT

Westwick Street (between St Margaret's Street and St Lawrence Little Steps) is a modern development, which takes its name from the old city gate on Westwick Street.

HEN & CHICKENS YARD

28 St Mary's Plain, was named after the Hen & Chickens pub at 28 St Mary's Plain from 1760 and closed in 1912. By 1925 the yard was under the site of Sexton's boot factory.

HERRING'S YARD

Magdalen Street. *White's Directory* of 1845 lists Robert Herring, gardener and seedsman, at Magdalen Street.

HEWITT'S YARD

103–113 Ber Street. *Hunt's Directory* of 1850 lists George Hewett (sic) at Ber Street. The yard was lost 1970–74.

HILL'S YARD

184 St George's Street. *White's Directory* of 1883 lists Eric Hill, grocer, near here. The yard was lost 1935–41.

HINDE'S YARD

26–30 Botolph Street. *Pigot's Directory* of 1830 lists Ephraim Hinde & son, bombazine & crape manufacturer, near here. The yard may also have been known as Crape Factory Yard. The yard was lost by 1925.

HINDES' YARD

13–15 St Augustine's Street. *Pigot's Directory* of 1830 lists Daniel Hindes, shopkeeper, near here.

HINDES' (or HINDS') YARD

70 St Benedict's Street. *Kelly's Directory* of 1900 lists William Hinds, rope maker, at 70 St Benedict's Street.

HIPPER'S YARD
Three King Lane, exact location unknown. *White's Directory* of 1854 lists Mary Ann Hipper and Co, drapers, nearby at St Benedict's Street.

HOBROUGH LANE
133–135 King Street. *Hunt's Directory* of 1850 lists Henry Hobrough, coal merchant, at King Street. 'The Ferry' is also listed here from 1920–25.

HODDS' YARD
west side of Ber Street, exact location unknown. *Robson's Commercial Directory* of 1839 lists Richard Hodds, cheesemonger and grocer, at Ber Street.

HODD'S YARD
46–48 Botolph Street. The yard was lost in the mid to late 1960s for the Anglia Square development.

HOLE IN THE WALL LANE
7 Bedford Street, was the former name of School Lane. It took its name from the Hole in the Wall pub, listed there from 1760. The pub was built into the chancel of the disused Church of St Crouch (demolished in 1515, except for the chancel). The pub closed in 1825 and was demolished. (See School Lane.)

HOLKHAM STREET
Castle Ditches (Castle Meadow), exact location unknown, took its name from the Holkham Arms pub, which was recorded there from 1819 and closed in 1850. It was also known as Holkham Lane in 1854, and there was a school there in 1830. The street was lost by 1883.

HOLL'S YARD
127 Oak Street; see Hall's Yard. The yard was lost during air raids in World War Two.

HOLLAND COURT
The Close, was built in 1961–64. The first building there was the Diocesan office; when further buildings were added, it took the name 'court'. It was named after the Right Reverend Herbert St. Barbe Holland, who was the Dean of Norwich from 1946–52; he revived the Friends of the Cathedral to help raise funds and abolished the 6d admission fee to the east end of the cathedral so that the people of the city could enjoy it and feel closer to the church.

HOLMES' YARD/COURT
58 Westwick Street. *Kelly's Directory* of 1912 lists Thomas William Holmes, newsagent, at 30 Westwick Street. The yard was lost by 1935–41.

HOLME STREET
Former name for Bishopgate.

HOLTOR LANE
Former name for Dove Street.

HOOD'S BUILDINGS
23 Market Lane. *White's Directory* of 1854 lists Jonathan Hood, victualler and landlord of the Globe, nearby at Globe Lane. (See Globe Lane for information about the Globe pub.)

HOOK'S WALK
The Close, was named after the Very Revd Norman Hook, who was Dean of Norwich from 1956–69.

HOOK'S (or CROOK'S) YARD
53–55 Colegate. *White's Directory* of 1883 lists Samuel B. Hook, tailor, at Colegate. *Kelly's Directory* of 1900 lists Mrs Hook at 51 Colegate. The yard was lost 1935–41.

HOSPITAL LANE
Former name for Bishopgate.

HOSPITAL YARD
Bishopgate, is referenced in *Chase's Directory* of 1783; the master of the Great Hospital lived there. The yard was lost by 1830 – presumably seen as part of the hospital grounds.

HORNS LANE
Horns Lane ran originally from 68–70 Ber Street to 140–142 King Street; now it ends in a cul-de-sac before it reaches King Street. The Jewish community once had a burial ground on the slope between Horns Lane and Mariner's Lane. Horns Lane was Skeygate in the 13th century (which Sandred and Lingström suggest could mean 'the road on the ridge'), then became St Bartilmew's Lane in the 16th century after St Bartholomew's Church. According to Kirkpatrick it took the name of Hors Lane from a pub sign on Conesford Street (King Street).

Streets off Horns Lane:
Pegg's Opening (11–13)
Burleigh Street (formerly William Street) (27–29)*
Royal Oak Court
Prospect Place or Lane (12–14)
Garden Street (no longer reaches Horns Lane) (18–20)
Bartholomew Street*
St Julian Street (30–32)
St Julian's Church Alley
Spencer's Yard*

THE HORSEFAIR
Runs off St Faith's Lane; it was the site of the mediaeval horse fairs. Horsefair Loke leads from here to the Close.

HORSEMAN SQUARE
Timberhill, exact location unknown. The Light Horseman pub is recorded at 20 Westlegate, which may have backed on to Horseman Square. The yard was lost by 1854.

HORTON'S YARD
113–115 Oak Street. *Pigot's Directory* of 1830 lists Thomas Horton, Bombasin dresser, near there. The yard was lost 1935–41.

HOSIER GATE
Former name for London Street.

HOUGHTON'S YARD
65–67 Ber Street. *White's Directory* of 1845 lists Robert Houghton, baker and flour dealer, at Ber Street. The yard was lost 1935–41.

HOUGHTON'S YARD
Recorded at Elm Hill in 1845, exact location unknown. *Harrod & Co's Directory* of 1877 lists Mrs E. Houghton, dyer, at Elm Hill. The yard was lost by 1883.

HOVELL COURT/HOVEL'S YARD
54–56 Pottergate, is now known as Kingsgate Court.

HOWARD TERRACE
27 Sussex Street.

HOWARD'S YARD
42–44 Botolph Street. The yard was lost 1896–1900.

HOWARD'S YARD
14 Bull Close. *White's Directory* of 1890 lists Thomas Howard, grocer. The yard was lost 1890–96.

HOWES BUILDINGS
120–122 Ber Street. *White's Directory* of 1883 lists Mrs Anne Howes & Son, Tallow chandlers, near there. The yard was lost when the area was cleared for redevelopment in the 1960s.

HOWES' COURT
Pottergate, exact location unknown. *Peck's Directory* of 1802 lists Gordon Howes, Esq, resident at 53 Pottergate.

HOWLETT'S COURT
14–16 Botolph Street. *Robson's Commercial Directory* of 1839 lists P. Howlett, horsehair manufacturer, at Botolph Street. The yard was lost in the mid to late 1960s for the Anglia Square development.

HOWMAN'S YARD
75–77 Oak Street. *Harrod & Co's Directory* of 1877 lists George Howman, butcher, at Oak Street. The yard was lost 1970–75.

HUBY'S YARD
104 Magdalen Street. *Chase's Directory* of 1783 lists John Huby, whitesmith, at 104 Magdalen Street; *Pigot's Directory* of 1830 also lists him. The yard was lost by the mid-1800s.

HUGGINS' ROW
St Benedict's Street, exact location unknown. *Peck's Directory* of 1802 lists John Huggins, 'currier', at St Benedict's Street.

HUNGATE (STREET)
Former name for Prince's Street.

HUNT'S YARD
25–27 St Stephen's Street. *White's Directory* of 1883 lists Hunt, son & Co mineral water manufacturers near there. It was formerly King's Head Yard. The area was known as the Archway by 1912 and was lost by 1964.

IMPERIAL ARMS YARD
King Street, was named after the Imperial Arms pub, which is recorded at Upper King Street from 1806 and was closed by 1865; the yard was lost with it.

INDIGO COURT
1 Oak Street, is a development from the late 20th century. Oak Street was the area of the city where the dyers and cloth manufacturers lived, so the court takes its name from the a dark-blue dye.

INFIRMARY SQUARE
57 Magpie Road.

INKERMAN COTTAGES
23 Bishopgate.

ISELIN'S COURT
45 St Giles' Street. *Chase's Directory* of 1783 lists John Iselin, gentleman, at 45 St Giles' Street. The court was lost by 1830.

IVORY SQUARE
Scoles Green, exact location unknown.

JACK OF NEWBURY YARD

17–19 Fye Bridge Street, was named after the Jack of Newbury pub, which is recorded at 19 Fye Bridge Street from 1760 and closed in 1971.

JACK OF NEWBURY YARD

Pottergate, exact location unknown. The yard was lost by 1830.

JARRETT'S YARD

8–10 Bull Close. *Harrod & Co's Directory* of 1877 lists John Jarrett, shopkeeper, at Bull Close. The yard was lost 1935–41.

JAY'S COURT

30–32 Bethel Street. *Robson's Commercial Directory* of 1839 lists Joshua Jay, dyer, at Bethel Street. In April 1933 the building was knocked down to make way for the new city fire station.

JAY'S COURT

Fisher's Lane, first alley. The yard is referenced in *White's Directory* of 1845 but is lost by 1896.

JAY'S SQUARE

15 Rose Lane. *White's Directory* of 1854 lists George Jay, fishmonger, at Upper Market Street and victualler at the Free Trade inn in Rose Lane. The Free Trade tavern is recorded at 41 Rose Lane from 1854; it closed in 1967. Jay's Square was lost 1900–12.

JECKELL'S YARD

179–185 Ber Street, formerly Blacksmith's Yard. *White's Directory* of 1854 lists George Jeckell, cooper, at Ber Street. The yard was lost 1935–41.

JENKIN'S LANE

114–116 Oak Street. Chatham Street runs from here to Sussex Street.

JENNINGS' YARD

131–133 Magdalen Street, former name for Gillings' Yard. *Harrod & Co's Directory* of 1868 lists Thomas Jennings, hat manufacturer, at Magdalen Street.

JERMY'S YARD

Lower Westwick Street, exact location unknown. *Harrod & Co's Directory* of 1868 lists William Jermy, shopkeeper, nearby at St Swithin's Church Alley.

JOHNSON'S YARD

Barrack Street, exact location unknown. *Robson's Commercial Directory* of 1839 lists William Johnson, stationer, at Barrack Street. The yard was lost by 1854.

JOLLY BUTCHERS' YARD

123–125 Ber Street, was named after the Jolly Butchers' pub, which is recorded at 125 Ber Street from 1822. The pub was converted into offices after it was closed in 1989. It was known locally as 'Black Anna's' after the landlady, Antoinette Hannent (née Carrara), who took over the pub in 1935 and held jazz sessions there on Tuesday nights. Anna got her nickname because she dressed in black and said she hadn't worn colours since she was a girl. The US airmen called her 'the English Sophie Tucker' because of her deep, husky voice, and she was known in the city as the queen of jazz. She died in 1976.

Jolly Butchers' Yard. (Photograph by author)

JOLLY SAWYERS YARD

26–28 Fishergate, was named after the Sawyers' Arms pub, which is recorded at 22 Fishergate from 1845 and closed some time before 1877. The yard was lost by 1935.

JOLLY SAWYER'S YARD

Off St Paul's Opening, exact location unknown, took its name from the Jolly Sawyers pub, which is recorded at Norman's Lane, St Paul's Plain, from 1806; the address is also shown as Peacock Street. The pub closed in 1888 and was demolished.

JONES' YARD

Oak Street, exact location unknown. *Robson's Commercial Directory* of 1839 lists J.S. Jones, grocer, at Coslany Street (which may have been in the section renamed as Oak Street after 1890).

JUBILEE YARD

21 Ber Street, was named after the Jubilee inn, which is recorded at 21 Ber Street in 1850 and closed in 1891. The yard was lost 1912–25.

JULIAN'S PLACE
Chapel Field Road, exact location unknown.

KEEL & WHERRY YARD
Just Wherry Yard in 1783. 214–216 King Street, was named after the Keel & Wherry pub, which is recorded at 214 King Street from around 1763. It was closed in 1964 and demolished; the yard was lost with it.

KENSINGTON ROW
St Catherine's Plain, exact location unknown.

KERRISON'S YARD
3–4 Tombland. *Robson's Commercial Directory* of 1839 lists R. Kerrison, agent to Alliance Fire Office, at Tombland.

KEY & CASTLE YARD
105–107 Oak Street, was named after the Key and Castle pub, which is recorded at 105 Oak Street from 1851; the pub closed in 1958. William Sheward, who became the landlord in 1868, murdered his wife in 1851, chopped her into little bits and distributed the pieces around the city. He confessed almost 20 years later and was the first person to be privately executed at the city gaol. The yard is now the site of new flats and houses, though the pub's name has been kept.

KING STREET
King Street runs from the junction of Tombland and Queen Street to Bracondale (where Conesford Gate used to be). It's thought to be the oldest street in Norwich and it's definitely the longest, as it's a mile from the Ethelbert Gate to Bracondale. The name in the 12th century was Cunesford

King Street, viewed from the Millennium Bridge. (Photograph by author)

or Cungesford Street, meaning 'King's Ford'; Conesford was also the name of that particular district (or mediaeval leet) of the city. The name gradually changed to King Street in the 18th century, and the section between Rose Lane and Tombland is sometimes known as Upper King Street. The area became very run down by the mid-1900s, but has undergone a huge amount of regeneration in the early 21st century.

Streets off King Street
East:
Griffin Yard, (1) (Upper) King Street*
Prince of Wales Road
Greyfriars (formerly Greyfriars Priory) (25–27)
Rose Lane (39–41)
Allcock Yard (45)
Murrell's Yard (53–55)
Oby's or Obey's Yard (61–63)
Lifford's Yard*
Lewis' Yard*
Watson's Yard (71–73)*
Bird in Hand Yard (75–77)*
Lane's Yard (83–87)
Mountergate (97–99)
St Ann's Lane, or St Anne's Staithe Lane (109)
Old Barge Yard (123)
Green Man Yard (131)*
Hobrough Lane and The Ferry (133–135)
Websdale Yard (135–139)*
Abbey Lane (137)
Greenland Fishery (141)*
Thompson's Ferry and Wright's Ferry (157–175)*
Wickham's Yard (193–195)*
Norwich Corporation Yard (213)*
Half Moon Yard (241–243)*
Ferry Yard (243–247)
Cellar House Yard (near 249)

West:
Bank Street
Agricultural Hall Plain
Cattle Market Street (48–50)
Three Tuns Court (formerly Tuns Yard) (60)
Watson's Court (64)
Nelson's Monument Yard (66)
Swan Yard (68–70)
St Peter's Court (80)
Old Raven Yard (82–90)
Stepping Lane (90–92)
King's Quarter (92–122)
Thorn Lane (no longer runs to King Street) (100)
Fuggle's yard (102)

Strike's Yard (102–108)*
Watson's Yard (108–110)*
Elephant & Castle Yard (110–112)*
Dray's Yard (116)
St Julian's Alley (120–122)
Horns Lane (no longer reaches King Street) (140–142)
Music House Lane (144 – leads to Rouen Road)
Waterman Yard (142–144)*
Baxter's Court or Yard (152–164)*
Little Ship Yard (166)
Ship Yard (168)
Sherborne Place (now off Rouen Road rather than King Street) (184)
Mariners Lane (formerly after 182)
St Etheldreda's Church Alley
Lincoln's Court (182)*
Rainbow Yard (186)*
Baxter's Garden*
Beaney's Garden*
Rayner's Yard (190–192)*
Argyle Street (no longer runs that far) (204–206)
Keel & Wherry Yard (214–216)
Rouen Road (216)
Southgate Lane (footpath which runs to Bracondale)
Stuart Road (238)
Alan Road (252)
Cinder Ovens Yard (266)*
Winkle's Row (272–274)
Carrow Road (after 280)
Bracondale

Exact location unknown:
Anchor Yard*
Cook's Lane*
Dowson's Yard*
Friar's Lane*
Imperial Arms Yard*
Harper's Yard*
Mission Place*
Northumberland Place*
Old Durham Wharf*
Tuck's Court*

Buildings on King Street

City wall
Conesford Gate (sometimes known as the South Gate) was sited near the end of King Street. Part of the City Walls were in a pleasure garden called Richmond Hill, named after a pub. The gate was demolished in 1794.

Churches
St Clement Conesford, see Abbey Lane.

St Cuthbert's Church was on the site of 7 King Street in the 13th century. It was demolished in 1530.

St Edward's Church, Conesford, stood on the west side of King Street, and its churchyard adjoined Hildebrond's Hospital. According to Blomefield, the parish was added to St Julian's after the death of Robert, the rector, some time between 1269 and 1305.

St Etheldreda's Church dates from the 12th century, and according to *White's Directory* of 1845 there was still a small anchorage at the church after the Reformation. It was the last church in city to lose its thatched roof, when it was restored in 1883. It has been redundant since 1975 and has been used as a sculptor's workshop; the church is in the care of the Norwich Historic Churches Trust.

St Etheldreda's Church, King Street. (Photograph by author)

St Michael Conesford was sold to the Augustinian friary in 1360 and demolished.

St Olave's Chapel was originally built on the site of Read's Flour Mill, but was demolished in the early 1500s. At the time of writing, in early 2005, Read's Mill is about to be developed into flats.

St Peter Parmentergate Church dates from 1486. According to Blomefield, the name comes from 'the gate by the churchyard at the foot of the mount'. It has been redundant since 1979 and has been used as an organ builder's workshop; the church is in the care of the Norwich Historic Churches Trust.

St Peter Parmentergate Church. (Photograph by author)

Exterior of Dragon Hall, King Street. (Photograph copyright Norfolk and Norwich Heritage Trust)

Hildebrond's Hospital – According to Kirkpatrick, Hildebrond's Hospital stood on the west side of King Street (Conesford Street, as it was then), just north of St Peter Southgate. It was founded in 1216 by Hildebrond (a mercer in the city) and his wife Maud as a common hall for poor people. The site was later used by Norwich Brewery.

Howard House, 97 King Street, was the home of Henry Howard, Duke of Norfolk, in 1677. It was built on land that once belonged to the Austin Friars. The house originally had orchards and a pleasure ground, which led to the river, known as 'My Lord's Garden'; the gardens were there until the 1930s and the house was derelict by 1995.

Jurnet's House (now Wensum Lodge), 167 King Street, is the oldest surviving house in the city, built about 1175, and has a 12th-century undercroft. It belonged to the Jurnet family until King John seized it. Sir John Paston (see Elm Hill) lived there around 1478, and Lord Chief Justice Coke lived there in 1613. The City Waits rehearsed there in the 18th century, when the house was known as the Music

Remains of St Peter Southgate, King Street. (Photograph by author)

St Peter Southgate was founded before 1827 and fell into ruin in 1887. The remains are still visible.

Carrow Abbey is a Benedictine nunnery which was established in 1146. Julian of Norwich may have been educated there. The abbey was dissolved at the Reformation and the site has been used as part of Colman's.

Other buildings of note
Dragon Hall – see Old Barge Yard

Jurnet's House (Music House), King Street. (Photograph by author)

House. The Waits were the five official musicians for the city; they played the sackbut, hautboys and recorders, and their instruments were presents from Elizabeth I. Drake asked for them to be on his expedition to Portugal in 1589, but three of them died. The City Waits were paid off in 1790, and the building was divided into tenements. It was bought by the brewing family of John Youngs, who built a maltings there in 1851. It was sold to brewers Bullard & Sons in 1958, and converted to an adult education centre in 1997.

The Old Barge on King Street was at one point known as the Meddyz inn, named after Roger Medday, bailiff of Norwich during the reign of Edward III.

Norfolk Club, 17 King Street, was the Crown Bank from 1792 until the bank moved to Hardwick House in 1866.

People linked with King Street

Francis Arnam, mayor in 1732, lived at 4–6 Upper King Street.

William Ashwell, merchant and mayor in 1441 and 1448, left a bequest in his will to 'Yvihall in Conisford' (aka Hildebrond's Spital near St Peter Southgate).

Roger Best (or Beast), a grocer and mayor in 1467 and 1472, lived in a house called Basits Place on the corner of Mariner's Lane and King Street.

Sir William Boleyn was the man who partitioned Dragon Hall – see Old Barge Yard.

John Caius, the doctor who refounded Gonville Hall, Cambridge, in 1557, lived at 168 King Street (formerly known as the Ship inn). His family name was Keys, but John changed it to the Latin spelling of Caius when he went to Gonville at the age of 19. He was supposed to become a clergyman but studied medicine in Padua; he was the first person to write a systematic description of the 'sweating sickness' or the plague. He became Master of Gonville Hall, but he was a Catholic and his fellows were Protestants – they burned his rooms and he had to resign. He became physician to Edward VI, Mary Tudor and Elizabeth I and died in 1573.

William Clarke, mayor in 1739, lived in Upper King Street (in a house later known as Messrs Overbury's office). He caused the dissolution of St George's Company in the city.

Thomas Codde, brewer and mayor in 1549 and 1555, lived in King Street opposite the Church of the Greyfriars. He sympathised with Kett's rebels but urged them to moderation. Codde told Kett ' I will give the blood and life out of my body before I will by villainy treacherously forsake the city or through fear or cowardice cast off my allegiance to my king.'

Jeremiah James Colman, mayor from 1867–68, went into partnership with his uncle, Jeremiah, in 1851 and moved the firm of Colmans to Carrow in 1856. By 1893 the firm had over 2,000 employees. Colman was an extremely enlightened employer – he employed the first industrial nurse (Phillipa Flowerday), built schools for the children of his employees and introduced paid holidays and subsidised meals. He also introduced a lending library, a clothing club, a savings bank and social benefits.

Elizabeth Elvin was a midwife who delivered over 8,500 children. She was buried at St Etheldreda's in King Street.

William Robert Crow Howlett, mayor from 1906–07, lived in King Street in 1890. His family's music business was based at 11 Market Place.

James Hudson, a banker who became mayor in 1794, lived at 17 King Street; his firm was originally known as Hudson & Hatfield and became Harvey & Hudson.

The Jurnet family was the wealthiest family of Jews in 12th-century England; they built the house on King Street and lived there from 1170–1210.

William Taylor, scholar and revolutionary, lived in King Street. He was the son of the secretary of Norwich's Revolution Society (also called William), and contributed to the local newspaper, *The Cabinet,* and tended to make up words – including 'rehabilitation'! He edited a newspaper called *The Iris* in 1803–04, and tried to persuade the Lakeland poet Robert Southey to move to Norwich to become its editor. He said of Norwich Literary Society, 'Contented mediocrity is always the ultimate destiny of us provincials.' His contemporary Harriet Martineau called him a 'wild rover'.

Nockold Thompson was an attorney and brewer; he was mayor in 1759. His form was the Old Brewery in King Street (the site of Morgan's in 1938) and brewed a particularly strong ale called Tompson's Nog.

Robert Toppes, a mercer or textile merchant, built Dragon Hall in 1450. He was mayor of the city four times, and was in the Fleet prison for six weeks in 1441 for supporting Gladman's insurrection.

Events at King Street

The first artesian well was sunk in the city at King Street; in 1893 the city's first electric-powered factory was built there. There have been a few large fires on the street; Jackson's brewhouse (at 146 King Street) caught fire in December 1770 and again in November 1773, but there was no material damage. But from then on the fires got worse – in July 1804 a malt kiln, granary and house at Prentice & Co, King Street, were destroyed by fire, and the cost of the damage was estimated at £1,000 (more than £57,000 in today's money). In 1876 there was a severe fire at Albion Mills (which was originally built for spinning yarn, and was converted in 1932 to Read's Flour Mills), and on 30 June 1881 the fire in the mustard-packing department at Carrow

Works was so huge that it was reportedly seen as far away as Ely, as a light in the sky!

There was also a tragedy in May 1845 when Walter Morgan of Morgan's Brewery was inspecting his vats of beer; he was overcome by the fumes, fell into the beer and drowned.

King Street also saw a number of firsts in the city. The first screw steamboat built in Norwich was launched from Field's boat-building yard at Carrow Abbey on 10 March 1868; it was called the *Alexandra*, and was owned by John Hart Boughen. On 21 February 1878 the first long-distance phone call in the city was made from Colman's to Liverpool Street Station – a distance of 120 miles. The *Norfolk Chronicle* said 'Parties of ladies and gentlemen at both ends were able to converse freely with each other, the words being clearly understood and distinctly heard. This was considered to be a very successful experiment, although it does not appear that at present the telephone can be adapted to public use.' I wonder what that journalist would think of the mobile phones of today? On 17 December 1881 the first phone wire was recorded in Norwich, listed as being installed by the United Telephone Company; it went from Morgan's Brewery in King Street to Mousehold House. And on 13 April 1883 Carrow Works was first lit by electric light; the machinery in the printing works was also first driven by electric power.

Part of King Street was demolished when Rouen Road was built in the 1960s, and there was further demolition in the 1970s. However, the area is now undergoing substantial regeneration and will no doubt take its old position as one of the leading streets in the city.

KING'S HEAD LANE

Runs from 42–44 Calvert Street to 63 St George's Street. It was named after the King's Head inn, which is recorded at 49 St George's Street from 1760 (number 63 from 1904). The pub closed in 1932 and the lane was lost as part of the Anglia Square development in the late 1960s.

KING'S HEAD YARD

42 Magdalen Street, was also linked with Marshall's Yard in 1883; *White's Directory* of 1883 lists Robert Marshall, fish salesman, and Mrs Martha Marshall, marine store dealer, on Magdalen Street. King's Head Yard was named after the King's Head pub, which is recorded at 42 Magdalen Street from 1760 and is still open.

KING'S HEAD YARD

25–27 St Stephen's Street, was named after the King's Head pub, which is recorded at 25 St Stephen's Street from 1760 but closed by 1864. It became known as Hunt's Yard and then as The Archway, but was lost by 1964.

KING'S QUARTER

King Street, is a new development on the site of the old Morgan's Brewery. The yards in this section take their names from brewing terms, and include: Fuggles Yard (102); Dray's Yard (116).

KING'S YARD

2 Cow Hill. *Peck's Directory* of 1802 lists Thomas King, carpenter, at 7 Cow Hill.

KINGSGATE COURT

54–56 Pottergate, was formerly Hovell's Court.

KNIGHT'S COURT

Near 21 St Benedict's Street. *Pigot's Directory* of 1830 lists James Knight, tailor and draper, at St Benedict's Street. The yard was lost 1883–90.

KNIGHT'S YARD

122–124 Ber Street. *Harrod & Co's Directory* of 1877 lists Mrs Charlotte Knights, pawnbroker, at Ber Street. Knight's Yard was also known as Watson's Yard and was lost 1925–35.

LABOUR IN VAIN YARD

Guildhall Hill, was named after the Labour In Vain pub, which is recorded at 2 Market Place from 1830. It shared a yard with the Guildhall Stores (with which it seems to have amalgamated in 1877). The Guildhall Stores closed in 1934. The sign of the Labour in Vain was apparently painted by Crome – and was fairly distasteful by today's standards, with two women trying to scrub a Negro white.

LACEY'S COURT

18–20 Prince's Street, former name for Plumbers' Arms Alley. *Kelly's Directory* of 1912 lists William Lacey, banker, at 11 Prince's Street.

LADY'S SQUARE

11–21 Lady's Lane. The square was lost when the new library was built in the 1960s.

LADY'S LANE

Lady's Lane ran from 15–17 Bethel Street to 17–19 Theatre Street. It takes its name from the 'Chapel of Our Lady in the Fields'. When the library was built in the early 1960s, the street name changed to Esperanto Way, although the name found no favour with the citizens of Norwich. According to Blomefield, there was a lane called Old Ladies' Lane, which led to the churchyard of St Mary's College; in 1383 this lane was 'put by' and a new 'Ladies Lane' was built.

Streets off Lady's Lane
East:
Southern Court (formerly Sotheron's Buildings) (after 12)*

West:
Lady's Square (also known as Lady's Row) (11–21)*

Buildings on Lady's Lane
The Medical Institute was founded in 1872 and closed just before the National Health Service began. It burned down on 4 January 1952.

The Methodist Chapel (St Peter's) was built in 1824; the foundation stone was laid on 14 April by the Revd William Gilpin and the building opened on 21 October. In 1938 the chapel was demolished to make way for the new library.

People linked with Lady's Lane
Edward Samuel Bignold was the city coroner and was also the son of Thomas Bignold (see Surrey Street); his house was at Lady's Lane.

Henry Z.T. Flowers, mayor in 1904–05, was a printer; his business was located in Lady's Lane.

Bartholomew Gattey: the *Norfolk Chronicle* describes him as 'the eccentric but clever flute-player at the Theatre Royal'. He became mentally ill, and in December 1863 his friends arranged a benefit which kept him in funds until his death in October 1865, aged 64.

Events at Lady's Lane
There was a huge fire at Lady's Lane on 4 January 1952, when the Michelin Tyre depot (formerly the Medical Institute building) caught light. Twenty thousand motor tyres and tubes went up, worth £25,000 (over £400,000 in today's money), and it took firemen an hour to control the blaze.

LADY'S SQUARE
Also known as Lady's Row, 11–21 Lady's Lane.

LAMB INN YARD
Orford Place, was named after the Lamb (or Holy Lamb) pub, which is recorded at the Market Place from 1574. The landlord, John Aggas, was murdered by his brother-in-law in 1787 in a row over free drinks for the brother-in-law's friends. There was more trouble in store on 5 January 1939 when a fire caused £1,500 of damage and the windows were splintered by the heat. John William Hubbard, the grandson of the licensee), jumped out of the bedroom window to raise the alarm – clad only in his pyjamas! He also saved Jimmy the cat, but the canary in the kitchen was killed by smoke. The Lamb was renamed the Rat and Parrot in 1996, then renamed Henry's at the Lamb in 2002.

LAMB YARD
Haymarket, is the other yard linked to the Lamb at Orford Place (see above).

LAMB YARD
28–30 Ber Street. The Lamb pub was listed at 135 Ber Street from 1806–45, was renamed the Jolly Drovers and closed in 1871. The yard was lost 1970–74.

LAMB'S COURT
Golden Ball Street, exact location unknown. *Robson's Commercial Directory* of 1839 lists D.T. Lamb, dressing machine maker, at Golden Ball Street. The yard was lost by 1883.

LANCASTRIAN SCHOOL YARD
Probably in College Court, 21–23 Palace Street. Jeremiah Colman (the uncle of J.J. Colman – see King Street) founded the Lancastrian School in Norwich in 1810. He also founded the *Norfolk News* and was the mayor of Norwich from 1846–47. According to *White's Directory* of 1845, the school educated 250 boys. The yard was lost by 1935.

LANE'S YARD
83–87 King Street, led to 8–10 Mountergate, which was known as Lane's Buildings in 1890.

LANSDOWNE PLACE
Quayside, exact location unknown.

THE LATHES
Formerly Cross Street, 40–42 Sussex Street.

LATONER ROWE
Former name for London Street.

LAWSON'S YARD
St George's Street, exact location unknown.

LEACH'S YARD
St Martin's Lane, exact location unknown, *Robson's Commercial Directory* of 1839 lists William Leech (sic), carpenter, at St Martin's Lane.

LEACHE'S COURT
Near 9 Elm Hill, is listed in *White's Directory* of 1883 but appears to be lost by 1890.

LEONARD STREET
Links Esdelle Street and Edward Street.

LEOPARD COURT

98 Bull Close Road, was named after the Leopard pub, which is recorded at 98–100 Bull Close Road, from 1840. The court was briefly known as Leopard Opening towards the end of the 19th century.

LEWIS'S YARD

King Street, is listed in *White's Directory* of 1833 but appears to be lost by 1890.

LIBRARY COURT

North side of St Andrew's Street, was named after the Free Library. It was lost as part of the road-widening scheme in 1964.

LIFFORD'S YARD

East side of King Street, exact location unknown. *Robson's Commercial Directory* of 1839 lists Thomas Lifford, beer retailer and collector of rents, at King Street. The yard appears to be lost by 1890.

LIGHT HORSEMAN YARD

161 Barrack Street, was named after the Light Horseman pub, which is recorded at 161 Barrack Street from 1830. It was closed in 1920 and the yard was lost 1925–35.

LILY'S COURT

49–51 Magdalen Street, may have taken its name from a pub. It is listed as Ling's Court/Yard from 1883. The yard was lost by 1964.

LILY TERRACE

Originally ran from Ashbourne Street but today runs from 130–156 Ber Street. Pub historian John Riddington-Young says that Lily Terrace was named after the Lily pub, which is recorded at 152 Ber Street. The pub was closed in 1964 and demolished. The landlord in 1930, Edward Cubitt, killed himself before the end of his first year as a publican because he was worried about the business.

LINCOLN'S COURT

182 King Street. *Pigot's Directory* of 1830 lists James Lincoln, baker and flour dealer, near there; *White's Directory* of 1883 lists Christopher T. Lincoln, practical brewer, near there. The court was lost some time after 1975.

LINCOLN'S COURT

104–108 Pottergate. *White's Directory* of 1883 lists James Lincoln, boot and shoe manufacturer, at Pottergate. The yard was lost by 1925.

LINCOLN'S YARD

19 Grapes Hill. *Kelly's Directory* of 1900 lists Alfred George Lincoln, chimney sweep, at 21 Grapes Hill.

LINCOLN'S YARD

Pump Street (off Buffcoat Lane), exact location unknown. *Robson's Commercial Directory* of 1839 lists John Lincoln, pipemaker, at Common Pump Street.

LING'S COURT/YARD

49–51 Magdalen Street, formerly Lily's Court. *Kelly's Directory* of 1912 lists John Ling, draper and postmaster, at 23 Magdalen Street. The yard was lost by 1964.

LING'S YARD

Pottergate, exact location unknown. *Robson's Commercial Directory* of 1839 lists Ling & son, upholsterers and cabinet makers, carpet and paper warehouse, at Pottergate and Bridewell Alley. The yard was lost by 1854.

Weaver's cottage, Lion & Castle Yard. (Photograph by author)

LION & CASTLE YARD

23 Timberhill, was named after the Lion & Castle pub, which is recorded at 27 Timberhill from 1822 and closed in 1925. The Lion and Castle is also the Norwich coat of arms. All Saints Alley runs from Lion & Castle Yard to 20 Westlegate.

LIPFIELD'S YARD

East side of Magdalen Street, was listed as Lipfield's Court by 1883; it may be a misprint for Zipfel's Court.

LITTLE ARABIAN HORSE YARD
70–72 Oak Street. See Arabian Horse Yard.

LITTLE BARRACK YARD
114 St George's Street. See Barrack Yard, 114–116 St George's Street. The yard was lost 1935–41.

LITTLE BETHEL COURT
29–31 Bethel Street, was formerly Bell's Court or Yard.

LITTLE BETHEL STREET
Runs from 37–49 Bethel Street to Chapel Field North. It was opened in 1792 and was known as Short Bethel Street in the early 1900s.

LITTLE BREW YARD
120 Oak Street. The yard was lost 1935–41.

LITTLE BUCK'S YARD
139 Oak Street – see Buck Yard, Oak Street, for the origin of the name.

LITTLE BULL CLOSE
35 Cowgate.

LITTLE CARDINAL'S CAP YARD
84–86 St Benedict's Street – see Cardinal's Cap Yard.

LITTLE CHERRY TREE YARD
160–162 St George's Street – see Cherry Tree Yard.

LITTLE COW YARD
14–16 Cow Hill – see Cow Yard.

LITTLE CROWN YARD (also known as **OLD CROWN YARD**)
91 Oak Street, was named after the Crown & Sceptre pub, recorded at Oak Street from before 1678 and closed by 1861. The yard was lost by 1935.

LITTLE FOX & HOUNDS YARD
155 Ber Street – see Fox & Hounds Yard.

LITTLE LONDON STREET
Little London Street runs from 11–13 London Street to 6 Bedford Street. According to Sandred and Lingström, it used to connect Hole in the Wall Lane (later School Lane) to St Andrew's Street. It was called Smythy Row in the 14th century, then Smithy Lane, (after the goldsmiths who worked there); at that time London Street was known as Cockey Lane. The street was known as Little London Street by 1845.

Buildings on Little London Street
According to Blomefield, there was a Goldsmith's Hall in 'Smethy Lane'; at one point it was known as the Stone Hall, and in 1286 it was owned by John le Brun (who also owned St Mary's College in Chapelfield). The door from this hall is now part of the Guildhall.

People linked with Little London Street
Robert Craske, grocer, was mayor in 1623. He lived in Benjamin Wrench's house in Little London Street (then known as Smythy Row), which was demolished to make way for the new corn hall.

William Hart (or Herte), mayor in 1512 and 1519, lived in Little London Street.

William Moore was a partner in a London Street ironmonger's called Moore & Barnard. He lived at 4 Theatre Street but his office was on Little London Street (later the site of Garland's department store). He was mayor in 1835 and his Guild Day was the last one held.

LITTLE ORFORD STREET
Former name for Orford Place.

LITTLE PLOUGH YARD
56–58 St Benedict's Street. See Plough Yard.

LITTLE QUEEN CAROLINE YARD
63 Oak Street. See Queen Caroline Yard.

LITTLE SHIP YARD
166 King Street. See Ship Yard, 168 King Street.

LITTLE WATER LANE
Runs from St George's Street to Water Lane (Colegate). The Norvic Shoe factory was located there.

LITTLE WHITE HORSE YARD
13 Botolph Street. See White Horse Yard, Botolph Street.

LITTLE WHITE LION YARD
104–106 St Benedict's Street – see Great White Lion Yard.

LIVINGSTONE PLACE
172–174 Ber Street. The yard was lost 1970–75.

LIVINGSTONE'S COURT AND TERRACE
Gaol Hill (exact location unknown), is listed at the Market Place in *Chase's Directory* of 1783; the name is Livington's in 1830 and Livingstone's by 1839, but it's not referenced after 1845.

LOBSTER LANE
Lobster Lane runs from 22–24 Exchange Street to

Pottergate. It was named after the New Lobster pub, which is recorded at Lobster Lane from 1811 and may have been known as the Old Lobster in 1761. The Old Lobster closed in 1873. Bedford Street was also known as Lobster Lane in the 1830s. In the 1950s a tailor's shop on Lobster Lane had a circle painted on the wall with the legend 'The North Pole is in a direct line from this spot.' Lobster Lane is very, very narrow – as a lorry driver discovered in spring 2005 when he got lost, tried to turn into Lobster Lane from Exchange Street – and got stuck for several hours!

People linked with Lobster Lane

The boxer Ned Painter became the landlord of the Sun & Anchor tavern in 1820; his ad in the local paper said 'he intends to give private lessons in sparring in the most scientific style and at reasonable terms at all hours of the day'. In July 1820 Painter fought against Oliver near Mousehold Heath and won after 12 rounds – despite the huge thunderstorm in the middle of it. George Borrow wrote about the fight in his novel *Lavengro*; and Painter said that this was his last appearance in the prize ring. In April 1843 Painter was involved in a court case, when Jeremiah Cross sued him for assault; Cross claimed that Painter thrashed him with an ash stick so severely that he needed medical treatment for a long while afterwards. Painter pointed out that Cross had grossly insulted his daughter – perhaps not a sensible thing to do to a woman whose father was a prize boxer! Painter was found guilty but was only fined one shilling, and his friends rallied round to give him a 'benefit' exhibition of boxers at the Royal Victoria Gardens to cover his court costs.

LOBSTER YARD

Pottergate, exact location unknown. The (Old) Lobster inn was recorded at Pottergate from 1761.

LOCK & KEY YARD

89–91 Ber Street, was named after the Lock & Key pub, which is recorded at 89 Ber Street from 1806; the pub closed in 1913.

LOCK'S COURT

Ran from 60–64 St Stephen's Street to St Stephen's Back Street. *White's Directory* of 1854 lists Henry Lock, shoemaker, at St Stephen's Street. The yard was lost 1960–64.

LOCKET'S COURT

North side of St Andrew's Street before number 15. *Pigot's Directory* of 1830 lists Henry Lock, engineer, at St Andrew's Street. The court appears to be lost by 1890.

LOCKET'S YARD

St Andrew's Street, north side of St Andrew's Street after Locklet's Court. The court appears to be lost by 1890.

THE LOKES

128 Barrack Street, were lost by 1964.

LONDON STREET

London Street runs from the Market Place (number 10–11, at the junction of Gentleman's Walk and Guildhall Hill) to Bank Plain. According to Sandred and Lingström, it was known in the 13th century as Hosiergate, after the stocking manufacturers. Blomefield says it was known as Cuteler Rowe in the 14th century (after the cutlers), then Latoner or Timme's Rowe (after the metal works that used an alloy called 'latten'). Again according to Blomefield, the street became known as Cockey Lane in the late 17th century after the *cloacae sive gurgites publicae*, because two of the common sewers or watercourses in the city met here: one which ran from Nedham Street (St Stephen's) and one which ran from St Giles'. These waterways were open and had bridges over them until the reign of Edward IV, and then the streets were paved and the cockeys were covered over. In the 18th century the street became known as London Lane – according to Kirkpatrick, 'possibly from the number of Shops of all Trades & the great traffic and passage of Peoples Horses, Carts, Coaches, &c, through it' (sic).

Streets off London Street

North:
Little London Street (11–13)
Swan Lane (27–29)
Bedford Street (51–53)
St Andrew's Hill (53)

South:
Castle Street (22–28)
Opie Street (54–56)

Exact location unknown:
Cattermoul's Lane*

Buildings on London Street

Jarrolds department store was originally architect George Skipper's offices, and the building was designed by him.

Gap was formerly the London & Provincial Bank (built by George Skipper in 1907).

The Natwest Bank was built in 1924 by F.C.R. Palmer and W.F.C. Holden.

People linked with London Street

Richard Beatniffe kept a bookshop at 6 London Lane in the

London Street, former London & Provincial Bank. (Photograph by author)

18th century. In 1795 he advertised a stock of 6,000 books; he also had a printing press and published his *Norfolk Tour* there.

George Birch, apothecary, was mayor in 1621. He lived on the corner of London Street and Swan Lane – the location of the shop opposite jeweller's Winsor Bishop (sic spelling, no d in Winsor).

Laurence Goodwin, grocer, was mayor in 1697. Dean Prideaux described him as 'a very honest quiet good man, but not soe fitt for business'. He died at the age of 92 and was buried in St Andrew's Church. He lived in London Street.

Thomas Lane, mercer, was mayor in 1603. It's thought that his house was on the site of 48 London Street.

Edward Manning, brazier, lived at London Street. He died in February 1838 at the age of 83 and was described as the 'oldest and weathiest retired tradesman in St Peter Mancroft' – he had £70,000 worth of property (over £4 million in today's money) and an annual income of over £2,100 a year (over £125,000 in today's money).

Louis Marchesi, restaurateur, founded the Round Table movement in 1927 – a club where young businessmen (aged 18–45) could meet, exchange ideas and join in the civic life of the city without being political or religious. Within a year there were 85 members and Round Tables were established nationally. Marchesi owned Langford's restaurant (now 50 London Street). Meetings of Round Table No.1 took place there, and possibly also at Suckling House.

John Rightwise, mercer, was mayor in 1501 and 1513. He lived in a house on the site of 18 London Street; its door was removed in 1877 to the gateway of the moat on Mannington Hall. He began building the Market Cross in 1501.

John Tesmond, goldsmith, was mayor in 1601. It's thought that his house was on the site of 44 London Street.

Events at London Street

In February 1763, according to the *Norfolk Chronicle*, workmen pulled down a decaying house and found two metal dies (one for French pistoles and one for guineas of Wm III) and two pairs of 'flacks' for caulking metals. It's thought they belonged to Samuel Selfe, a bookseller and stationer who lived there in 1710 and was arraigned in London for forging stamps. He was also suspected of counterfeiting gold coins – but clearly he hid his tools well!

In 1811 the Trafalgar Lodge of Oddfellows held a meeting at the Three Tuns (listed at 51 London Street from 1802). The floor of the upper room collapsed; luckily, no one was hurt.

In Feburary 1847 the shop of Mr Cooper, silversmith and jeweller, was broken into and £2,000 worth of goods were stolen.

On 13 January 1866 the Consolidated Bank (later the National Provincial Bank) opened. It cost £4,000, and was designed by local architect R.M. Phipson and built by Mr Hall of Pottergate. Just five years later it was the subject of scandal; in March 1871 Richard Hoskins, a clerk at the bank, was charged with stealing £1,835. He pleaded guilty, and was sentenced to 6 months' imprisonment with hard labour.

The arrival of the railway meant that the route between Thorpe and the market place needed to be improved. London Street was widened in 1856 to 15ft wide, and again in 1876 to 35ft – the latter was supervised by Edward Boardman, and the work cost £27,000. In 1967 London Street was pedestrianised – the first 'motor' street to be pedestrianised in England.

The street has also been the victim of fires. On 22 March 1873 James Darken's music warehouse at 6 London Street (which also sold harmoniums and pianos, and had a circulating music library) caught light, causing £1,500 of damage. The following year there was an even more damaging fire at Mr Dixon's the silversmith's, causing £2,000 of damage. But worse was to come: in August 1970, there was a disastrous fire at Garland's department store (now the site of Habitat and River Island). It started with a chip pan fire in the restaurant and turned into a million-pound blaze; it took nearly 70 firemen three hours to stop the whole of London Street being gutted, and the smoke was visible from five miles away.

LONG LANE

23–25 Charing Cross. According to Sandred and Lingström, it was originally known in the early 14th century as Craketayleshole – possibly from the fuller William Craketayle who is recorded in 13th-century documents – and was also known as Fullers Hole (Fullers Lane by 1766). The fullers (who cleaned cloth) were concentrated in the area around Charing Cross. It was referenced as Long Lane by 1845, but no longer exists.

LONG WALK

Bethel Street, exact location unknown. It's referenced in the street lists of White's 1845 and 1854, but was lost by 1883.

LONG YARD

Bishopgate, exact location unknown.

LONG YARD

4–16 Fishergate. One of its occupants had a very unusual profession – from 1883–1890, Thomas Russen was listed as a 'sheep's feet boiler'. The yard was lost by 1912.

LOOSE'S YARD

Known as Burrell's Yard before 1890. 41 Magdalen Street. *Kelly's Directory* of 1912 lists James Travers Loose, earthenware dealer, at 25 Magdalen Street.

LORD CAMDEN YARD

15–17 Charing Cross, was named after the Lord Camden pub, which is recorded at 15 Charing Cross from 1806. The pub had closed by 1927, and the yard was lost during street widening in the 1970s.

LORD HOWE YARD

6–8 St Benedict's Street, was named after the Lord Howe pub, which is recorded at 6–8 St Benedict's Street from 1806. The pub had closed by 1868.

LOVE'S YARD

33–37 Palace Street, was later known as Chiddick's Court.

LOVEL STAITHE

Is an early 21st-century development on the east side of Recorder Road, which runs to the river. *White's Directory* of 1845 lists James Lovelock, ferryman, nearby at lower Close.

LOVICK'S YARD

Before 2 Mariner's Lane. *Robson's Commercial Directory* of 1839 lists J. Lovick, plumber, painter and glazier, nearby at Ber Street.

LOVICK'S COURT

St Andrew's Street, exact location unknown. *Pigot's Directory* of 1830 lists Samuel Lovick's china and glass emporium at St Andrew's Street. The court was lost by 1854.

LOW'S YARD

12 St Giles' Street. *White's Directory* of 1883 lists Frederick Low, veterinary surgeon, and *Kelly's Directory* of 1900–12 lists Harry Vincent Low. The yard is now lost but was approximately where the city hall tower is now.

LOWE'S YARD

2–10 Calvert Street, is a development of modern flats which takes its name from a yard that was demolished here during the slum clearances of 1937.

LOWE'S YARD

37–41 St George's Street, runs to 2–10 Calvert Street. *Harrod & Co's Directory* of 1877 lists Joseph Lowe, baker, at Gildengate Street (aka St George's Street). See entry below.

LOWER GOAT LANE

Lower Goat Lane runs from 16 Pottergate to just before 1 St Giles' Street. It was originally known as Stonegate Magna, but by the 17th century it had taken its name from a pub sign. (see Upper Goat Lane).

Buildings at Lower Goat Lane

The 'East of England Music Hall' opened on the site of the Theatre Stores pub in 1878. It was renamed the Connaught Music Room and Palace of Varieties in 1893, and closed when the Hippodrome opened on St Giles' Street.

People linked with Lower Goat Lane

Robert Debney, scrivener, was mayor in 1624; he lived in Stonegate Magna and was buried in St Gregory's Church.

Events at Lower Goat Lane

On 3 March 1775 the *Norwich Mercury* reported a frightening accident in Lower Goat Lane – two servants narrowly escaped with their lives after the fall of a large beam, which had been supporting a room at James Darley's glass warehouse. On 1 May 1939 there was a fatal fire. William Frost, a hardware merchant, was out on his rounds when his house caught fire. His 51-year-old wife Ethel was unable to get out.

LOWER SQUARE

22 Thorn Lane, was lost by 1947.

LOYALTY COURT

34–36 St Stephen's Street, was originally known as Sardinian Court; when the pub changed its name to the Loyalty Stores in 1893, the court changed its name as well. The Loyalty Stores closed in 1911.

LUCKETT'S COURT

23–25 St Andrew's Street. *Pigot's Directory* of 1830 lists William Wright, dyer, at the court. The court was lost by 1896.

LUKE'S YARD

St Augustine's Street, exact location unknown. The yard was lost by 1900.

MACE'S YARD

Near 43 Barrack Street. *White's Directory* of 1883 lists Gilbert Mace, earthenware dealer, at 43 Barrack Street. The yard was lost by 1890.

MAGDALEN CLOSE

121–127 Magdalen Street, is a development from the mid-20th century that takes its name from the street.

MAGDALEN PLACE

Cowgate, exact location unknown.

MAGDALEN STREET

Magdalen Street runs from Fye Bridge Street to Bull Close Road and Magdalen Gate. It's thought to be the Saxon north-south road. It was originally known as Fye Bridge Street, but in the 19th century the name was changed to Magdalen Street after the chapel at Magdalen Gate.

Streets off Magdalen Street
East:
Peak's or Peeke's Court*
Thoroughfare Yard (13–15 – runs to Fishergate)
Red Lion Yard (19)
Gurney's Court (31)
Loose's Yard (formerly Burrell's Yard) (41)
St Saviour's Lane (45–47)
St Saviour's Alley (runs to St Saviour's Lane)
Ling's Court/Yard (also known as Lily's Court) (49–51)*
Bayfield's Yard (57–59)*
Fisher's Court (63–65)*
Abel's Court or Yard (65–67)
Woolcombers' Arms Yard (formerly Sutton's Yard) (77–79)*
Barnes' Yard (87–89)*
Cowgate (99–101)
Zipfel's Court (possibly known as Lipfield's Yard or Court) (111)
Addison's Yard (117)*
Magdalen Close (121–127)
New Yard (125–127)
Gillings Yard (also known as Jenning's Yard) (131–133)
Hartley's Court (formerly White Lion Yard) (135–137)
Paradise Place (139–141)
Two Brewers Yard (149–151)
Garden Place (formerly Red Lion Yard) (159)
Bull Close Road (163)

West:
Colegate (before 2)
Boswell's Yard (24)
Golden Dog Lane (32–34)
Runnymede (32, runs to Calvert Street)

King's Head Yard (also known as Marshall's Yard) (42)
Sackville Place (44–48)
Cobb's Yard (54–56)*
Sovereign Way (runs to Anglia Square) (58)
Elephant Yard (58–60)*
Bishop's Court or Yard (60–62)*
Botolph Street and Stump's Cross (68–70)
Anne's Walk (runs to Anglia Square)
White Horse Yard (84–86)*
Hacon's Yard (92)*
Edward Street (runs to Esdelle Street)
Minns' Court (formerly Pattison's Yard) (100–102)*
Huby's Yard (104)*
Cross Keys Yard (110–112)*
Beckham's Yard (formerly Shrimpling yard or Salter's Court) (116–118)*
The Archway (120a)
Throckmorton Yard
Bailey's Yard (formerly Royal's Yard) (136–138)
Webb's Yard (138–42)
Whiting's Court (formerly Clabburn's Yard) (150)*
Wall Lane (formerly Under the Walls) (152)

Exact location unknown:
Austin's Yard*
Cat & Fiddle Yard*
Dabson's Court or Yard*
Herring's Yard*
May's Court*
Mint Yard*
Pawsey's Yard*
Sweep's Yard*
Tawler's Court*

Buildings on Magdalen Street
City Wall
Part of the City Wall ran along the end of Magdalen Street. Magdalen Gate was the last gate in the City Wall to be fortified, in 1339. It was repaired in 1756, whitewashed in 1783 and was the last to be demolished in 1808. It was sometimes known as Fyebridge Gates. It was also known as Leper's Gate, because the lazar (or leper's) house built by Herbert de Losinga stood outside it; the lazar house was Norwich's first branch library. Finally, the gate became known as Magdalen Gate, named after the Magdalen Chapel outside the walls. There was also once a gallows at Magdalen Gate, and the people hanged there were buried in the Church of St Margaret. The Rush Fair was held at the Artichoke pub, just outside Magdalen Gates; this was where the citizens bought poultry and rushes from the Broads.

City Wall at Magdalen Street. (Photograph by author)

Churches

All Saints' Church, Fybriggate, was recorded by name in the Domesday book. The church stood on the north side of Cowgate at the junction with Magdalen Street. The parish was added to St Paul's and the church was demolished in 1550. According to Blomefield, the lepers from the lazar house outside Magdalen Gates were buried here.

St Botolph's Church – Blomefield places the church in Magdalen Street near Stump Cross. It was built in about 1300; the parish was added to St Saviour's in 1548 and the church was demolished in 1549. The Odeon Cinema was built on the site.

St Margaret *in Combusto* Church – also known as St Margaret, Fye Bridge or St Margaret by the Gates – was thought to be founded around 1100. The parish was added to All Saints' (see above) in 1468, and the church was demolished in 1547. According to Blomefield, it was known as 'in Combusto' because it was in the part of the city burnt in a fire in the Conqueror's time, and those hanged on the gallows outside Magdalen Gates could be buried there. The site was excavated in 1987.

St Mary the Burnt Church (also known as St Mary *Combuste* and St Mary Unbrent – because it was in the area that wasn't burnt in the fire around the time of the Conquest) was recorded by name before the Conquest. The parish was amalgamated with St Saviour's around 1540 and the church was demolished.

St Saviour's Church dates from the 15th century and was restored in 1727. It was rebuilt in 1853 by Richard Stannard, and partly restored again in 1923. It has been redundant since 1976 and is in the care of the Norwich Historic Churches Trust. It was used as a badminton hall in the 1990s.

Other buildings of note

Stump Cross was situated opposite St Saviour's Church; it was named after the 'Guylding Cross' at the junction of Magdalen Street and Botolph Street.

62 Magdalen Street was formerly Woodruffe's Dolls' Hospital.

According to cinema historian Stephen Peart, Norwich's first purpose-built cinema was the Cinema Palace at 114–116 Magdalen Street. It opened in 1912, despite the floods which affected its subway exit. The name changed to the Mayfair in 1946; it was closed in 1956 and demolished, and the site became a bowling alley in the 1960s. It's now part of Anglia TV studios.

People linked with Magdalen Street

Thomas Blosse, merchant and mayor in 1612, lived on the west side of Magdalen Street opposite Stump Cross. His wife Prudence left her houses at 20 and 22 Botolph Street as almshouses for widows.

Sir William Jackson Hooker, botanist, lived in Magdalen Street when young. He became Regius Professor of Botany at the University of Glasgow in 1820, and was appointed the first director of the Royal Gardens at Kew in 1841, where his innovations included the Palm House, the Herbarium and the Library.

Barnabas Leman, mayor in 1813 and 1818, lived on Magdalen Street and died there in 1835, aged 91.

James Martineau, Unitarian philosopher and minister,

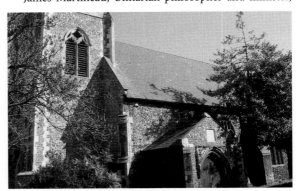

St Saviour's Church, Magdalen Street. (Photograph by author)

was born at 24 Magdalen Street in 1805. He was the seventh Martineau child and was educated at Norwich Grammar School (see The Close). His books included *A Study of Spinoza* (1882), *Types of Ethical Theory* (1885) and *A Study of Religion* (1888).

John Staniforth Patteson, brewer, was mayor in 1823; he lived in a house opposite the Cat & Fiddle in Magdalen Street, and his mansion later became Hurrell's Shoe Factory. In 1830 he had to read the Riot Act to a mob on Castle Hill. He moved to Cringleford in 1831 and died of heart failure in 1832.

Thomas Shipdam, mercer, was mayor in 1631. It's thought that he lived at 29 Magdalen Street, opposite Golden Dog Lane.

Joseph de Carle Smith, chemist, was mayor in 1877–78. He was born in Magdalen Street and was one of the original owners of the *Norfolk News*. He disliked ceremony, so when worshipping at the cathedral or his own parish church (St Mary's), he refused to wear his mayor's robes.

Thomas Tawell founded the Hospital and School for the Indigent Blind on Magdalen Street in 1805; in 1845 there were 15 aged blind and 30 pupils at the hospital and school.

Events at Magdalen Street
There were wide slum clearances in the 1930s; the street was given a 'facelift' in 1959 by the Civic Trust, and it was refreshed again in 1993. In 1972 a Tudor building at 77 Magdalen Street (formerly the Rose Tavern) was badly damaged by fire; the building was demolished.

There have been other notable fires at Magdalen Street; in April 1863 a fire broke out in the warehouse of Gabriel Plummer, ironmonger and carpenter, at 32 Magdalen Street, but there was little damage. More seriously, a fire at Smith's Druggist in 1853 killed four people, Hurrell's shoe factory at 96–100 Magdalen Street was destroyed by fire in air raids on 2 August 1942, and fireman Bruce Carter died while putting out the fire at Secondhand Land in 1985. But, on a lighter note, a puppy came to the rescue during a fire at JD Carpets in June 1973, by racing up to his owner's bedroom and warning her that there was a fire. Linda Bowers grabbed her three-year-old daughter Hayley and got onto the flat roof, while her husband raised the alarm – and there were no casualties.

MAGPIE ROAD
Magpie Road runs from St Magdalen's Gates (at the junction of St Augustine's Street) to 2 Magdalen Road. It takes its name from the Magpie pub, which is recorded at 34 Magpie Road from 1806. The pub was known as the 'Weighing Chains' at one point because it had a public weighing machine attached to the front, used for weighing wagons.

Streets off Magpie Street
Left:
Starling Road (9–35)
Infirmary Square (before 57)
Heath Road (57–61)

Right:
Catherine Wheel Opening (32–34)
Esdelle Street (62)

MAGNET SQUARE
28 St Stephen's Street. The Magnet coach ran between Norwich and London from April 1824; it left the Swan inn and Rampant Horse at 4pm and arrived in London at 7am. In October 1825 the Magnet overturned at Thetford and one of the passengers was crushed when the vehicle fell on her. The yard may have become Unicorn Alley.

MAIDSTONE ROAD
36–38 Rose Lane, is a Victorian development.

MALTHOUSE ROAD
Runs from 11 Rampant Horse Street along the back of St Stephen's Church to Coburg Street; the section between Chantry Road and Coburg Street was formerly known as St Stephen's Back Street or St Stephen's Church Street. There were two malthouses here, one on each side of the road; in 1820 the first Norwich Gasworks were built on Malthouse Road. One Post Alley and Barwell's Court link the road to St Stephen's Street. Chantry Road runs between Malthouse Road and 16 Chapel Field East

MALTHOUSE YARD
6 St Stephen's Street.

MALTHOUSE YARD
Peacock Street, exact location unknown.

MALTHOUSE YARD
6–10 Upper Goat Lane. The yard was lost by 1925.

MALTSTER'S YARD
15–23 All Saints Green; *White's Directory* of 1883 lists Mr Stephen Malster at All Saints Green. The yard was lost by 1912; the site was used as the Thatched Assembly Rooms.

MALTZY COURT
North side of St Martin's Lane (now off St Crispin's Road).

MANCROFT YARD
33 St Peter's Street (Mancroft). The yard takes its name from the city district of Mancroft, and was lost in the slum clearances at the beginning of World War Two.

MANDELA CLOSE

Is a post-1975 development on the west side of Oak Street, near New Mills Yard.

MANDELL'S OR MANDALL'S COURT

8–10 Prince's Street. *White's Directory* of 1883 lists Mrs Sarah Louise Mandall at Church Walk/Redwell Street (just round the corner). *White's Directory* of 1854 lists Robert Mandall, builder, at Mandall's Court in Prince's Street.

MANDELL'S YARD

2 Wensum Street. *Robson's Commercial Directory* of 1839 lists John Mandell, builder, nearby at Prince's Street. The yard was lost by 1890.

MANNING'S YARD

3–5 Golden Ball Street. *Harrod & Co's Directory* of 1877 lists Walter Manning, brush maker and dealer in carpenters' and joiners' tools, at Golden Ball Street. The yard was lost 193–41.

MANSFIELD'S YARD

41a St Stephen's Street, was known as Browne's Court from 1883. *Harrod & Co's Directory* of 1877 lists Robert E. Mansfield, painter, at St Stephen's Street.

MARINE STORE YARD

29–31 St Mary's Plain, became White Bear Yard by 1925.

MARINER'S LANE

Mariner's Lane originally ran from 124–126 Ber Street to 182 King Street, but since the building of Rouen Road has ended in a car park. Its original name in the 13th century was Hollegate, meaning 'street in the Hollow'. It was known as St John's Lane in the 16th century, after the church; in Blomefield's time, it was Holgate Lane, and by the 18th century it was known as Mariner's Lane, from the sign of the Mariners Tavern at 39 Mariner's Lane (which closed in 1962).

Streets off Mariner's Lane
South:
Old Friends Yard (before 1)*
Wood's Yard (7–9)*
Russell Street (before 11)*
Arthur Street (9–11)
Compass Street (39–41)
Gladstone Place (43–45)

North:
Lovick's Yard (before 2)
Nelson Place (22–24)

Burleigh Street (ran to Thorn Lane) (34–36)
Sherborne Place (ran to King Street)

People linked with Mariner's Lane
The knight Robert de Salle lived in a house on the north side of Mariner's Lane. He was of humble birth but King Edward made him a knight because of his bravery. During the Peasants' Revolt, John Litester and the rebels asked Salle to be their leader. When he refused, calling them traitors, they killed him and took control of the city. However, their power didn't last long because the 'fighting bishop' of Norwich, Henry Despenser, fought them and regained control of the city.

MARJORIE HINDE COURT

Runs from 61a Bethel Street to Chapel Field North and was built some time after 1960.

MARKET AVENUE

Runs from the junction of Bell Avenue and Rose Lane to the junction of Castle Meadow and Agricultural Hall Plain.

Buildings on Market Avenue
The Shire Hall was built in 1822, designed by William Wilkins jnr. The assizes and quarter sessions were held there, and there was an underground tunnel to the castle so that prisoners could be brought to trial; the first county sessions were held there in October 1823. In 1846 the walls cracked and the building started sinking, so Joseph Stannard jnr put it on a raft of concrete 10ft thick. The building was Norwich Crown Court until 1978; since 1990 part of it has been used as the Regimental Museum.

Shire Hall. (Photograph by author)

MARKET LANE

Was named after the cattle market; it ran from 6–8 Scoles Green to 26–28 Thorn Lane. The lane was lost in the 1960s when Rouen Road was developed. There were two yards running from it: Paradise Row or Place (32 – ran to Thorn Lane) and Prospect Place (40–42).

MARKET PLACE

The market place runs from London Street in the north-east to the Haymarket in the north-west, and from St Peter's Street in the south-west to Dove Street in the north-west. It was originally known as Mancroft ('common enclosure'). According to Blomefield, the west side of the market was called Vuere, Over or Upper Market. The south side was the linen drapery; behind this was the barley market yard. Barley Market Lane led from Upper Newport and the barley market and Helleyn's Lane led from the butchery. There were also two other lanes here; one was called Coysn's Lane, and the other was called Elmeswell's Lane, which led to John de Elmeswell's house (also known as Kisthalle). The middle row had a fish market on the west side and the market place on the east side. There was also a morage house or murage loft.

By the Guildhall, there was a common well at the east end. In 1404 a new pillory was built by it and a cage underneath it. During the reign of Edward IV part of the house was turned into a cage with stocks in it; and in 1479 the well was railed in.

Streets off Market Place:
North: (Guildhall Hill):
Chamberlin's Court
Labour In Vain Yard (near 2)
Dove Street (6)
Chronicle Office Court (8)

Norwich Market in the early 20th century. (Photograph courtesy of Norwich City Council)

Exchange Street (10–11)
London Street (10–11)
Gaol (or Goal) Hill

East (Gentleman's Walk):
Old Post Office Court/Yard (15–17 – runs to Castle Street)
Davey Place (19–20)
Royal Arcade (24)
White Lion Street (30)
Haymarket (31)

South:
Weaver's Lane (32–33)
St Peter's Alley or Steps (33–34)
St Peter's Street (39)

Stall at Norwich Market. (Photograph courtesy of Norwich City Council)

City Hall lit up. (Photograph courtesy of Norwich City Council)

West:
Half Moon Court (38–39)*
Pudding Lane (just after 38)
Butchery (42–43)
Fishmarket (44)

Other streets whose exact locations could not be placed include:
Marston's Court (possibly near 13)*
Livingston's Court* (north side as in 1845 it's listed at Goal Hill)
Matchett's Court*

Buildings on the Market Place
Churches
St Peter Mancroft church – see St Peter Street

Other buildings of note
City Hall is built on the site of the first Norwich bank; it is also the site where James Smith sold the first ready-made shoes in Norwich. Architects Charles James and Stephen Pierce won a competition for the best design, and it was built by Sir Lindsey Parkinson's firm. The foundation stone was laid by the Lord Mayor in September 1936, and it was opened by George VI on 29 October 1938. The tower is 185ft high and the bell is sometimes known as 'Death Nelly' because of its deep tone. The striking was silenced during World War Two because the tower was a spotters' post, in connection with the factory alarm system of air raid warnings.

Market Cross – according to Blomefield, this was first put up during Edward III's reign. It was repaired during the reign of Henry IV, by which time it had a chapel and four

City Hall clock tower. (Photograph by author)

shops. In 1501 it was pulled down and rebuilt by the mayor, John Rightwise, because it had fallen down. The new building had an oratory, which was turned into a storehouse at the Dissolution; the sealed measures of the city were also kept there. In 1646 the whole city was taxed to repair the cross; in 1732 it was sold, pulled down and the site was paved over. An iron pillar holding four gas lamps was put up near the site in 1837.

Statues: a marble statue of Nelson was put up in the market place in 1852, but was moved to The Close in 1856. A bronze statue of Wellington was put up in 1854 and unveiled by Sir Samuel Bignold in front of a crowd of 20,000 people; the statue was moved to The Close in 1937.

War Memorial – during Sir Robert Bignold's mayoralty Sir Edwin Lutyens designed the War Memorial, which was placed in front of the east wall of the Guildhall; it was unveiled by a Norwich ex-serviceman, Private B. A. Withers, on Sunday 8 October 1927, in front of a crowd of 50,000 people. The memorial was moved on 17 October 1938 to the front of the new City Hall, and the Bishop of Norwich rededicated it on 28 September 1947 to include the dead from World War Two.

People linked with the Market Place

Sir James Edward Smith – see Surrey Street.
Nathaniel Roe, goldsmith and jeweller, was mayor in 1777; at one point he lived at 9 Market Place.

Events at the Market Place

The market place was paved in 1731; it was first lit with gas in 1820, although the first gas light in the city was introduced at the shop of Mr Harrison in the Market Place; the newspaper reported that '16 brilliant lights were kept burning for 5 hours at a cost of 9d in coals'. Joseph Oxley & Sons, who traded as hatters and hosiers at 5 Gentleman's Walk, were the first to introduce gas light into a Norwich factory. On 13 October 1818 they had a midnight trial 'of a gasometer with complete apparatus erected by Messrs John and Philip Taylor of London'. The first gas pipes were laid in the Market Place in January 1820, and on 10 May 1820 street lamps in several shops were lit with gas for the first time. In 1881 the Market Place was lit by electric lights, and most gas lamps in the city were changed over to electric

Market Place in 1938. (Photograph courtesy of Norwich City Council)

from 1910 to 1913. In May 1883 the first steam fire engine in the city was tested in the Market Place – it cost £600, partly funded by public subscription and partly funded by Norwich Union.

The market place itself was revamped completely in 1938, after the building of City Hall – before then, there were houses and lanes between St Peter and the Guildhall. Though there was a tragedy there in December 1859 when the new fishmarket was being built; three of the arches beneath the 'promenade' fell down and killed workman William Powley.

The market place was revamped again in the 1970s; the market place underwent yet another revamp and archaeologists found some very interesting things during excavations, including the footings of the old Market Cross.

As it's been one of the main gathering points in the city, the Market Place has seen several riots in its time. In February 1803 20 shoemakers who had been fined by the mayor for making shoes 'contrary to an Act of Parliament' symbolically burned 100 pairs of shoes in the market place.

In May 1816 there was a serious riot where the crowd threw fireballs and broke the windows of the Guildhall, then broke into New Mills and threw flour into the river before smashing windows in St Andrew's Street, Bank Street, Tombland and Magdalen Street; although the mob dispersed, the riot started again two days later and the mob had to be dispersed 'by the military'. In March 1856, after the peace treaty signed with Russia, the bells of St Peter Mancroft were rung and flags put on the tower. There were fireworks in the Market Place, and a bonfire was lit against police regulations – but when police put it out the mob went wild! They broke windows in the Market Place, threw a lit squib into a wagon of straw in Castle Meadow, and when firemen tried to douse the flames the rioters stoned them! There was also a serious riot on 14 January 1887, when socialists Mowbray and Henderson 'harangued' a crowd of unemployed workmen; they said they could not starve and must 'procure food for themselves'. The rioters raided shops on the Walk; the magistrates were called, and Mowbray was sentenced to nine months' imprisonment with hard labour, and Henderson to four.

The Market Place has also been a place of celebration; in October 1801 there was a general illumination 'in celebration of the Peace' with France, and a huge bonfire was lit. In 1813, as part of the city's celebration of the victories over France, a bullock was roasted whole in the Market Place, and 600 2d loaves were given away with 10 barrels of stout, followed by a huge bonfire. There was another bullock roasted and distributed with loaves and barrels of beer at the coronation of George IV in July 1821, followed by fireworks and a brilliantly lit triumphal arch set up near the Guildhall. Queen Victoria's coronation in July 1838 was celebrated in the Market Place with a 'feu de joie' by the 4th Dragoon Guards, and there was a grand display of fireworks in the evening. However, there was a problem with a similar firework display to celebrate the marriage of Queen Victoria to Prince Albert in February 1840, when a rocket went through the shutters of a shop in the Market Place and another went through the second-storey window of a house in London street; several people were injured.

As well as celebration, the Market Place has seen a lot of entertainment. Mr Peck's Coffee House at the Church Stile in the Market Place was the scene of some unusual exhibitions in the 19th century, including in April 1801 'the largest Rattlesnake ever seen in England… he has not taken any sustenance for the last 11 months' and in August 1806 'a most surprising crocodile from the Nile… he is so remarkably tame that any lady or gentleman may touch him with safety'. In 1868 Mr Simmon 'the aëronaut' thrilled crowds when he ascended in a balloon from the Market Place but, according to *White's Directory* of 1890, he 'lost the balloon and narrowly escaped with his life'.

MARQUIS OF GRANBY ROW OR OPENING
161–171 Barrack Street, was named after the Marquis of Granby pub, which is recorded at 171 Barrack Street from 1763; it closed in 1969. It became known as the Marquis of Granby Opening in 1925, and was renumbered as 239 Barrack Street in 1964; opening was lost some time after 1970.

MARSHALL'S YARD
42 Magdalen Street – see King's Head Yard. *Harrod & Co's Directory* of 1877 lists Maria Marshall, baker, and Robert Marshall, fishmonger, at Magdalen Street.

MARSHAM'S YARD
21 St Benedict's Street. The yard was lost 1883–90.

MARSTON'S COURT
Market Place, exact location unknown. *Harrod & Co's Directory* of 1877 lists Richard Marston, confectioner, at 13 Market Place. The yard was lost by 1890.

MARTIN'S COURT
4–6 St Benedict's Street to 37–39 Pottergate, was also known as Pipe Burners' Yard. *Robson's Commercial Directory* of 1839 lists George Martin, bootmaker, at St Gregory's Churchyard; *White's Directory* of 1890 lists Benjamin Martin & Son, boot manufacturers.

MARTIN'S YARD
Pitt Street, exact location unknown.

MARY CHAPMAN COURT
Is a new development on the west side of Duke Street after the bridge. The name commemorates Mary Chapman – see Bethel Street.

MASON'S COURT
16–18 Ber Street. *White's Directory* of 1883 and *Kelly's Directory* of 1900 list basket maker George Mason at 16 Ber Street. The yard was lost during air raids in World War Two (although the area is currently an outside pottery shop).

MASON'S YARD
14–16 Ber Street *White's Directory* of 1883 and *Kelly's Directory* of 1900 list basket maker George Mason at 16 Ber Street. The yard was lost during air raids in World War Two.

MASON'S YARD
Lower Westwick Street, exact location unknown.

MASTER'S COURT
63 Bethel Street – see Ninham's Court. *White's Directory* of

1854 lists Alfred Master, surgeon, at Bethel Street; he's also listed as a JP in *Kelly's Directory* of 1890.

MATCHETT'S COURT
Market Place (exact location unknown) takes its name from Matchett, Stevenson & Matchett, booksellers and patent medicine vendors. It's listed in *Pigot's Directory* of 1830 but not after.

MATTHEWS YARD
Thorn Lane, exact location unknown.

MAUDE'S COURT
St Benedict's Street, exact location unknown.

MAUDE GRAY COURT
33–35 St Benedict's Street, was formerly Self's Yard.

MAY'S COURT
Magdalen Street, exact location unknown.

MAYS COURT
5–6 Upper St Giles, was formerly known as Hayes' Court (83–85 St Giles' Street). *Harrod & Co's Directory* of 1877 lists James May, boot and shoemaker, at 5 Upper St Giles, and the show rooms of Mrs May, milliner, at 84 St Giles' Street.

MAYES' COURT
40–42 St Benedict's Street. *Pigot's Directory* of 1830 lists William Mayes, builder, at St Benedict's Street. The yard was lost 1890–96.

MERCHANT'S COURT
Is a late 20th-century development on the west side of St George's Street, near the Colegate junction.

MIDDLE ROW
33–35 Chapel Field Road. The row was lost by 1960, firstly for a car sales outlet then for the office block of Norvic House.

MIDDLE SQUARE
20 Thorn Lane, was lost by 1947.

MIDDLE STREET
Former name for St George's Street.

MIDDLETON'S COURT
St Benedict's Street. *Pigot's Directory* of 1830 lists Chas Middleton, hot presser, at the court.

MILLARD'S YARD
Prince's Street, exact location unknown. *White's Directory* of 1845 lists William Millard, Salter & Son, land agents, at Prince's Street. The yard was lost by 1925.

MILLER'S COURT
Surrey Street, was also known as Quantrill's Court. *Robson's Commercial Directory* of 1839 lists Henry Miller, solicitor and registrar of the Borough Court of Requests, at Surrey Street.

MILLENNIUM PLAIN
Is the area between Theatre Street and the corner of Bethel Street/St Peter's Street; it's the site of the former Lady Lane and Norwich Central Library, which burned down on 1 August 1994; it was the worst library fire in the country since World War Two and much archive material, along with thousands of books, was lost in the 1,000-degree blaze. It took 15 fire engines to subdue the blaze, and the smoke was visible from at least six miles away. During excavations, archaeologists found a gold Viking ingot on the site.

Buildings at Millennium Plain
The Forum houses the Norwich Central Library (with seven miles of shelving) and the BBC. The building opened to the public in November 2001 but was officially opened by Queen Elizabeth II on 18 July 2002, where she sent the largest group email she'd ever sent – to over 114,000 children at 452 schools in Norfolk.

The Forum in the evening. (Photograph courtesy of Norwich City Council)

MINNS' COURT
100–102 Magdalen Street, was formerly known as Pattison's Yard. *Harrod & Co's Directory* of 1877 lists John Minns as the landlord of the Queens Arms in Magdalen Street (which was located at 102 Magdalen Street – he had been landlord there since at least 1839). The yard was lost by 1964.

MINN'S YARD

31–33 St Augustine's Street, former name for Nunn's Yard.

MINT YARD

Magdalen Street, exact location unknown.

MINT YARD

3–5 Fishergate. The yard was referenced in *Kelly's Directory* of 1890 but lost by 1925.

MINT YARD

Thorn Lane, exact location unknown.

MISCHIEF YARD

46 Peacock Street, was named after the Mischief Tavern pub, which is recorded at 44 Peacock Street from 1720; the tavern closed in 1914, although the yard is listed in Kelly's Directories of 1927 and 1935. The yard was lost by 1941.

MISSION PLACE

King Street, exact location unknown. The yard was listed in *White's Directory* of 1845 and 1854 but does not appear after then.

MITCHELL'S YARD

79–81 Pitt Street. *White's Directory* of 1883 lists Robert Mitchell, basket maker. The yard became known as Cattermoul's Yard by 1890 and was lost by 1925.

MODEL SCHOOL YARD

15 Prince's Street, formerly National School Yard. *White's Directory* of 1845 lists the Central or Model School for Boys at Prince's Street. The yard was lost by 1925.

MOLLETT'S YARD (also known as MOLLETT'S STAITH)

At the junction of Fye Bridge Street and Magdalen Street. *White's Directory* of 1854 lists Rizen Mollett, coal director, at Mollett's Staith.

THE MONASTERY

Formerly Monastery Yard, 8 Elm Hill, was previously known as Goss Court. It took its name from the monastery that Father Ignatius tried to set up at 14 Elm Hill in 1864–66. Ignatius's real name was Joseph Leycester Lyne; he was the son of a merchant from Barking. He was always a strange child; at the age of eight he apparently saw the ghost of a schoolmate who died in the room next to his, and he left his school suffering from nervous shock after being caned for looking at pictures of the Holy Land instead of at his textbook.

He took holy orders in Scotland and then became a self-appointed monk. He established the Priory of St Mary and

St Dunstan in Elm Hill: at the start it was just Ignatius, another monk and a dog, and they lived on bread and potatoes. He converted the rector of St Lawrence's Church in St Benedict's Street and several other citizens; he held up to eight services a day and his penances were harsh. For example, one magistrate's wife and daughter had to lie face down in ashes on the church floor because they'd attended a dance. After breaking a rule of silence, some young men had to trace the outline of the cross on the floor with their tongues.

The Monastery, Elm Hill. (Photograph by author)

Norwich folk didn't take kindly to him, but when they protested about him some very strange occurrences were reported. One woman who cursed him in the street fell dead in a doorway. Another teased him about his tonsure, and her child's hair fell out – though Ignatius restored it when she begged him to help. A churchwarden complained to the bishop about Ignatius and his attitude to church furniture – and died. And when a mob tried to burn his house down, a thunderstorm put out the flames! Ignatius left the city in 1866 and established a monastery in the Brecon mountains.

MOON & STARS YARD

54 Colegate, was named after the Moon & Stars Yard pub, which is recorded at Colegate from 1783 – one of the residents in 1783 was James Forster, bricklayer and 'chimney doctor'. The address appears to be listed as 23 Duke Street from 1830. The pub closed in 1958 and the yard was lost.

MORRIS'S COURT or TOOLEY YARD

24–26 Thorn Lane, was lost by 1947.

MOUNSER'S YARD (also known as **MOUNTSEAR'S or MOUNTSEER'S COURT**)

22 Prince's Street. *Robson's Commercial Directory* of 1839 lists Robert Mounsear (sic), upholsterer, at Prince's Street. The yard was lost by 1935–41.

MOUNSER'S YARD

14–16 Timberhill. *Harrod & Co's Directory* of 1877 and *Kelly's Directory* of 1900 list William Mounser, cutler, at 14 Timberhill. The yard was lost during air raids in World War Two and the site is now part of the Castle Mall development.

MOUNTERGATE

Mountergate runs from 97–99 King Street to 67 Rose Lane. According to Sandred and Lingström, it was known in the 13th century as Inferior Cunesford (see King Street for the name derivation) or Nether Conesford, but was known as St Vayst Lane in the 16th century (from St Vedast's Church), which gradually corrupted to St Faith's Lane. It became known as Mountergate by about 1890 – probably a corruption from Parmentergate, as St Peter Parmentergate's Church is nearby on King Street. The area by King Street has undergone regeneration in the early 21st century and is becoming known as Nether Conesford again.

In the 18th and 19th centuries there were pleasure gardens at Mountergate – known as the Spring Gardens in 1783 and Hop Pole Gardens in the mid to late 1800s.

Weaver's house at Mountergate. (Photograph by author)

Streets off Mountergate

South:
Fish market
Synagogue Street (37–39)
Prince of Wales Road

North:
Lane's Buildings (8–10) 1890
Orchard Street
Parmentergate Court
St John's Street (36–38 – led to St Ann's Lane but is now a cul-de-sac)
Prince of Wales Road (Eastbourne Place)

Buildings on Mountergate

The Fishmarket opened on the north side of the street on 24 December 1913 to replace the one on St Peter's Street.

New Museum of Contemporary Art at Nether Conesford (at 93–95 King Street; but the entrance is in Mountergate).

St Faith's House was the home of John Hotblack, JP, in 1890; it is now a business centre which specialises in mentoring and 'business incubation'.

St Faith's House at Mountergate. (Photograph by author)

People linked with Mountergate

John Addey, a linen draper who was also a partner in merchants Addey & Herring and was mayor in 1773, lived at St Faith's Lane (later Mountergate). There was a fire at his house in September 1778 but luckily there was little damage. William Herring, who was an alderman of the city for 32 years, also lived there.

Events at Mountergate

In January 1830 John Wright had vitriol thrown into his face at Mountergate (then known as St Faith's Lane); he shot at his assailant, who escaped. Richard Nockolds, who was executed 9 April 1831 for arson, confessed to the crime. In April 1833 a private still was discovered on the street; 15 gallons were seized, the owners were fined £30 (today's equivalent of nearly £2,000) each, and when they didn't pay up they were sentenced to 3 months' imprisonment!

'Pedestrian feats' (or foot races) were particularly popular at the Hop Pole Gardens at Mountergate. In July

1884 Madame Angelo walked 1,000 miles in 1,000 hours. The report in the *Norfolk Chronicle* said that 'during last week she showed signs of flagging, her limbs swelling, and considerable difficulty was experienced in keeping her awake'. Madame Angelo was going to walk the last mile with her baby in her arms, but she was so exhausted that she could only manage to carry the baby for the last four laps. In the August Bank Holiday 1884 London entertainer Dan Leno performed 'step dancing' to delight the crows.

There was a major fire in Mountergate on 14 October 1928, when Ranson's timber mills went up; it spread to Harrison & Sons' marine storeyard and Mountergate Saw Mill, and the Georgian House in Spring Gardens was also burned. The fire was brought under control – but not before the yard and sawmills were gutted.

MOUNTSEAR'S YARD/COURT
See Mounser's Yard, 22 Prince's Street.

MOUNTSEER'S COURT
See Mounser's Yard, 22 Prince's Street.

MOWEY'S COURT
Runs from Grapes Hill (formerly known as St Giles' Hill) to the south side of St Benedict's Street, exact location unknown.

MULBERRY CLOSE
Off Robert Gybson Way, Westwick Street, is a late 20th-century development.

MULBERRY TREE YARD
73–85 St Benedict's Street. *Pigot's Directory* of 1830 lists Robert Atterton, whitesmith, at the yard. The yard appears to be lost by 1890 but may be linked to the name Mulberry Close nearby on Robert Gybson Way.

MURRELL'S YARD
53–55 King Street. *Pigot's Directory* of 1830 lists Robert Murrell, baker, at King Street. The yard was lost by 1960 (when Norwich Lads' Club was built on the area) and now lies beneath buildings of the Cotman Housing Association put up in 2001.

MUSEUM COURT
On the corner of Duke Street and St Andrew's Street, housed the Norfolk and Norwich museum (founded in 1825), the Norfolk and Norwich Literary Institute and the Norwich Free Library. The court was a chapel with an adjoining house, which was built in 1764 by the 10th Duke of Norfolk. It was let to the Norwich subscription library in 1794 until the library moved to Guildhall Hill in 1839; the

Literary Institute opened there in 1822. The site was then used for the Norwich Free Library, which was the first ever purpose-built public library. The foundation stone was laid by Samuel Bignold, and the library was opened on 16 March 1857. The building was decorated with the head of Homer and the city arms; it was demolished in 1964 when St Andrew's Street was widened, and the Duke Street car park was built.

MUSEUM COURT
Haymarket, took its name from the Norfolk and Norwich Museum (when it moved from St Andrew's Street).

MUSEUM STREET
Former name for Post Office Street. It took the name from the Norfolk and Norwich Museum (see Museum Court).

MUSIC HOUSE LANE
144 King Street, was named after the Old Music House pub, which is recorded at 167 King Street from 1760. The pub closed in 1932. The building is also known as Jurnet's House (see King Street). The lane leads to the north side of Rouen Road.

MUSPOLE COURT
23 Muspole Street, is a new development which takes its name from the street.

MUSPOLE STREET
Muspole Street originally ran from St George's Plain to the top of Pitt Street; nowadays it runs from Colegate to the junction of Duke Street and St Mary's Plain. The street's name is referenced as far back as 1250 – and different spellings include Muspall and Muspoll. It's thought to come from Moss Pool or Mouse Pool; Sandred and Lingström suggest the possibility of 'Must Pool', meaning 'muddy stream', and the curve of the street may be skirting the old marshy area. Part of the street was once known as Soutergate (or Southgate), after shoemakers who lived in the area.

Streets off Muspole Street
Right side:
Wiseman's Yard*
St George's Alley
Alms Lane (9 – runs to 88 St George's Street)
Muspole Court (23)
Wright's Foundry Yard (29–31)

Left side:
Woolpack Yard (2)
Old Yeast Yard (8)*

Dunk's Court (18)*
Tubby's Yard (28–34)*
Archer's (or Arches) Yard (36)*
Cock House Yard*

Buildings on Muspole Street

The Woolpack pub (2 Muspole Street) was formerly the town house of the Augustinian Prior of Our Lady Of Walsingham, and was conveyed to John the Prior in 1298. It was used as a place where the prior could conduct business and entertain guests. The current building dates from the 15th century and it is thought that there was once a connecting tunnel to St George's Church.

The Woolpack, Muspole Street. (Photograph by author)

MYHILL'S YARD

8–10 Whitefriars Street. The yard was lost by 1964.

NAILOR'S LANE

Charing Cross, exact location unknown. The yard was referenced in 1845 and 1854 but lost by 1883.

NASH'S YARD

At the junction of Charing Cross and Lower Westwick Street. *Peck's Directory* of 1802 lists John Nash, importer and dealer in wines, at 33 Wymer Street (aka Lower Westwick Street). *Harrod & Co's Directory* of 1877 lists W.S. Nash, wholesale stationer, at Charing Cross. The yard is not mentioned after 1883 – although *Kelly's Directory* of 1941 lists William Nash, wholesale paper merchant, at 25–29 Charing Cross.

NATIONAL SCHOOL YARD

15 Prince's Street, former name for Model School Yard.

NEALE'S SQUARE

Ran from 117 Pottergate to St Benedict's Street, was destroyed in air raids in 1942 and was replaced by

Wellington Green. *White's Directory* of 1845 lists Lawrence Neale, gardener and seedsman, at St Benedict's Street. One notable resident was Susannah Stevenson, who died in January 1874 aged 105. Her obituary in the *Norfolk Chronicle* said that 'a few days ago she repeated no less than 30 verses which she had learned at school 95 years ago' – so clearly she was sharp-witted right to the end.

NELSON PLACE

22–24 Mariner's Lane.

NELSON TAVERN YARD

Timberhill, was named after the Nelson Tavern, which is recorded at 45 Timberhill from 1930. The yard is now lost.

NELSON'S MONUMENT YARD

66 King Street, was named after the Nelson's Monument pub, which is recorded at 66 King Street from 1822 and closed in 1908.

NEW MILLS LANE

41 Oak Street (Coslany Street before 1890). See New Mills Yard.

NEW MILLS YARD

New Mills Yard runs from 98 Westwick Street to 41–43 Oak Street. It takes it name from the New Mills (formerly Appleyard's Mills), which were rebuilt in 1430; the city bakers all had to grind their wheat there. There is a metal gauge in the yard which shows the levels of the floods over the years 1570–1912. The pumping station itself is late Victorian, and the River Wensum is not tidal at this point.

Events at New Mills Yard

The Mills were the subject of a huge row in the 1400s, partly due to Thomas Wetherby, the mayor in 1427 and 1437. Wetherby was described as being of 'grete goodes and grete pryde' and tried to fix the election of his successor in 1433. He was fined £100 (over £32,000 in today's money) and stripped of all his offices; in revenge, he persuaded the abbot of St Benet's to claim that the mills were obstructing the river. The Earl of Suffolk got an award in 1442 ordering the city to pull down the mills and enter into a bond with the bishop saying they'd be fined £100 if they rebuilt the mills. The townspeople were furious and the result was Gladman's insurrection. The mayor was summoned to London and thrown into the Fleet prison; in the meantime, Wetherby seized the city's seal and sealed the bond. The city threw itself on the king's mercy, but the city's liberties were seized and Sir John Clifton was appointed *custos* until the row settled down again.

There is a flood marker at New Mills Yard showing the

View from St Miles'
Bridge during 1912
floods, picture courtesy
of Norfolk County
Council Library and
Information Service.

levels of the floods – the stone is quite a bit higher than the river. On 27 April 1762 the waters rose a frightening 12ft in 24 hours, and 328 parish churches were inundated – and this clearly wasn't the first time, as the newspaper reports that this was 15in higher than 1691 and 15in lower than 1614. On 28 January 1809 there was a flood after a rapid thaw; boats were rowed in St Martin's Street, and the lower part of the city was 6–7ft under water. In July 1853 there was a huge thunderstorm and rain fell for three hours, resulting in the lower parts of the city being flooded. But the two floods that will always live on in the city's memory are those of 1878 and 1912.

Flood marker at New Mills. (Photograph by author). The road level has changed, although the market has stayed in the same place. Half the marker is actually buried and the level of the 1912 floods would go two bricks above Christopher's head on the right.

On 16 November 1878 there was a rapid thaw after snow and continuous rain, plus high tide at Yarmouth. The river burst its banks at New Mills and flooded the streets; several hundred people had to leave their homes, and the Guildhall was opened as a store house, with 2,600 loaves of bread and hundreds of blankets. The *Norfolk Chronicle* reports that Grant's factory lost several thousand pounds of silk, and the gasometer in Barn Road was surrounded by 3ft of water. Bullards' store room (aka Anchor Brewery on Westwick Street) was flooded, and the casks (which had been plugged) floated and were 'a seat of refuge for a great number of washed out rats'. Sadly, three people died: 17-year-old George Churchyard, who was found in the warehouse of Wills the fellmonger in Heigham Street; Robert Rudrum from Carrow Works; and 'carman' Thomas Arnup, who'd been out delivering coal and hadn't known about the city floods when he tried to come home; his horse was also drowned and his cart was smashed.

NEW YARD

125–127 Magdalen Street. The yard was lost by 1960.

NEWBEGIN'S YARD

18–24 St Mary's Plain, former name of Atkinson's Yard. By 1925 the yard was under the site of Sexton's boot factory.

NEWMAN'S YARD

93–95 Ber Street. *Pigot's Directory* of 1830 lists Elizabeth Newman, flour dealer and baker, and Richard Newman, baker, in Ber Street. The yard was lost 1935–41.

NICHOL'S YARD

19–21 St Augustine's Street. *Pigot's Directory* of 1830 lists John Nichols, rope and twine maker, in St Augustine's Street.

NICKALL'S BUILDINGS

63–75 Barrack Street. *White's Directory* of 1883 lists William Nickalls, tailor, at Barrack Street. The area became known as Priory Square by 1935.

NICKALL'S YARD

36 Barrack Street and 45–47 Barrack Street. *White's Directory* of 1883 lists Matthew J. Nickalls jnr, whitesmith, and *Kelly's Directory* of 1900 lists Clara Nickalls, milliner, both at Barrack Street. The yard at 45–47 was lost by 1890 and the yard at 36 was lost 1935–41.

NIGHTINGALE'S YARD

24–26 Colegate, was named after the Nightingale pub, which is recorded at 26 Colegate from 1870 (previously known as the Mechanic's Tavern). The pub was closed in 1907 and the yard was lost.

NINHAM'S COURT

Runs from 63 Bethel Street to 10–11 Chapel Field North; it was previously called Master's Court, but was renamed in honour of artist Henry Ninham, who lived at 12 Chapel Field North and often sketched the court. Ninham was an heraldic painter and copper-plate printer, and also painted coasts of arms on carriages. He was interested in old buildings, particularly doorways, and many of his etchings gives us a glimpse of parts of Norwich that are now lost. He died in October 1874 aged 82; his father was also an artist and sketched the gates of Norwich in 1782.

Walter Nugent Monck lived at Ninham's Court for nearly 40 years. He was a drama student at Liverpool Academy; after he left, he met William Poel, who wanted to produce Shakespeare's plays in the form in which they were originally shown. Monck liked the idea, and when he visited Norwich he produced plays with friends at the Music House in King Street. He moved to Dublin as producer at the Abbey Theatre, then moved back to Norwich in 1919 and built a replica Shakespearean theatre in St John

Ninham's Court. (Photograph by author)

Maddermarket at a cost of £3,300, raised entirely by supporters. Even today, his tradition is kept that the actors in plays produced there are anonymous.

NORGATE'S COURT

St Stephen's Street, exact location unknown. *Harrod & Co's Directory* of 1877 lists Norgate, England & Co, wine and brandy importers, at St Stephen's Street. The Norgates took over the Boar's Head, so this may be an alternate name for Boar's Head Yard.

NORMAN'S BUILDINGS

Is a cul-de-sac at the end of Rouen Road; its original address was Stepping Lane.

NORRIS GARDENS

Formerly Norris Court or Yard, 35–37 Elm Hill, was known as Norris Yard in 1883 and Norris Court in 1890. *Pigot's Directory* of 1830 lists John Norris, cabinet maker, there.

NORTHUMBERLAND PLACE

King Street, precise location unknown. The yard was referenced in *White's Directory* of 1845 and 1854 but lost by 1883.

NORWICH CORPORATION YARD

213 King Street. At the time of writing, early 2005, the area is being redeveloped into flats.

NOWHERE YARD

South side of Westwick Street, exact location unknown, was named after the Nowhere Tavern, which is recorded at Lower Westwick Street by 1811. In March 1888 the house is recorded as a 'cottage, owned by Charles Crawshay, formerly a public house called Nowhere'.

NUNN'S COURT OR YARD

31–33 St Augustine's Street, was formerly known as Minn's Yard. *Harrod & Co's Directory* of 1877 lists John Nunn, corn dealer, and Rachel Nunn, florist, at St Augustine's Street. The yard was lost by 1960.

OAK STREET

Oak Street runs from the junction of Colegate and Coslany Street to the junction of St Martin's Road and Baker's Road. Before 1890, part of Oak Street was actually Coslany Street – 1–41 on the west side and 2–32 on the east. The street was known as St Martin's at Oak Street from 1783–1845, but was Oak Street by 1854. The name came from the church, which had a large oak tree growing in the churchyard.

At the time of writing, there are new developments which have been recently built (or are currently being built!) on the west side of the street from Indigo Court up to New Mills Yard.

Streets off Oak Street

West:

Indigo Court (1)
Dial Yard/Court (5)*
Tuns or Tim's Yard (9–11)*
Saw Mill Yard (13–15)*
Distillery Yard (25–27)*
Reeves' or Reed's Yard (29–31)*
Betts' Yard (31)*
Buck's Yard (35–37)*
Unicorn Yard (39)*
New Mills Yard or Lane (41–43)
Barker's Yard (57–59)*
Queen Caroline Yard (61)*
Little Queen Caroline Yard (63–65)*
Bloomsbury Place (67–71)*
Mandela Close
White Lion Yard (71–73)
Howman's Yard (75–77)
St Crispin's Road (77–87)
Hawkes' Yard (79–81)*
Station Road (before 83)*
Little Crown Yard and Old Crown Yard (before 91)*
Bath House Yard (97–99)*
Ragged School Yard (before 105)*
Key & Castle Yard (105–107)
Robinson's Yard (111–113)*
Horton's Yard (113–115)*
Saddler's or Sadler's Yard (115–119)*
Suffolk Arms Yard (119)*
Smith's Yard (121)*
Flower Pot Yard (127)
Holl's or Hall's Yard (127)
Buck Yard and Little Buck's Yard (139–141)

East:
St Miles' Alley (before 12)
Eight Ringers Yard (12–14)*
Sun Yard (14–26)*
Pearce's Yard/Court (14–24)*
Scholar's Court (14)*
Greenland Fishery Yard (30–32)* (address formerly Coslany Street)
Rudd's Yard (32–34)*
St Mary's Plain (40–42 – leads to Duke Street/Muspole Street)
Gay's Yard (formerly Bream's Yard) (48–50)*
Dolphin Yard (54–56)*
Rayner's Yard (64)*
St Martin's Lane (68–70)
Arabian Horse Yard (70a)*
Little Arabian Horse Yard (70–72)*
Osborne's Yard (82a)*
Fellmongers' Yard (90)*
Talbot Square (formerly 90–96)
Baldwin's Yard (runs to 10 Quaker's Lane) (94–96)
Goat Yard (96–102)*
St Crispin's Road
Dog Yard (104–106)
Talbot Yard (108–110)
Jenkin's Lane (114–116 – ran to Chatham Street)
Little Brew Yard (120)*
Old Brew Yard (122)*
Royal Oak Yard (130)*
Angel Yard (140–146)*
Sussex Street (154–56)
Ebenezer Terrace (formerly Osborne's Buildings) (166–176)
Swan Yard (178–180)*
St Martin's at Oak Wall Lane (182–184)
Baker's Road (192–194)*

Exact location unknown:
Bidle's Yard*
Brew Yard*
Fuller's Hole, St Martin's Gates*
Jones' Yard*
Oak Yard*
Plummer's Yard or Court*

Buildings on Oak Street

City Wall

St Martin's Gate was originally known as Coslany Gate. Richard Spynke (see Barn Road) covered and leaded St Martin's Gate, had a portcullis made for it and provided bars and chains. The gate was taken down in 1808.

Churches

St Martin at Oak's Church took its name from an oak in the churchyard, which had a figure of the virgin (Our Lady) in its branches. According to Pevsner, the church dates from before 1441. *White's Directory* of 1890 says that in 1882 'part of the churchyard was thrown into St Martin's Lane' to widen it. The church was damaged in World War Two and was rebuilt by J. P Chaplin in 1953. The church has been redundant since 1976 and is in the care of the Norwich Historic Churches Trust; it was converted into a night shelter for the homeless in 1978.

St Martin at Oak's Church. (Photograph by author)

Other buildings of note

Empire cinema – according to cinema historian Stephen Peart, the Empire was opened at 79 Oak Street in 1913 and was closed in 1940. It was destroyed in an air raid in April 1942.

The Great Hall (see Flower Pot Yard).

Public urinal – Pevsner dates this from 1919 and says it is unusual as it is made from patterned concrete.

People linked with Oak Street

Peter Finch, brewer and mayor in 1827, lived at 41 Oak Street; his brewery was located there too.

William Sheward was the landlord of the Key and Castle at 105 Oak Street. He opened a pawnbroker's shop in St Giles in 1938 but went bankrupt. Perhaps influenced by something he'd read in a London newspaper, he murdered his wife Martha at their home in Tabernacle Street on 15 June 1851 and chopped her body into pieces, then scattered them around the city and moved to London. When the limbs started appearing, the city authorities believed that it was a prank by medical students; everything was found except her head. However, by January 1869 Sheward could no longer live with the guilt and confessed in a London police office. He was found guilty at his trial in Norwich and was hanged on 20 April 1869; this was the first private execution in Norwich Castle.

Events at Oak Street

In January 1827 a bull entered the Bess o' Bedlam pub, rushed upstairs and 'made its way into a room where a musical party was held'. According to the report in the *Norfolk Chronicle*, 'the animal was dislodged with great difficulty'.

The area was badly bombed during World War Two but also suffered from fires. On 17 June 1935 there was a severe fire at the new dye works of Fras. Hinde & Hardy. Mrs Pughe, the manageress of the Empire Cinema next door, told the audience to go home, and 81-year-old Mrs Jex was taken from her home in Howman's Yard to a safe place. The factory covered a large area of Oak Street; the *Eastern Daily Press* reported that the flames at their worst were as high as the chimneystack.

A more tragic case occurred on 23 October 1946. Mrs Esther Dunt of 134 Oak Street had already been bombed out once during the war; but that night her house caught fire. The neighbours heard her screams and tried to help, but were forced back by smoke. Esther escaped – but sadly her children didn't. Eight-year-old Barry, two-year-old John, one-year-old Michael and three-month-old Carl perished in the house.

OAK YARD

Oak Street, exact location unknown.

OBY'S OR OBEY'S YARD

61–63 King Street.

OCTAGON COURT

Calvert Street, was named after the Octagon just round the corner in Colegate.

OLD BANK OF ENGLAND COURT

Off Queen Street, was named after the Bank of England branch which was set up there in 1828 but was closed in May 1852. The court was used as the headquarters for Norwich Art Circle. Legend has it that in 1810 Sir Lambert Blackwall had a bet that he could drive a four-in-hand coach into the yard, turn it round without touching the sides and drive out again. Amazingly, he won the bet!

OLD BARGE YARD

Runs from 123 King Street to the river. The Old Barge inn incorporated the entrance to Meddays Hall (Meddyz inn) by 1906. The building was damaged in air raids in April 1942, and the Old Barge was closed in 1969. The building was originally built by Robert Toppes, *c.*1450. The great hall – 88ft by 22ft – was used as a goods showroom. It was then partitioned by William Boleyn and used as worker's cottages. It has also been used as a rectory, a butcher's shop

and a training centre. In 1979 the city council bought it and restored it, and it has been converted to a heritage centre known as Dragon Hall (named after the dragon in one of the spandrels).

OLD BREW YARD

122 Oak Street. The yard was lost 1935–41.

OLD CAT & FIDDLE YARD

See Cat & Fiddle Yard, 8 Botolph Street.

OLD CROWN YARD

91 Oak Street – see Little Crown Yard.

OLD DURHAM WHARF

King Street, exact location unknown.

OLD FRIENDS YARD

Before 1 Mariner's Lane, was named after the Old Friends pub, which is recorded at 119 Ber Street from 1854 and closed in 1908. (There was also another Old Friend's pub at 136 Ber Street, which was recorded there before 1865 and closed in 1953.) The yard was lost by 1960.

OLD MEETING HOUSE ALLEY (or YARD)

17 Colegate, takes its name from the Old Meeting House and Sunday School. The Old Meeting House was a Congregationalist church, built in 1693 on the site of the Dominican Friars' Church, which was destroyed by fire in 1449. It is the oldest remaining nonconformist chapel in Norwich and was restored in 1970 and 1993. *White's*

Old Meeting House, Colegate. (Photograph by author)

Directory of 1845 says that Balderstone's School was here; it was founded by Bartholomew Balderstone, who left £1,000 for a school to teach 20 poor children. The school building plus a large day school and Sunday school were built there in 1842.

OLD POST OFFICE COURT

Known as Old Post Office Yard in 1845–54. Runs from 6–8

Castle Street to 15–17 Market Place. It was originally part of the Half Moon pub but became a thoroughfare in the early 19th century. Sandred and Lingström suggest that the post office here may have been replaced by the one in Exchange Street, which was in turn replaced by the one in Prince of Wales Road (in the old Crown Bank).

OLD POST OFFICE YARD
19–21 Bedford Street, was named after the office where letters were posted in Georgian times. *White's Directory* of 1845 lists a News Room there.

There was a nasty incident there on 18 July 1864, when John Hamblington stabbed Virtue Anderson at Mr Calton's Club House Tavern in Old Post Office Yard. She'd been living apart from her husband George for the previous four years; during that time, she'd spent nine months living with Hamblington and had his baby. Hamblington stabbed her in the throat and simply left; a neighbour raised the alarm and called the doctor, who said the wound was 2½in long but shallow, and Virtue was more shocked than hurt. Police Constable Edward Lawrence found Hamblington in Magdalen Street the following day and arrested him; Hamblington was found guilty of unlawfully wounding and sentenced to 12 months' imprisonment with hard labour.

OLD RAVEN YARD
82–90 King Street, was named after the Raven inn, which is recorded at 32 Lower King Street from 1760. The pub closed in 1873. *White's Directory* of 1845 says that a Lancastrian School was established at Raven Yard in 1845; in 1845 it had 73 scholars.

Old Raven Yard, King Street. (Photograph by author)

(OLD) STAMP OFFICE YARD OR COURT
27 St Andrew's Street, takes its name from a Georgian office located there that sold stamps for official documents.

OLD SWAN YARD
27 St Peter's Street, took its name from the White Swan pub which is recorded at St Peter's Street from 1648. It was the principal centre for cock-fighting in Norfolk; and in 1762 an ox weighing more than 100 stone was exhibited there. The pub closed in 1895 and was demolished in the 1960s; the site became part of the car park in front of the Central Library (now the site of Millennium Plain and the Forum).

OLD YEAST YARD
8 Muspole Street. The yard was lost 1935–41.

ONE POST ALLEY (or PASSAGE)
Runs from 26–28 St Stephen's Street to Malthouse Road (St Stephen's Back Street). It was also known as Stocking's Alley in 1885 (see Stockings Court).

OPIE STREET
Runs from 25–27 Castle Meadow to 54–56 London Street; it was formerly known as the Devil's Steps, Gropecunte Lane and Evil Whore's Lane, and sedan chairs could be hired there at one point. It was renamed Opie Street after the writer Amelia Opie, who lived there in the 19th century. Amelia was the only child of physician John Alderson; she was sympathetic to the French Revolution and was interested in murder trials. She married the painter John Opie and moved to London. Sir Walter Scott said of her first novel, *Father and Daughter*, that he 'cried over it more than he had ever cried over such things'. The *Edinburgh Review* was less appreciative, calling it 'an appalling piece of domestic tragedy', and Thomas Love Peacock satirised her in *Headlong Hall* as Miss Philomena Poppyseed, 'an indefatigable compounder of novels written for the express purpose of supporting every species of superstition and prejudice'. When she was widowed in 1807, Amelia returned to Norwich and lived in Colegate with her father. After her father's death in 1825, she decided to be a Quaker (although her friends, the Gurneys, thought that this was a ploy to get John Joseph Gurney to marry her – a plot that didn't work!). She moved to Scotland and then to Cornwall before returning to Norwich; she lived in a house in Opie Street and died at the age of 84.

ORCHARD STREET
Former name for St John Street, Mountergate.

ORFORD HILL
Orford Hill runs from the corner of White Lion Street/Back of the Inns to 11 Orford Place. It was known as the Swynemarket in the late 13th century (when the market moved from All Saints Green to here), and Hog Hill by the end of the 17th century; but was renamed in the early 1800s after George Walpole, the 3rd Earl of Orford, who (according to the plaque on the street) 'gave generously to

public subscriptions for planning improvements made in his time'.

Streets off Orford Hill

York Alley or Passage (1)
Castle Meadow (2–3)
Orford Street (5–6)
Timberhill (6–7)
Red Lion Street (11–12)
Orford Place (11–12
White Lion Street (after 17)

Buildings on Orford Hill

A concrete stag was placed on top of Darlow's gun shop in 1890 by Mr Jeffries, an eccentric; it was removed after a fire but replaced in 1970 thanks to the Norwich Society.

The stag on Orford Hill. (Photograph by author)

People linked with Orford Hill

John Greene Cross, surgeon, lived in a house on Orford Hill later known as the Livingstone Hotel.

George Walpole, the 3rd Earl of Orford, was sometimes known as the 'mad Earl'. He inherited the title in 1751 at the age of 21, and lived a life devoted to pleasure – although he also gave very generously to public subscription to improve Norwich and became Lord Lieutenant of Norfolk. He once harnessed four deer to a coach and drove to Newmarket, and also tried to breed a very fast type of greyhound. He also bet a friend that he could get geese to London quicker than his friends could get turkeys to London – and he won, as the turkeys roosted on trees at night. However, not all of his bets were successful as he had to sell priceless paintings to Catherine the Great of Russia for £40,000 to pay his gambling debts. When his favourite mistress died, he wouldn't let her body be buried and hid it under pile of old boots in a cupboard. It was said that he died of grief at her death, but in reality he died after a fall from his horse.

Events at Orford Hill

In October 1826 Mr Hart's house on Orford Hill was supposedly haunted. Crowds gathered in the evenings to watch for the ghost; but then police officer Mr Martin explored unoccupied premises next door and found the hiding place of the 'ghost'.

In the late 19th century, the ironmonger's shop next to the Bell on Orford Hill was demolished to allow the laying of a tram route.

ORFORD PLACE

Formerly Little Orford Street, runs from 11 Haymarket to the junction of Red Lion Street and 11–12 Orford Hill. See Orford Hill for the derivation of the name). The Lamb Yard runs off the north side of the street; Toll's Court also ran from here to Brigg Street.

There was a frightening incident here on 1 December 1860 at Marrison's gun maker shop. There was a gunpowder explosion which wrecked the front of the shop as well as that of the photographer Mr Frankland next door. Frankland's sister was sitting in a room over Marrison's shop; the explosion threw her to the ceiling, and then she fell through the floor to the burning ruins below and was killed. Charles Hill, Marrison's shop boy, was also killed. The explosion also blew out the windows of the Bell Hotel and other houses; however, the insurance didn't pay for all of the damage because it turned out that Marrison kept more gunpowder on the premises than the terms of his contract allowed.

ORFORD ROAD

Leads from the junction of Red Lion Street and Orford Place to the junction of Orford Place and Orford Hill. See Orford Hill for the derivation of the name.

ORFORD STREET

Runs from Farmer's Avenue to Timberhill (at the junction with Orford Hill). See Orford Hill for the derivation of the name.

ORFORD YARD

25 Red Lion Street (Anchor Buildings), was named after the Orford Arms pub, which is recorded at 21 Magdalen Street from 1865 and closed in 1974.

OSBORNE SQUARE (also known as OSBORN'S COURT/YARD)

10–12 Timberhill. *Chase's Directory* of 1783 lists M. Osborne, grocer and tallow chandler, at 33 Timberhill. The court was lost by 1900 (when George A. Boston's furniture factory was on the site).

OSBORNE SQUARE
4 Cattle Market Street, is referenced in 1890 but not after.

OSBORNE'S YARD
82a Oak Street. *Robson's Commercial Directory* of 1839 lists Samuel Osborn, land steward at Coslany Street (aka Oak Street after 1890). This may also be linked with Osborne's Buildings at 166–176 Oak Street (see Ebenezer Terrace). The yard was lost 1935–41.

OXFORD STREET
St Catherine's Plain.

PAGE'S COURT
Church Street, Haymarket (now William Booth Street), exact location unknown. *Harrod & Co's Directory* of 1877 lists S.D. Page and Sons, wholesale brush, patten and paper bag manufacturers, at Haymarket and Theatre Street.

PAGE'S YARD
10 St Peter's Street. *Chase's Directory* of 1783 lists Page & Christian, watchmakers and gunsmiths, at 10 Upper Market Street (aka St Peter's Street). The yard was lost by 1830.

PALACE STREET
Palace Street runs from 20 Tombland to St Martin's at Palace Plain. It was known in the 18th century as St Martin's Street, and as St Martin's Palace Street by 1839. It takes its name from the Bishop's Palace on the south side of the street.

STREETS OFF PALACE STREET
Bedding Lane (3)
Pigg Lane (13–15)
College Court (may also have been Lancastrian School Yard) (21–23)*
Chestnut Place (25–27)*
Chiddick's Court (formerly Love's Yard) (33–37)*
St Martin at Palace Plain (37)

Exact location unknown:
Ringer's Court*

Buildings off Palace Street
The Bishop's Palace was built by Herbert de Losinga; it was restored in the 1850s and since 1960 has been part of the Norwich School.

PALACE YARD
79 Barrack Street, takes its name from St James' Palace, which was nearby.

PALMER'S YARD
19 Timberhill. *White's Directory* of 1883 lists William Palmer, boot tree maker, at 19 Timberhill.

PARADISE PLACE
139–141 Magdalen Street.

PARADISE ROW OR PLACE
32–40 Market Lane (the address is Scoles Green in 1911, so it clearly runs between the two). Now it is a small development off Thorn Lane.

PARAGON BUILDINGS
Castle Meadow, exact location unknown. The buildings were referenced in 1845 and 1854 but lost by 1883.

PARMENTERGATE COURT
Runs from the north side of Mountergate to St John's Street; it's a modern development which takes its name from the nearby Church of St Peter Parmentergate.

PARK'S YARD
112–114 Ber Street. The yard was lost before 1960, when King's metal merchants had a building on the site.

PARSONAGE SQUARE
Runs from 9–11 Bedford Street to 35–37 Exchange Street; it may have been the site of the Duke of Wellington pub. On 13 May 1900 Thomas Milham died here, aged 65; he was the last of the old watchmen, and used to 'shout the hour' at Gurney's Bank at 11pm. He was also the doorkeeper at the Corn Hall, and his obituary in the *Norfolk Chronicle* called him 'a man of great integrity'.

PATTESON'S CUT (The Cut)
70 Barrack Street. *Pigot's Directory* of 1830 lists Steward, Patteson and Steward, brewer, at Barrack Street.

PATTISON'S YARD
100–102 Magdalen Street, former name of Minns' Court. The name is after John Staniforth Patteson (whose surname isn't spelled the same as the yard!) Patteson was a brewer who lived here in the 1820s. The yard was lost by 1964.

PAUL'S YARD
154–156 Ber Street. *Harrod & Co's Directory* of 1877 lists Charlee (sic) Paul, fishmonger, at Ber Street. The yard was lost by 1941.

PAWSEY'S YARD
Magdalen Street, exact location unknown. *Pigot's Directory*

of 1830 lists Pawsey and Smith, cabinet makers and upholsterers, at Magdalen Street.

PEACOCK STREET

Runs from 47–49 Fishergate – originally to 20–22 Cowgate, but it was cut in half by St Crispin's Road. It was known in the 14th century as Tolthorp Lane, which Kirkpatrick says is after Sir Gilbert de Tolthorpe (who took his name from the manor there). By the end of the 17th century it was known as Rotten Row, which Kirkpatrick says is from 'several old cottages on the East side of this lane towards Fishergate', By 1830 it was known as Peacock Street, which may have been after a resident or after the Peacock pub, which was recorded in Pitt Street in 1845. The section between Fishergate and St Paul's Opening is now called Blackfriars Street.

Streets off Peacock Street

East:
Harvey's Yard (21)*
St Paul's Opening (31)
Waller's Yard (near 33)*
Barrack Street (formerly Church Street (St Paul's)) (45–47)
Willis Street (75)

West:
Webster's Court (12)*
Mischief Yard (46)*
St Saviour's Lane (22 – now off Blackfriars)
Albion Yard (64)
Roe's Yard*

Exact location unknown:
Burrell's Yard *
Malthouse Yard*

Events at Peacock Street

On 5 March 1926 there was a major fire on the street, which destroyed the factory of Williams Ltd and four cottages.

PEACOCK YARD

1 Red Lion Street, was named after the Peacock pub, which is recorded at 1 Red Lion Street from 1760; there was a fire there in September 1777, but the pub survived until 1958. The yard was lost with the pub.

PEAK'S COURT or PEEKE'S COURT

Is listed at both the east side of Fye Bridge Street and Magdalen Street (i.e. where the streets merge). The court is referenced in *White's Directory* of 1845 but was lost by 1854.

PEARCE'S YARD or COURT

14–24 Oak Street (Coslany Street before 1890). *Harrod &*

Co's Directory of 1877 lists J. Pearce, Grocer, at Coslany Street. The yard was lost during slum clearances in the 1930s.

PEEL MEWS

Robert Gybson Way (off Westwick Street), is a late 20th-century development which takes its name from Peel Yard (see below).

PEEL YARD

69 Westwick Street. *Robson's Commercial Directory* of 1839 lists Edmund Peel, shopkeeper, at Lower Westwick Street. Peel Yard was lost by 1941 but the name lives on in Peel Mews, off Robert Gybson Way.

PEGG'S YARD or OPENING

Ber Street, at the junction with 11–13 Horns Lane. *Harrod & Co's Directory* of 1877 lists W.B. Pegg, builder, at Horn's Lane, Ber Street. Another Pegg's Yard is listed on the opposite side of the road at 95–101 Ber Street; the yard was lost 1883–90.

PELICAN YARD

31–33 Pitt Street, was named after the Pelican pub, which is recorded at 33 Pitt Street from 1760. The licensee in 1794, Isaac Saint, was taken to London for questioning by a privy council because he was secretary of a United Society for Parliamentary Reform which met at the Pelican; the government of the time was nervous because of the recent revolution in France. The pub closed in 1867 and the yard was lost by 1941.

PERCY'S COURT

73–75 Pitt Street. The court was lost 1890–96.

PESTELL'S or PESTLE'S YARD

110–112 Cowgate. The yard was lost 1935–41.

PETER'S COURT

12–14 Calvert Street, was formerly known as Hall's Yard.

PHOENIX YARD

71 Cowgate, was named after the Phoenix Cellars and Phoenix Brewery, which is recorded at 96 Magdalen Street. The pub and brewery were closed in 1905 and became the site of the Phoenix Shoe Works; the shoe works was demolished in the 1960s for the Anglia Square development.

PIGG LANE

Runs from 13–15 Palace Street to 5–8 Quayside. It was originally called Norman's Lane in the 13th century, probably after the fisherman Robert Norman who had a house there. By the end of the 14th century it was called Hornynges Lane; by the end of the 15th century it was known as Wateryng Lane, because it was a watering place for horses at Quayside. By 1626 it had become Piggs' Lane, after Henry Pigg, Tudor constable and property owner.

PILGRIM'S COURT
Brigg Street, exact location unknown.

PIPE BURNERS' ROW
29 Bull Close. The row appears to be lost by 1935–41 or to have merged with the yard in the directories.

PIPE BURNERS' YARD
31 Bull Close, was also known as Pipe Makers' Yard in 1890. *White's Directory* of 1883 lists Samuel Lovett, tobacco pipe maker, at the yard.

PIPE BURNERS' YARD
37 Pottergate to 4–6 St Benedict's Street, was formerly known as Martin's Court. The archaeologist Brian Ayers says that evidence of pipekilns was found here. By 1971 the yard had become dilapidated.

PIPE BURNERS' YARD or ROW
42–44 St Stephen's Street to St Stephen's Back Street. The yard was lost by 1941–47.

PIPE YARD
73–75 Westwick Street. The yard was lost 1935–41.

PITT STREET
Pitt Street originally ran from the end of Muspole Street (at the Duke Street junction) to the junction of St Augustine's Street, Botolph Street and Gildencroft. Nowadays, it runs from the St Crispin's Road roundabout to St Augustine's Street. It was known in the 16th century as Olave's Street, from St Olave's Church, but took the name Pit Street from an open pit at the end of the churchyard. A second 't' was added in honour of William Pitt in the 18th century.

Streets off Pitt Street
East:
Whip & Nag Yard (3)*
Ely's or Eley's Yard (23–27)*
Pelican Yard (31–33)*
Percy's Court (73–5)*
Cherry Lane (formerly Cherry Tree Yard and Tooley Street) (35–43 – used to run to St George's Street)
Dark Entry Yard (43–51)*
Adelaide Court (51–53)*

Adelaide Yard (57–59)*
Gibson's Court (69)*
Cattermoul's Yard (formerly Mitchell's Yard) (79–81)*
Clabburn's court (79)*
Mitchell's Yard (79–81)*
Botolph Street
St Augustine's Street

West:
St Mary's Alley (formerly Soutergate Street and Southgate Street) (6)
Blakeley's Yard (12–14)*
Cattermoul's Yard (14)*
St Martin's Lane (26–28)
Gilbert's Yard (48–52)*
Winter's Yard (82–84)*

Exact location unknown:
Martin's Yard*
Primrose's Yard
Shuttle Yard
Tooley Street

Buildings on Pitt Street
Churches
St Olave's Church on Pitt Street was probably in ruins by 1482. The parish was added to that of St George Colegate in 1546, and the church was demolished.

Events at Pitt Street
Pitt Street was badly bombed during the Baedeker air raids of April 1942.

PLAIN YARD
St Stephen's Street, exact location unknown.

PLASTERERS' ARMS YARD
Bull Close, took its name from the Plasterers' Arms pub (which may have become the Bricklayers' Arms, recorded at 38 Bull Close from 1836). The Bricklayers' Arms was closed in 1938, was rebuilt in 1939 and was closed in 1978. The yard has since been lost.

PLAYFORD'S COURT
65–67 Pottergate. *Pigot's Directory* of 1830 lists Robert Playford, Patten & Trunk Maker, not far from there at 4 Dove Lane.

PLOUGH YARD
58–60 St Benedict's Street, was named after the Plough pub, listed at 58 St Benedict's Street from 1822; the yard may

have stretched as far back as Ten Bell Lane. The pub was damaged during air raids in April 1942. See also Little Plough Yard.

PLUMBERS' ARMS ALLEY

Runs from 18–20 Prince's Street to Wagon & Horses Lane. It was named after the Plumbers' Arms pub, which is recorded at 18 Prince's Street from 1822 to 1868. Although the pub was closed, the yard is still there. It was listed as Lacey's Court in 1883. Sandred and Lingström say that it was the same as Princes Inn Lane in 1845, but Prince's Inn Lane was also a former name for Waggon & Horses Lane. It was briefly known as Lacey's Court from 1883–90.

House in Plumbers' Arms Alley. (Photograph by author)

PLUMMER'S YARD or COURT

Oak Street, exact location unknown. *White's Directory* of 1845 lists Samuel Plummer's academy at Oak Street.

POPE'S BUILDINGS

9 Calvert Street.

POPE'S HEAD YARD

7 St Peter's Street, takes its name from the Pope's Head pub, which dated back to the 1500s and was mentioned in the trial of the Royalist rioters following the Great Blowe of 1648 (see Bethel Street). The pub's address has also been

given as 12 Upper Market Street. The pub was closed in 1912 and was demolished in 1935 to make way for City Hall.

PORTER'S YARD

Before number 6 World's End Lane. *Pigot's Directory* of 1830 lists Robert Porter, builder, nearby at St Martin at Palace Plain. Porter's Saw Mills on Fishergate were also close by.

POST OFFICE COURT

Pottergate, exact location unknown. In 1783 the post office and its court were in Jack of Newbury Yard; Elisha de Hague was the postmaster. The yard was lost by 1830.

POST OFFICE STREET

Was the lower half of Exchange Street (from Lobster Lane to St Andrew's Street); it took its name from the main post office on the south side of the street. This part of the street was formerly known as Museum Street.

POTTERGATE

Pottergate runs from Lobster Lane to Wellington Lane; according to Sandred and Lingström, it originally ran from Heigham Road to London Street (i.e. was also Lobster Lane and Bedford Street). It's one of the oldest streets in the city, and its name, from the 13th century, comes from its association with pottery work; Saxon kilns have been excavated here, although according to Sandred and Lingström there were no longer any potteries in Norwich by the 13th century. As with the other streets whose name ends in 'gate', Pottergate was known as Pottergate Street by 1783, but had dropped the 'street' by 1839.

Streets off Pottergate
North:
St John (Maddermarket) Street and Alley (7)
Stranger's Court (formerly Emms' Yard) (17–21)
Emms' Yard (formerly Cott's Yard) (19–21)*
Cook's Court (before 27)
St Gregory's Alley (27 – runs to St Benedict's Street)
Martin's Court (also known as Pipe Burners' Yard) (37–39)
St Lawrence Lane (51 – runs to St Benedict's Street)
Colman Court (formerly Baker's Yard) (57–59)
Playford's Court (65–67)
Three King Lane (79–81 – runs to St Benedict's Street)
Ten Bell Court (83–87)
Ten Bell Lane (95)
St Benedict's Alley (or St Benedict's Church Alley) (105–111)*
Neale's Square (117)*
Wellington Green (formerly St Benedict's Alley)
Wellington Lane (formerly Duck Lane)

South:
Dove Street (2)
Bagley's Court (6)
Lower Goat Lane (16 – runs to St Giles' Street)
Upper Goat Lane (20–22 – runs to St Giles' Street)
Wooden Entry (or Wood Entry) Yard (34)*
Boarded Entry Yard (46)*
Fisher's Lane (48–50 – runs to St Giles' Street)
Kingsgate Court (formerly Hovell Court or Hovel's Yard) (54–56)
Cow Hill (92–94 – runs to St Giles' Street)
Lincoln's Court (104–108)*
Pump Yard (108)*
Wellington Square (now Damocles Court) (108)
Copeman Street (108)
Damocles Court
Seeley's Court (116–20)
Wellington Lane (132)

Exact location unknown:
Browne's Yard or Court (ran to St Benedict's Street)*
Excise Office Yard*
Howes' Court*
Jack of Newbury Yard*
Ling's Yard*
Lobster Yard*
Post Office Court*

Buildings on Pottergate

Colman House (63a Pottergate) dates from the 17th century. It was the eye infirmary from 1854–1913, and in 1845 it could accommodate 8–9 in-patients and saw 300 out-patients each year. It then became a shoe factory and was converted to flats in 1984.

The dispensary was set up in Pottergate in 1804, as medical and surgical aid for the sick; Robert Thompson was the surgeon and apothecary.

Jenny Lind Infirmary for Sick Children was established in Pottergate in 1853, after the opera singer Jenny Lind gave two concerts in Norwich in 1849 and donated the proceeds of £1,253 to establish the hospital. The hospital was moved to Unthank Road in 1900. There was also a playground there and the site was given to the city by J. J. Colman in 1900, in memory of his son Alan who had died the previous year. In 1972 the playground was moved to Union Street.

Kinghorn House is a 17th-century building named after Joseph Kinghorn, the minister of St Mary's Baptist Church from 1789–1832, who lived there until his death in 1832. Towards the end of his ministry, he introduced Sunday evening meetings lit by gas – these were the first gas-lit evening meetings in Norwich.

Kinghorn House, Pottergate. (Photograph by author)

The Penny Library was established at Mr Quinton's at 36 Pottergate in 1822 and was adopted as a public institution in 1824. By 1845 it had 2,000 volumes; 200 readers paid 1d a week or a shilling a quarter to belong to the library.

People linked with Pottergate

Starling Day was a wool factor, merchant and banker who was mayor in 1782 and 1812; he lived at 103 Pottergate and in 1813 opened a subscription fund to help Russian provinces who were suffering because of Napoleon's invasion. His bank, Starling Day and Son, opened at 103 Pottergate in 1806. There were financial problems in 1825, but Gurney & Co came to the rescue and stopped a run on the bank by placing a pile of £1 notes on the counter. His son, also named Starling Day, was mayor in 1808, and his grandson, Thomas Starling Day, was mayor in 1825 – his mayoral procession passed through a new opening in the City Wall at the end of Pottergate.

Sarah Ann Glover, the inventor of the tonic sol-fa system, lived at 91 Pottergate. Her system was developed from the Italian 'solfeggio', where a key note is used from tuned glasses and all the other notes alter in pitch accordingly. She didn't want to profit from it as she was happy teaching; she ran a school for gentlewomen in Colegate with her sisters, Christina and Margaret, teaching arithmetic, drawing, sewing and music to poor children. John Spencer Curwen published the sol-fa system and took the credit of introducing it to teach singing.

Thomas Pye, a grocer, was mayor in 1597. He founded six almshouses in 1614, originally on the site of St Gregory's Churchyard; they were rebuilt in West Pottergate in 1827 and became known as Pye's Terrace.

William Stevenson was a painter of miniatures; he opened a drawing academy at 100 Pottergate by 1784, and became the proprietor of the newspaper the *Norfolk Chronicle*.

John Tolye (or Tooley), a merchant, was mayor in 1638 and 1644. In 1638 he gave a house called Sawyer's (part of 54 Pottergate) to Anguish's Boys Hospital. He was a royalist supporter during the Civil War, and was brought before the House of Commons in 1648. They declared him delinquent, and he was fined £1,000 (nearly £82,000 in today's money) and committed to the Fleet Prison for three months.

Charles Turner, a schoolmaster who was mayor in 1834, lived at 63a Pottergate.

Edward Willett, mayor in 1840–41, owned a weaving factory in Pottergate; he was one of the founders of the Norwich Crape Company in 1856.

Events at Pottergate

In January 1825 a new roadway through the City Wall at the west end of Pottergate was completed; it was opened for traffic two days later. Mr Blyth, who was instrumental with alderman T.S. Day in getting the road built, and his wife were the first people to travel on the new road.

There was a severe fire in the street on 14 July 1859 at Mr Noble's the organ builders; his entire stock was destroyed. The building next door was the hospital for invalids of the West Militia and, according to the *Norfolk Chronicle*, '10 sick Militiamen escaped… in great alarm, only partially dressed'. Pottergate fire station opened nearly 40 years later in September 1898.

Number 60 saw a murder in December 1896. John George Foster was a labourer at Arnold's brewery, and he staggered into the police station bleeding from a wound in his throat, saying that he tried to kill himself after murdering a woman. That woman was Alice Maria Newby, known as Mrs Nadin – although she'd refused to marry bricklayer William Nadin, despite living with him. Foster stabbed Newby through the throat with a shoemaker's knife; he was found guilty of manslaughter and sentenced to penal servitude for life.

PRIEST COURT

Rampant Horse Street, exact location unknown. *Robson's Commercial Directory* of 1839 lists George Priest, watchmatcher, nearby at 2 Brigg Street.*

PRIMROSE'S YARD

Pitt Street, exact location unknown. *White's Directory* of 1845 lists Mary Primrose, baker, at Pitt Street.

PRINCE OF WALES ROAD

Prince of Wales Road runs from the bottom of Agricultural Hall Plain to the top of Thorpe Road. It was named after the Prince of Wales and was built in 1860 on the site of the hopfields and orchards of the Austin Friars. It was opened for public traffic on 9 November 1862.

Streets off Prince of Wales Road

North:
Wales Square (58–60)
Cathedral Street (formerly Cathedral Street North – runs to St Faith's Lane) (72–74)
St Faith's Lane (after 98 – runs to Tombland)

Prince of Wales Road. (Photograph courtesy of Norwich City Council)

Foundry Court (runs to Recorder Road)
Recorder Road

South:
Crown Road (once ran to Rose Lane)
St Vedast Street (formerly Cathedral Street South) (61–63)
Eastbourne Place (87 – now links Prince of Wales Road to Rose Lane)
Rose Lane (after 89)
Mountergate

Buildings on Prince of Wales Road

Alexandra Mansions, 86–98 Prince of Wales Road, was built in 1890 as the first block of residential flats in Norwich; it had shops on the ground floor.

Foundry Bridge was built in 1885, named after the foundry which once stood on the site of the Hotel Nelson – although it had also been known as Station Bridge. The original bridge was cast by Barnard, Bishop & Barnard and has been moved to the Barn Road roundabout. It's the third bridge on the site; the first was built in 1810 and the second was built in 1844 at a cost of £800.

The Electric Cinema was opened at 102–104 Prince of Wales Road in 1912; it had a resident orchestra. It was taken over and reopened as the Norvic in September 1949 and closed in 1961.

The Greyfriars (Austin Friars) Church was on the site of 44 Prince of Wales Road from 1292–1539.

The Prince of Wales cinema was opened at 110a Prince of Wales Road, in June 1912; it closed in 1922 and was turned into a dance hall called the Grosvenor Rooms. The Beatles played here in May 1963 – then queued up with fans at Rose Lane for a bag of chips! It's now an office block called Grosvenor House.

The Regent cinema was built in 1922 and opened in 1923; it became the ABC in 1961, then the Cannon and became the Mercy nightclub.

People linked with Prince of Wales Road

David Hodgson, artist, lived on Prince of Wales Road (and possibly also King Street). He was part of the Norwich School and is known for his paintings of street scenes, particularly that of the fish market. He died in April 1864, and his obituary in the *Norfolk Chronicle* says that he 'excelled in architectural subjects, which he painted with great care and truthfulness of detail'. His father Charles was also an artist and was friendly with Crome and Ladbroke.

Events at Prince of Wales Road

There was an enormous fire at Foundry Bridge on 9 September 1917 at Norwich Components Ltd. The fire started at midnight and the building quickly became five storeys of flames. The night shift there – including 150 women – managed to get out, but the factory was gutted in 20 minutes, causing thousands of pounds worth of damage.

On 20 September 1923 number 40 and 42 Prince of Wales Road were being converted into a shop and warehouse when they collapsed with no warning. Five workmen were buried in the rubble; one of them escaped with shock, one had a broken leg and one had a fracture at the base of his skull. Thomas Arthur Pointer died, and Philip Matthew was buried face-down under 6ft of rubble – luckily, rescue workers managed to dig him out, but unsurprisingly he suffered badly from shock.

PRINCE OF WALES YARD

32–34 St Benedict's Street, was named after the Prince of Wales pub, which is recorded at 48 St Benedict's Street, from 1845. The pub was damaged during air raids in 1942 and was closed in 1965.

PRINCE OF WALES YARD

39 St Augustine's Street, was named after the Prince of Wales pub, which is recorded at 39 St Augustine's Street from 1763. The pub closed in 1969. The yard may also have been known as Stone Mason's Yard.

PRINCE OF WALES YARD

Tombland, was named after the Prince of Wales pub, which is recorded at 8–10 Prince of Wales Road since 1870 (and backs onto the yard); the pub was damaged during an air raid in 1942 but was restored and is still open today.

PRINCE'S INN LANE

Prince's Street (exact location unknown); was named after the Prince's inn, which is mentioned in city records as far back as 1391 and was listed in 1811 at Hungate Street. It may be linked with Plumbers' Arms Alley or with Waggon & Horses Lane.

PRINCE'S STREET

Prince's Street runs from St Andrew's Hall Plain to the middle of Tombland. It was known as Hundegate (or Hungate Street) in the 13th century; tradition says that the bishop's hounds were once kept there. It was renamed Prince's Street by 1830, after the Prince's inn (see Prince's Inn Lane). The road numbering system here switched between 1890 and 1900 (after work was done on the tram system), and originally the north side of the street was odd-numbered, with Elm Hill at 19–21.

Streets off Prince's Street

North:
Elm Hill (2–6)

Mandell's Court (8–10)
Plumbers' Arms Alley (also known as Lacey's Court) (18)
Mounser's Yard (also known an Mountseer's or Mountsear's Court) (20–22)*
Tombland Alley (formerly St George's Church Alley) (after 26)

On the south side, the street has included:
Redwell Street (after 9)
Model School Yard (formerly National School Yard) (15)*
St Michael at Plea's Alley (runs to 10 Redwell Street)
St Michael at Plea's Court

Other streets whose exact locations could not be placed include:
Millard's Yard*
Prince's Inn Lane*

Buildings on Prince's Street
Churches
St Christopher's Church – the pre-Conquest Church of St Christopher was sited at 3 Prince's Street. It was destroyed by fire in the late 1200s and the parish was added to St Andrew's.

Congregational Church (United Reform Church) was built in 1869 by Boardman, to replace a small chapel which dated from 1819; the foundation stone of the original chapel was laid by Revd John Alexander in March 1819, and the building opened in December 1819.

St Peter Hungate Church was renovated in 1458 by John and Margaret Paston; it has an angel hammerbeam roof and squints in the transept piers. The chancel roof collapsed in 1604; the chancel was in such bad condition by 1906 that the city considered demolishing it, but it was restored. Further restoration took place in 1931 and it has been a church history museum since 1933.

St Peter Hungate Church, Prince's Street. (Photograph by author)

Other buildings of note
Garsett House – also known as Armada House – was probably named after Robert Garsett, an alderman who lived there in the 1570s. Some of the wooden beams in the house were thought to have come from ships of the Spanish Armada wrecked off the East Anglian coast (hence the alternate name). In the 19th century it housed the Kent family's legal firm; Ernest Kent bequeathed the house to the Norfolk and Norwich Archaeological Society. When St Andrew's Street was extended in 1898, part of the southern wing was demolished.

Garsett House, Prince's Street. (Photograph by author)

People linked with Prince's Street
Robert Bendish, a grocer who was mayor in 1672, lived in a house on the corner of Elm Hill and Prince's Street, opposite St Peter Hungate.

Richard Harman, a skinner who was mayor in 1639, lived in Oxford House on Prince's Street in 1626. In 1643 he refused to subscribe for Parliament's fund to regain Newcastle.

Richard Tolye (or Tooley), a scrivener who was mayor in 1620, lived in Prince's Street.

PRINCES YARD
Botolph Street, exact location unknown.

PRIORY SQUARE

63–65 Barrack Street, formerly Nickall's Buildings. The square was lost 1964–75.

PRIORY YARD

109–111 Cowgate, was also known as Priory Playground, and takes its name from the priory that used to be there (the site is now known as Whitefriars). It was lost by 1964.

PROSPECT PLACE

12–14 Horns Lane, was named after Prospect Road and the Prospect pub. It ran to 40–42 Market Lane at one point.

PROSPECT ROAD

2–4 Scoles Green, was named after the Prospect pub (no details available).

PUDDING LANE

38 Market Place, leads to Weaver's Lane and Gentleman's Walk.

Pudding Lane. (Photograph by author)

PUMP LANE OR YARD

9–10 Fisher's Lane, is referenced in *White's Directory* of 1890 but was lost by 1941.

PUMP STREET

Pump Street, off Buffcoat Lane, contained Lincoln's Yard and Wales Yard. It was known as Common Pump Street from 1783–1830 and took its name from a pump that stood there. The street was demolished in 1861 for the extensions to the cattle market, although it may have run along the northern side of the present-day Cattle Market Street.

Events at Pump Street

There was a major fire at the street on 28 February 1778; the Crispin Alehouse, the house of baker Mr Smith, and four other houses were destroyed. The *Norwich Mercury* reported that one man managed to save his sheets and bed – but then they were stolen from the poor chap!

There was also a nasty murder there in April 1851 when James Flood killed his lover, Jane Field. That particular evening he'd been out drinking and she'd gone to find him. When he returned to their home in Pump Street, drunk, and discovered she wasn't there, he went out in a temper. The cry of 'murder' was heard and witnesses said he knocked Jane down between the pump and the pipemaker's shop and proceeded to kick her in the head. Jane threw up amounts of blood; Mr Day, the surgeon, was called, and she died later that night.

PUMP YARD

Just after 146 Cowgate. The yard was lost by 1964.

PUMP YARD

108 Pottergate. The yard was lost by 1890.

PUMP YARD

Quaker's Lane, exact location unknown. The yard appears to be lost by 1900.

PYE'S YARD

Runs beneath the arch leading to Cotman House at 8 St Martin's at Palace Plain through to the end of Bedding Lane; it takes its name from Samuel Pye, who built Cotman House.

QUAKERS LANE

Originally ran from 47–59 St Martin's Lane, but now runs from St Crispin's Road to Chatham Street; it was referred to from the early 17th century as Gildencroft Lane, but by the mid-18th century was known as Quakers Street. It takes its name from the Quakers' meeting house in Gildencroft, which was built in 1699 but destroyed during an air raid in 1942 and rebuilt in 1958. Local historian George Nobbs says the lane was known as 'Chaff Lug Alley' because it's so narrow. Two yards run off it: Baldwin's Yard (from number 10 through to 98 Oak Street); Pump Yard, exact location unknown.

QUANTRILL'S COURT

22–24 Surrey Street. *Pigot's Directory* of 1830 lists baker Robert Quantrell at Surrey Street. It was also known as Miller's Court in 1883; it was lost by 1964.

QUAYSIDE

Quayside runs from 27 Wensum Street to Bedding Lane; the name comes from its function.

Streets off Quayside:
Cock & Pie (or Pye) Yard (3–5)
Pigg Lane (5–8)
Beckwith's Court (13–14)
Bedding Lane (sometimes known as Thoroughfare Yard) (25–26)

Exact location unknown:
Lansdowne Place*
Roshier Court*

The area is undergoing extensive redevelopment at the time of writing.

Buildings on Quayside
According to local historian George Nobbs, there was once a ducking stool here.

People linked with Quayside
Jacob Henry Tillett, a solicitor who was mayor from 1859–60 and 1875–76, was born at Quayside. He was the son of dyer Jacob Tillett and was educated at Norwich School. He founded the *Norfolk News* in 1845 and was its chair and editor until his death in 1892. He was elected as the city's MP in 1870 but was unseated over bribery claims, even though he was believed to be innocent. He was re-elected MP in 1880 and was known as the Norwich Robespierre. When he died in January 1892 the *Norfolk Chronicle* said 'he was naturally of a kind, considerate and affectionate disposition'.

QUEEN ADELAIDE YARD

See Adelaide Yard, Pitt Street.

QUEEN ANN'S YARD

59 Colegate, was named after the Queen Anne pub (albeit spelled slightly differently), which is recorded at 57 Colegate from 1806 and was closed in 1909.

QUEEN CAROLINE YARD

61 Oak Street, was named after the Queen Caroline pub, which is recorded at 61 Oak Street from 1763. The pub was closed in 1925 and the yard was lost shortly after. Little Queen Caroline Yard was at 63 Oak Street.

QUEEN ELIZABETH CLOSE

Bishopgate (opposite the Adam & Eve pub), is a development of 24 flats built in 1973 on the site of St Matthew the Apostle's Church.

QUEEN OF HUNGARY YARD

47–49 St Benedict's Street, was named after the Queen of Hungary pub, which is recorded at 49 St Benedict's Street from 1760. It was closed in 1913.

QUEEN'S HEAD YARD

Cowgate (exact location unknown), was named after the Queen's Head pub, which is recorded at Cowgate from 1807. The pub closed in 1881.

QUEEN STREET

Queen Street runs from the junction of Redwell Street and Bank Plain to Tombland. It was originally known as Redwell Street; at the end of the 19th century there were several changes of street name, and when Redwell Street became Queen Street, St Michael's Street became Redwell Street.

Buildings on Queen Street
St Mary the Less Church was formerly known as St Mary at the Monastery Gate; the name was changed to Mary the Less to distinguish it from St Mary Coslany. By 1744 it was known as the 'French Church'. It became redundant at the Dissolution and the parish was added to St George Tombland in 1542. In 1623 it was used as a hall for the sale of yarn; in 1637 it was leased by the Walloons. In 1862 it was let out again, first to followers of Swedenborg and then to Catholics. In the mid-1990s it was used as a Flemish study centre.

St Mary the Less Church, Queen Street. (Photograph by author)

St Michael at Plea Church took its name because the mediaeval church plea courts were held there; other names included St Michael Motstow or Much Stow (i.e. head or chief church of St Michael, because of the plea courts held there) and St Michael of Muspole (because there used to be a pool where the well is now). The church was originally built in the form of a cross. It was restored in 1887 at a cost of £3,000 and has St Michael and the Dragon in its spandrels; a sundial was removed during the restoration. It has been redundant since 1974 and has been used as an antiques centre.

St Michael at Plea Church, Queen Street. (Photograph by author)

People linked with Queen Street

The Ferrour family dominated Queen Street; their family home was Ferrour House at 3 Queen Street. Robert Ferror (sic) was a wool trader who was mayor in 1526 and 1536. William Ferrour (or Ferrer) was a draper who was mayor in 1562 and 1575. His son Richard Ferrour, a dornix weaver, was mayor in 1596 (and was both baptised and buried in St Michael at Plea).

Charles Weston (jnr), a brewer who was mayor in 1789, lived at 4 Queen Street. His brewery was near St George's Bridge; he sold it in 1864 to Youngs, Crawshay & Youngs, and the site was later used for the Norwich Mercury Company printing works.

Events at Queen Street

In September 1807 a strange parcel was found in the churchyard of St Michael at Plea; according to the newspaper report, a child found 'concealed behind a gravestone, covered with a tile, a parcel containing more than £90 in forged Bank of England notes and £14 in counterfeit shillings' (the equivalent of almost £5,000 and £750 in today's money).

There was a large fire on 5 September 1892 between Bank Street and Queen Street, which started at the Queen Street premises of confectioner R.A. Cooper. During the rescue operation, police constable Hook was struck by falling masonry; it fractured his spine and he died five days later.

RACKHAM COURT

23 St Peter's Street, was formerly known as St Peter's Court. *White's Directory* of 1883 lists W.S. Rackham & Sons, Manchester Warehousemen, and Rackham & Co, drysalters, at St Peter's Street. *Harrod & Co's Directory* of 1877 also lists Rackham & Co, analytical chemists, at St Peter's Street. The yard was lost for the City Hall development in the early 1930s.

RAGGED SCHOOL YARD

Just before 105 Oak Street, took its name from the Sunday School which was set up in the 19th century for the children of poor people. The yard was lost by 1960.

RAINBOW YARD

186 King Street, was named after the Rainbow pub, which is recorded at 185 King Street from 1760. The pub closed in 1959; it was reported to have a large metal ring in one corner that was used to restrain a performing bear in the 1800s. The yard was lost with the pub.

RAMPANT HORSE STREET

Rampant Horse Street runs from St Stephen's Plain to the beginning of Theatre Street. The street was originally known as the Horsemarket (from the late 13th century); the the Ramping Horse inn (later the Rampant Horse) stood on the north side of the street from the 13th century. The street became known as Rampant Horse Lane by the mid-18th century and Rampant Horse Street by 1830. The Rampant Horse was closed in 1892 and the building was demolished before 1900.

Streets off Rampant Horse Street

South:
Malthouse Road (formerly St Stephen's Church Lane) (11)
Cartwright's Court (15–17)*

North:
Unthank's Court (near 2)*
Brigg Street (12–18)

Exact location unknown:
Back Rampant Horse Street*
Priest Court*
Thatched House Yard*
Thompson's Yard*

Buildings on Rampant Horse Street
Churches
St Stephen's Church was founded before the Conquest as the parish church for Nedeham. The ground floor of the church dates from the mid-14th century, though the top half was remodelled in 1604 and restored again in 1859. The tower at the side of the chancel also acts as a porch, and there are misericords under the choir stalls and poppy-head designs on the pews. According to *White's Directory* of 1890, the church has a curious carving of nine male saints, similar to the one in St Peter Mancroft's of nine female saints. The church was restored in 1859 at a cost of £1,500, and the churchyard was re-laid in 1882.

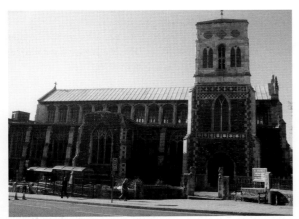

St Stephen's Church, Rampant Horse Street. (Photograph by author)

Other buildings of note
After World War Two, a static water tank was put up on the site of Curl's (now Debenham's). It contained 270,000 gallons and was one of the largest water tanks in the country at the time. It was drained and used as a car park.

People linked with Rampant Horse Street
Robert Brasier was a bellfounder who was mayor in 1410.

Richard Brasier, a goldsmith who was mayor in 1456 and 1463, lived in a house on the site between Red Lion Street, Little Orford Street and Rampant Horse Lane (where Debenham's is now). There was a foundry there, and his father Robert (also mayor, in 1410) was a bellfounder. In 1720, the site was the brewery of Benjamin Nuthall.

Richard de Castre or Castor was the vicar of St Stephen's in 1402. He was a follower of Wycliffe, and was called 'Castor the Good'; he was known as a prophet and apparently miracles occurred at his grave in the church after 1419, which led to pilgrimages there.

The Mingay family, who were prominent in local government, had their family home (Mingay House) at 14 Rampant Horse Street. William Mingay, a mercer and notary, was mayor in 1561. John Mingay, an apothecary, was mayor in 1617, and Roger Mingay, an ironmonger, was mayor in 1658. They are all buried in St Stephen's Church.

Events on Rampant Horse Street
The Rampant Horse inn was fairly notorious. In 1785 Parson Woodforde said he saw a 'learned pigg' there; this was a boar with a 'magic collar', who could spell and add figures. Dr Katterfelto, a quack doctor and conjuror, came to the Rampant Horse as part of a very long tour and gave performances of 'perpetual motion and occult secrets', which included raising his daughter to the ceiling with a hidden giant magnet. And in 1823 the resurrection men used the Rampant Horse as a place to post stolen corpses (mainly from Lakenham Churchyard) to London medical schools. In June 1861 Herr Kolisch, a famous chess player of the time, played 13 games simultaneously against some of the best local players at the Rampant Horse Hotel; he won eight of them, lost three and drew two.

On 17 July 1901 there was a major fire at Snelling's candle factory. The fire started in the lard room, and everyone thought it would destroy the neighbours (Goose, the printer and stationer, and Thompson the tinsmith). Rescue workers got barrels of tallow out of the factory, but the heat caused the wood to swell; the barrels burst and liquid tallow ran all over the road. And the firemen had a narrow escape when the roof fell in – one was stunned when the roof fell onto him, but clearly wasn't badly hurt as the newspaper reported that he soon got back to work.

The street was pretty much flattened in the air raids of 1942 and rebuilt.

RAMPANT HORSE YARD
31–33 Fishergate, was named after the Rampant Horse pub, which is recorded at 31 Fishergate from 1839. The pub closed in 1912 and was demolished; the yard was lost with it.

RATCATCHER'S YARD
71 Ber Street, was apparently named after a pub. It became Brook's Yard at the end of the 19th century, as it was apparently an 'ancient name' for the yard.

War damage in Rampant Horse Street, picture courtesy of Norfolk County Council Library and Information Service.

RAVEN YARD

86–90 King Street, is a housing development built in the 1970s over the old Raven Yard. See Old Raven Yard.

RAYNER'S YARD

190–192 King Street, is listed in *Kelly's Directory* of 1900 but was lost by 1964.

RAYNER'S YARD

64 Oak Street. *Harrod & Co's Directory* of 1877 lists G. Rayer (sic – no n), grocer, at Oak Street. The yard was lost by 1912.

RECORDER ROAD

Recorder Road runs from James Stuart Gardens to Prince Of Wales Road and was laid out in 1907. Sandred and Lingström suggest the name may be linked with the office of City Recorder.

Streets off Recorder Road
East:
Riverway Court
Lovel Staithe (runs to river)
Stuart's Court

West:
Foundry Court (runs to Prince of Wales Road)
Cavendish Court

Entrance to James Stuart Gardens, Recorder Road.
(Photograph by author)

Buildings
Blickling Court is a development of flats built in 1934 by Frank M. Dewing; they were built on the site of the old Horse Fairs held during the reigns of Edward I and Edward II. The Horse Fairs were moved to the castle ditches by Henry VII in 1500.

The Church of Christ Scientist, designed in 1934 by Herbert Ibberson, is now the Greek Orthodox Church of the Mother of God.

James Stuart Gardens, a memorial to J.J. Colman's son-in-law (through his daughter Laura Elizabeth Stuart, the city's first female JP), were opened in July 1922.

Vinegar Works, 1865; St Faith's Lane was temporarily called Vinegar Lane after Hill's vinegar works.

RED COW YARD

149–151 Barrack Street, was named after the Red Cow pub, which is recorded at 118 Barrack Street from 1760. The pub became known as the Brown Cow (or Dun Cow) by 1900; it closed in 1936 and was demolished as part of the slum clearance scheme.

RED LION STREET

Red Lion Street runs from the junction of 11–12 Orford Hill and Orford Place to the bottom of St Stephen's Street. It was called Westlegate from the 14th century, but became known as Red Lion Street in the late 17th century after the Red Lion pub, which is recorded at 15 Red Lion Street from at least 1776. The pub closed in 1938; according to pub historian Walter Wicks, the famous Elizabethan clown Richard Tarleton appeared there in 1583.

Streets off Red Lion Street
West:
Back Rampant Horse Street
Bird's Court (6)*

On the east side, the street has included:
Peacock Yard (1)*
Gynne's Yard (17)*
Orford Yard (25)

Buildings on Red Lion Street
The Anchor Buildings were the site of the first Norwich nightclub.

Events on Red Lion Street
John Browne, the landlord of the Yarmouth Bridge pub on Red Lion Street, died in February 1840 at the age of 39. He apparently suffered from a form of narcolepsy, as he was prone to falling asleep in the middle of conversations and could keep awake only for a few minutes at a time. Although

he lived on dry toast and tea, he was thought to be the heaviest man in the city, weighing 27 stone.

The street was demolished in 1899 so it could be widened for the trams. It was rebuilt by George Skipper and Edward Boardman between 1900 and 1903.

RED LION YARD

26 Coslany Street, was named after the Red Lion pub, which is recorded at 26 Coslany Street from 1760. It was closed in 1970 and later demolished, along with the yard. In the late 19th century the pub held an early morning licence so it could serve the employees of Barnard & Bishops.

RED LION YARD

19 Magdalen Street, was named after the Red Lion pub, which is recorded at 21 Magdalen Street from 1806. It was renamed the Viking Stores around 1955 and was closed by 1961.

RED LION YARD

155–157 Magdalen Street, was also known as Garden Place. It was named after the (second) Red Lion pub in Magdalen Street, which is listed at 157 Magdalen Street from 1760. The pub was closed in 1937.

RED LION YARD

14–18 St George's Street, was named after the Red Lion pub, which is recorded at 18 St George's Street from 1811 (and was also known as the Red Lion Stores). It is thought to be the first Norwich pub to feature a skiffle group, and was important in pop music circles in the 1950s and 1960s. The pub closed in 2004.

REDWELL PLAIN

Former name of Bank Plain.

REDWELL STREET

Redwell Street runs from the end of Bank Plain to 9 Prince's Street. It was known as St Michael's Street until around 1783 when it was renamed Red Well Street (which became Redwell Street by 1845). The name comes from the Red Well on the corner of St Michael at Plea's Churchyard; a pump was placed over the well in 1629.

Streets off Redwell Street
Clement Court (2–3)
St Andrew's Street (6–8)
Brady's Yard (6–8)*
Church Alley or Walk (10, runs to Prince's Street)

Exact location unknown:
Brundell's Court or Yard*

Buildings on Redwell Street
Churches
St Michael at Plea – see Queen Street.

People linked with Redwell Street
Dr Robert Hull, physician of the Norfolk and Norwich Hospital, lived at Redwell Street in the mid-1800s.

REED'S YARD

Oak Street – see Reeves' Yard, Oak Street.

REEVE'S YARD

49–51 St Benedict's Street. *White's Directory* of 1883 lists Job Reeve, victualler, at number 51, and Charles Reeve, confectioner, next door.

REEVES' YARD

29–31 Oak Street (Coslany Street before 1890), was also known as Reed's Yard. *Pigot's Directory* of 1830 lists John Sayer Reeve, baker, near there. The yard was lost by 1925.

RIBS OF BEEF YARD

24 Wensum Street, was named after the Ribs of Beef pub, which is recorded at 24 Fye Bridge Street from 1760. It was known as the Fye Bridge Tavern from 1915 and closed in 1959, but it reopened as the Ribs of Beef in 1985.

RICE'S COURT

14 Wensum Street; *Harrod & Co's Directory* of 1877 and *White's Directory* of 1883 list John Jethro Rice, stationer. The yard is now known as Roache's Court and appears to run to Elm Hill.

RIFLEMAN YARD

29 All Saints Green, was named after the Rifleman pub, which is recorded at 29 All Saints Green from 1806. The pub closed before 1867 and the yard was lost with it.

RIGBY'S COURT

Formerly Pit Lane, runs from 52–54 St Giles' Street to 64–66 Bethel Street. It was called Pit Lane in the mid-18th century (after a refuse pit, which Kirkpatrick says was filled up and paved over in the early 18th century) but took its name in the mid-19th century from surgeon Edward Rigby, who lived at 29 St Giles' Street and had a surgery and apothecary's shop at Pit Lane. Rigby specialised in the removal of gallstones and also introduced vaccination to the city; he had his own smallpox hospital, as well as a licence to keep 'twelve lunaticks' in a house in Lakenham. He had 12 children, including quadruplets, by Anne, his second wife, when he was 70. He practiced as a surgeon in Norwich for 53 years, was a founder of the Norwich

Medical Benevolent Society in 1786 and was mayor of the city in 1805. He was also a keen naturalist, to the point where he threw his tenants out and demolished their houses to plant more trees! The epitaph on his tomb in Framingham Earl reads: 'A monument for Rigby do you seek? / On every side the whispering woodlands speak.'

RINGER'S COURT

Palace Street, exact location unknown. *Robson's Commercial Directory* of 1839 lists J.M. Ringer, grocer, at St Martin's at Palace Street. There was also a foundry at one point nearby at Bedding Lane, so it may be named after the bells. The court was lost by 1925.

RISING SUN LANE

Rising Sun Lane ran from 21 Golden Ball Street to Scoles Green. It was named after the Rising Sun pub, listed at Golden Ball Street in 1845 and 89 Buffcoat Lane in 1851. The pub was there from 1760, but had closed by 1867. The road was lost by 1964.

Streets off Rising Sun Lane

South:
Chittick's court (5)*
Shorten's Yard (15–17)*
Davison's Court (south)*

North:
Bleach Yard (4)
Globe Lane (22)

RISING SUN ROW

31 Chapel Field Road, was named after the Rising Sun pub, which is recorded at Chapelfield from 1836–1856. According to pub historian Walter Wicks, the landlord was horse dealer Jack Abel, who also kept 'Kensington Gardens' at Old Lakenham – a miniature menagerie of bears and monkeys. The yard was lost by 1960, firstly for a car sales outlet then for the office block of Norvic House.

RIVER LANE

Runs from 85 Barrack Street – originally to a staithe called St James' Staithe. It was originally called Water Lane; as there were other streets with the same name in the city, the Corporation changed the name to River Lane in 1900.

RIVERWAY COURT

Is an early 21st-century development on the east side of Recorder Road; it takes its name from the river it overlooks.

ROACHE'S (OR ROACH'S) COURT

30–34 Elm Hill, runs to Wensum Street. *Pigot's Directory* of 1830 lists Richard Roach, gentleman, as a resident of Elm Hill. According to local historian George Nobbs, the court contained a barn and stables.

Roache's Court, Elm Hill. (Photograph by author)

ROACH'S (OR ROACHE'S) COURT

Fisher's Lane, after number 10. *White's Directory* of 1845 lists John Roach, collector of debts and land agent, at Fisher's Lane; this may be the same John Roach who was a schoolmaster there in 1830. In June 1838 there was a serious fire there at Bush the cabinet maker's; the factory was destroyed, as was the house next door where the silk weaver lost his silk and machinery. The report in the *Norfolk Chronicle* was thoroughly disgusted: 'the fire engines were not in a state for such an emergency, and many of the leather pipes had to be tied up with handkerchiefs'. The yard was lost by 1941.

ROBERT GYBSON WAY

Runs from Westwick Street to Coslany Street, and takes its name from Robert Gibson (see Westwick Street). Peel Mews and Mulberry Close run off it.

ROBIN HOOD YARD

North Barrack Street. Named after the Robin Hood pub, which is recorded nearby at 84 Mousehold Street from 1760; the pub was knocked down and rebuilt further back in 1889.

ROBINSON'S YARD
111–113 Oak Street. *Pigot's Directory* of 1830 lists William Robinson (camlet, bombazine & crape manufacturer) at Calvert Street. The yard was lost 1935–41.

ROCK YARD
34 Barrack Street. *Chase's Directory* of 1783 lists Richard Rock, throwsterer, at St James' Street (aka Barrack Street). The yard was lost 1935–41.

RODNEY STREET
Former name for upper Surrey Street.

ROE'S YARD
West side of Peacock Street after 64. The yard was lost 1883–90.

ROGER'S YARD
Lower Westwick Street, exact location unknown.

ROSE AVENUE
Runs from Market Avenue to the junction of Cattle Market Street with Rose Lane and King Street. Crown Road runs off it. In 1905 it was a plain between Crown Road and the King Street/Rose Lane junction.

ROSE LANE
Rose Lane runs from 39–41 King Street to the south side of Prince of Wales Road. It was originally called St Faith's Lane, but by the 17th century it was known as Rose Lane, named after the Rose Tavern at 2 Rose Lane. The junction with King Street was also known as Rose Corner in 1783. The Rose Tavern closed in 1911.

Streets off Rose Lane
South:
Turner's Square (after 15)*
Jay's Square (after 15)*
Boulton Street
St John's Street (or John Street) (41–43 – now off Mountergate)
Watson's Buildings (55)
Heale's Building (59)*
Bloomsbury Place (63)
Mountergate (after 67)
Prince of Wales Road

North:
Foy's or Foyson's Yard (4)*
Greyfriars Road (4 – runs to King Street)
Maidstone Road (36–38)
St Vedast Street (formerly Cathedral Street South) (52–60)

Buildings on Rose Lane
Churches
St John the Evangelist Church stood at 2–4 Rose Lane. The parish was added to St Peter's Parmentergate in around 1300; the building was bought by the Grey Friars and demolished.

Other buildings of note
Cooke's Hospital (46 Rose Lane) was founded by Thomas Cooke. The court was built in 1700 with 10 tenements around it.

Tudor Hall, Rose Lane. (Photograph by author)

Tudor Hall is actually mock-Tudor; it was built in 1899 as an office for Boulton & Paul, using timbers from a 16th-century merchant hall that had been pulled down on King Street. At one point, the building was known as Peppermint Park nightclub.

People linked with Rose Lane
Thomas Cooke, a worsted weaver, was mayor in 1689. He lived at 31 King Street and built almshouses (known as Cooke's Hospital) at the bottom of his orchard next to Rose Lane. The building were demolished in 1892 as they were declared insanitary; new buildings were put up in Quaker Lane, off St Martin's Lane. Cooke's brother Robert also endowed the hospital.

Events at Rose Lane
In November 1847 there was a large fire at Mr Kitten's warehouse; the warehouse and its contents – barrels of grease and resin – were destroyed. There was a second fire there the following year.

In August 1876 there was a large fire at Boulton & Paul's in Rose Lane, which spread to Turner's Yard, causing damage of £10,000 (the equivalent of nearly £575,000 in today's money); there was another large fire in May 1890 causing damage of £4–5,000.

Rose Lane, picture courtesy of Norfolk County Council Library and Information Service.

ROSE TERRACE
35–41 Chapel Field Road. The terrace was lost by 1960, firstly for a car sales outlet then for the office block of Norvic House.

ROSE & CROWN YARD
35 Bishopgate, was named after the Rose & Crown pub, which is recorded at 35 Bishopgate from 1836; the pub closed in 1891 and the yard was lost.

ROSE YARD
7–9 St Augustine's Street, was named after the Rose tavern, which is recorded at 7 St Augustine's Street from 1762 (though there had been an inn on the site since the 14th century). One of the landlords was Bob Bunn, who set a record by running 15 miles (including jumping 100 hurdles) in 90 minutes. The pub closed in 1981. On 29 December 1930 Adcock & Michell's boot factory burned down; the fire started at around 1pm and within two hours the roof had fallen in and the factory was gutted.

ROSE YARD
Castle Street (exact location unknown), was named after the White Rose pub (sometimes known as the Rose Tavern), which is recorded at 10 Back of the Inns from 1822. The pub was rebuilt in 1900 (when the yard was lost) and was renamed the Arcade Stores; it closed in 1962.

ROSE YARD
57–59 St Stephen's Street, was named after the Rose Tavern, which is recorded at 59 St Stephen's Street from 1850 (although there is a sign of a rose on an engraving by Ninham of St Stephen's Gate in 1792). The pub closed in 1913, and the yard was lost by 1964.

ROSEMARY LANE
Rosemary Lane runs from 7–9 St Mary's Plain to St Miles Alley. It was known as Little Helsden Lane from the 13th century, but was known as Rosemary Lane by the early 18th century. The modern name comes from the Rosemary Tavern, which is recorded at 1 Rosemary Road from 1861. (See St Mary's Plain.) The pub closed in 1908.

Streets off Rosemary Lane
The street has included:
Cartwright's Yard (1–3)*
Barker's Yard (west side*
Cockell's Yard (west side)*
Hare's Yard (west side)*

ROSHIER COURT
Quayside, exact location unknown. *Harrod & Co's Directory* of 1868 lists William Roshier, carpenter, nearby at Prince's Street, and *Kelly's Directory* of 1900 lists William Roshier & Sons, builders, nearby at 25 Palace Street.

ROUEN ROAD
Rouen Road runs from Cattle Market Street to 216 King Street. The northern end follows the original line of Rising Sun Lane, and according to Sandred and Lingström the section between Stepping Lane and Thorn Lane follows a street that was known as Cow Lane in the 18th century (and Market Lane in the 19th century). They also place the section between Thorn Lane and Music House Lane as St Julian's Street, and from Music House Lane to Mariner's Lane as William Street or Burleigh Street. The street was built in 1962 to save widening King Street. It was named after Norwich's twin town in France.

Streets off Rouen Road
North:
Norman's Buildings and Stepping Lane
St Julian's Alley (runs to King Street)
Music House Lane (runs to King Street)

South:
Argyle Street
Thorn Lane (runs to Ber Street)

Buildings on Rouen Road
Prospect House was built in 1970.
Normandie Tower was built in 1965.

ROYAL ARCADE
Runs from 24 Gentleman's Walk. It was built by Edward Skipper on the site of the Royal Hotel (opened 25 May 1899).

ROYAL HOTEL STREET
Former name of Arcade Street, was itself a replacement name for Angel Street or Angel Yard.

ROYAL OAK COURT
Runs from Horns Lane. It may have taken its name from the Royal Oak pub on Ber Street (see below).

ROYAL OAK YARD
64–66 Ber Street, was named after the Royal Oak pub, which is recorded at 64 Ber Street from 1689. The pub closed in 1965. Royal Oak Yard is now off Horns Lane.

ROYAL OAK YARD
130 Oak Street, was named after the Royal Oak pub, which is recorded at 132 Oak Street from 1806. The pub was

Rouen Road being constructed in
1962, picture courtesy of Norfolk
County Council Library and
Information Service.

damaged during an air raid in April 1942 and did not reopen; the yard was lost by 1964.

ROYAL OAK YARD
62–64 St Augustine's Street, was named after the Royal Oak pub, which is recorded at 64 St Augustine's Street from 1806. The pub is also shown in Ninham's illustration of St Augustine's Gates in 1791. The pub closed in 1972.

ROYAL'S YARD
See Bailey's Yard, 136–138 Magdalen Street.

RUDD'S YARD
32–34 Oak Street. *White's Directory* of 1883 lists Henry Rudd, earthenware dealer, at 48 Oak Street and William Rudd, clog maker, at 40 Oak Street. *Kelly's Directory* of 1900 lists Henry Rudd as a newsagent and also Martha Rudd, dressmaker, at 52 Oak Street. The yard was lost by 1935.

RUNNYMEDE
35 Calvert Street to 32 Magdalen Street.

RUSSELL'S YARD
Formerly Cobb's Yard, 147 Ber Street. *Chase's Directory* of 1783 lists Jeremiah Russell, tripe dresser, at 141 Ber Street. The yard was lost 1947–60.

RUSSELL STREET
Ran from 146–152 Ber Street to somewhere before 11 on Mariner's Lane. It became known as Ashbourne Street in 1900.

ST ANDREW'S CHANCEL STREET
Runs between St Andrew's Hill and Bridewell Alley, between the church and the bridewell.

ST ANDREW'S STREET
St Andrew's Street runs from Charing Cross to 6–8 Redwell Street. Kirkpatrick says that it was known was vicus Sci Andree Apostoli (St Andrew's Street) in 1283. It was also known as Wymer Street in the 18th century to as late as 1839 (either named after one of the four city districts, or, as Sandred and Lingström suggest, after Wymerus, a steward of William de Warren's estate). It became known as St Andrew's Bridge Street and St Andrew's Broad Street in the 19th century, and the names are taken from the church. Part of the street between the museum and Duke Street was known as Museum Street before 1845 (after the museum), and as Post Office Street from 1839–54 (after the post office on Exchange Street).

Streets off St Andrew's Street
On the north side, the street has included:

Locket's Court*
Locket's Yard*
Library Court*
Museum Court (11–13)*
Golden Can Yard (15)*
Lucketts Court or Yard (23–25)*
Old Stamp Office Yard (27)*
St George's Street (after 39)

On the south side, the street has included:
St John Maddermarket
Grimmer's Court (6–8)*
Exchange Street (12–14)
Bazaar Court (24–26)*
Bridewell Alley (32)
St Andrew's Hill
Blod's Court (possibly Blogg's Yard)*

Exact location unknown:
Lovick's Court*

Buildings on St Andrew's Street
Churches
St Andrew the Apostle's Church dates from 1478; the tower is the oldest part, and the rest was rebuilt in 1506 when the windows were also glazed. There are 12 shields carved in stone outside, including the arms of Bishop Henry

St Andrew's Church. (Photograph by author)

Despenser. The church contains monuments to Robert Suckling, Francis Rugge and Sir John Suckling. Blomefield calls the church 'the best parochial church in the city, except St Peter of Mancroft'; there was a church on the site before the Conquest, and the nearby Church and parish of St Christopher was added to the parish in the late 1200s. In January 1779 a bad storm, according to *White's Directory* of 1845, 'rolled up the lead of St Andrew's Church and blew it to a considerable distance'. The Misses Stone gave the church a new organ in 1863, and a new clock was dedicated at the church on St Andrew's Day in 1882.

Other buildings of note

The Royal Bazaar stood near to where the telephone exchange is now (see Bazaar Court).

Stuart Hall was built in 1924 by Ethel and Helen Colman during the restoration of Suckling House. Since April 1978 it has been used as a cinema, and at the time of writing the building is undergoing further restoration.

Suckling House was built in the mid-14th century as a city merchant's house. It was the home of Sir Robert Suckling (see below) and contains the remains of an Elizabethan fireplace with the Suckling motto 'Thynk and Thank God' carved into it. Several mayors of the city lived there – see below.

The Theatre de Luxe cinema, opened in 1910, was converted to 'talkies' in 1931 and closed in 1957; the building was later demolished.

Victoria Hall was next door to the Theatre de Luxe, at the corner of Bridewell Alley; Poole's Myriorama gave their annual show there.

People linked with St Andrew's Street

Christopher Baret, a grocer who was mayor in 1634 (and was deputy mayor in 1647 when mayor Utting was in prison), bought Suckling House from John Suckling in 1595.

John Cambridge, mayor in 1430 and 1437, also lived in Suckling House.

Edward Clark, mayor in 1700, lived in Suckling House.

John Clerk, a mercer who was mayor in 1515 and 1523, lived in Suckling House.

John Custance, a manufacturer of Holland linen and weaver of worsted, was mayor in 1726 and 1750. He lived at 23 and 25 St Andrew's Street with partner John Kirkpatrick.

John Kirkpatrick, historian and antiquarian, lived at 23 St Andrew's Street. He was also a linen draper and was a partner of John Custance before becoming treasurer to St Helen's Hospital.

Thomas Layer, a grocer who was mayor in 1576, 1585, and 1595, lived in 23–27 St Andrew's Street. He also gave an orchard in Colegate to the parish – now known as 56–89 Calvert Street.

Francis Rugge (or Rugg), who was mayor in 1587, 1598 and 1602, lived in a house on the corner of Bridewell Alley and St Andrew's Street. The site became the Girls' Model School.

Ralf Segryme, a merchant who was sheriff in 1442, lived at 2 St Andrew's Street. He gave a rood screen to St John Maddermarket Church and paid for the alterations to the prison in the Guildhall in 1453, so there was one for men and one for women. He was also a founder of St Barbara's Chapel in the Guildhall. He left £10 in his will to clean the river, and his executors also offered the city 200 marks towards repairing the City Walls.

The Suckling family lived at Suckling house and included a couple of mayors – Sir Robert Suckling, a mercer who was mayor in 1572 and 1582, and John Suckling, a baker who was mayor in 1584; in 1564 it was recorded that his loaves were underweight!

Henry Watts, a hosier who was mayor in 1646, lived at 23 St Andrew's Street.

Events at St Andrew's Street

In 1688 Norwich's first fire engine was stationed at the New Hall (St Andrew's Hall – see St Andrew's Hall Plain). The street was widened in 1884 and extended to Redwell Street in 1899–1900; it was widened again in 1966 and further changes followed in the 1970s.

ST ANDREW'S BROAD STREET

Former name for St Andrew's Street.

ST ANDREW'S HALL PLAIN

St Andrew's Hall Plain, previously known as St Andrew's Plain, is at the junction of St Andrew's Hill, Prince's Street, St George's Street (formerly Bridge Street) and St Andrew's Street; it runs to Prince's Street. It was formed in 1899–1900 to accommodate the trams.

Buildings on St Andrew's Hall Plain

Blackfriars and St Andrew's Hall was originally the Church of St John the Baptist and is the largest remaining Dominican building in the country. As well as a church, the hall has been an assembly hall, a municipal chapel, a sealing hall for cloth, a granary, a library, a concert hall, a Dutch church, an artillery ground and the grammar school (until it moved to The Close in 1553). The Black Friars built their first church here in 1326, although the undercroft and brick vaulting dates from the late 13th century when the Sack Friars were there; there's also the remains of Becket's Chapel next door.

In 1413 the roof and much of the church was destroyed by fire, which also killed two friars. The church was rebuilt in 1440–70, and Sir Thomas Erpingham's son Robert (who was a friar there) paid for the restoration of clerestory windows in memory of his father.

After the Reformation, the city mayor, Augustine Steward, sent a petition to the king, asking 'to make of the churche a fayer and large halle, well pathed, for the mayor and his bretherne, with all the citizens of the same, to repair thereunto for their common assemblyes'. The king granted it by charter in 1540. The original price was £81; then the king demanded an extra £152 for the lead on the roof, even though the lead was specified in the original contract. The city library was set up in the south porch in 1608. The Dutch used the hall as their church until 1625, when the city granted them the chapel at a fee of 6 shillings and 8 pence a year. Charles II knighted Sir Thomas Browne at St Andrew's Hall. The hall was used as a mint in 1696–98, when silver coinage was struck by the order of William III – according to *White's Directory* of 1845, it struck £259,371-worth of coins. It was first lit by gas in November 1824, in preparation for the first Triennial Music Festival, and according to the newspapers of the time 'the pure bright flame… communicated a lustre to every part of the edifice more evident, perhaps, than what it receives from the light of day.'

In July 1849 Professor Isham Bagge of the Polytechnic Institute of London gave a lecture there about electric light; the newspaper reported of the demonstration that 'the gas seemed extinguished amid the new blaze of light'. The hall was restored in 1861 by J.S. Benest. The mayors gave banquets in the hall after the annual election, and the St George's Company held their meetings there. According to *Pigot's Directory* of 1830, a court of conscience (for recovery of debts under 40 shillings) was held at St Andrew's Hall every Monday, and the ensign of the French ship *Genereux,* which was captured by Nelson in February 1800, was also displayed there; the flag was presented to the city by Sir Edward Berry, one of Nelson's captains. The hall has been used as a place of entertainment. In June 1853 Mr King held a séance there and introduced 'the new cult of table-turning or spiritualism' to the city. In February 1856 Jenny Lind sang the *Messiah* there and gave a second concert two days later; as a result, she donated £354 to the Jenny Lind Infirmary.

Charles Dickens also gave public readings here. In October 1859 he read *A Christmas Carol,* the trial from *Pickwick* and *The Story of Little Dombey and Mrs Gamp*, which met with a good reception; the local newspaper reported, 'His voice was far from powerful, but he had remarkable expression and the power of exhibiting this in face as well as in voice'. However, in October 1861, when he read from *David Copperfield* and *Nicholas Nickleby*, the paper remarked that 'Mr Dickens as a reader fails to do justice to himself as an author.' In August 1867 an 'industrial exhibition' was held at the hall for a month: this was the Norfolk and Eastern Counties Working Classes Exhibition, which included works of art, industry and mechanical invention.

In August 1868 Chang the Chinese Giant was exhibited – the *Norfolk Chronicle* reported that he was between eight and a half and nine feet high, and his 'natural suavity of manner is very agreeable'. The cloisters were used as part of St Andrew's Workhouse, but by 1862 they were part of the Boys' Middle School. Richard Mackenzie Bacon, the proprietor of the *Norwich Mercury*, had a row with the architect restoring the hall in the 19th century; the architect got his own back by carving two little caricatures over the south door. One shows a pig playing an organ (i.e. Bacon and the *Mercury*) and the other is a pig playing a horn (i.e. Bacon blowing his own trumpet!).

People linked with St Andrew's Hall Plain

Thomas Back jnr, a banker who was mayor in 1809, held his celebratory dinner on the Jubilee of George III (5 October). Apparently four grenadiers carried a baron of beef (which weighed 172lbs) twice round St Andrew's Hall before dinner. Back had a tempestuous career. A libel was

St Andrew's Hall. (Photograph by author)

St Andrew's Hall cloister remains. (Photograph by author)

published about him in *Roope's Weekly Letters*; Back set up a legal challenge, and in response Roope challenged the city steward to a duel and was thrown in gaol, Roope died shortly after, and Back died from an apoplectic fit (probably a heart attack) in the council chamber in 1820.

Benjamin Nuthall was a worsted weaver and brewer who was mayor in 1721 and 1749, He lived in Prince's Street in a house whose garden is now St Andrew's Hall Plain. His son John Nuthall, who was mayor in 1740, had to read the Riot Act on 7 July 1740 when there were riots in the city to stop corn being sent to Yarmouth for export; the rioters threw stones at magistrates then broke into the prison.

Alfred Stannard lived here; he was the last survivor of the Norwich School of Artists and was the brother of Joseph Stannard.

ST ANDREW'S CHURCH ALLEY
Runs off St Andrew's Hill, by the church.

ST ANDREW'S HILL AND STEPS
St Andrew's Hill and Steps runs from the junction of 53 London Street/Bedford Street to St Andrew's Street (the section formerly known as Post Office Street). It was called Blackfriar's Street in the mid-18th century (after the Hall) and was also known as Seven Steps; the modern name is from 1845, and the steps were removed in 1761. The former entrance to the Bridewell is on St Andrew's Hill.

Streets off St Andrew's Hill
St Andrew's Chancel Street (runs to Bridewell Alley)
Flint House Yard (after 13)

People linked with St Andrew's Hill
John Mann, a mercer who was mayor in 1653 and the Sheriff of London in 1669, left his property at 53 London Street and 1–5 St Andrew's Hill to Anguish's hospital.

ST ANDREW'S LANE
Former name for Bridewell Alley.

ST ANN'S LANE
109 King Street, took its name from St Anne's Church, which once stood there – though one of the earliest references Kirkpatrick found was in 1391 as 'a Lane next the Austin Fryers'. The parish of St Anne was added to St Clement in 1370 and the chapel was demolished after around 1389. The lane has also been known as St Anne's Staithe Lane, after the wharf or staithe leading off it. The spelling seems to drop and recover the final 'e' of Anne almost at whim! There was a friary there from 1360–63, and extensive remains were found in 1970 during excavations.

ST ANN'S WHARF or STAITHE
Leads off St Ann's Lane. According to Blomefield, in 1458 St Anne's Staithe was made the city's 'common stathe', and a crane and pubs were built there. In 1550 the city sold the bells of St Anne's and the lead on the north aisle and the steeple to Leonard Sotherton and John Rede (all spelling sic).

ST AUGUSTINE'S CHURCH ROW
West side of St Augustine's Street, near to the church. The Tudor cottages were restored in 1956.

St Augustine's Church Row. (Photograph by author)

ST AUGUSTINE'S STREET
St Augustine's Street runs from the junction of Botolph Street and Pitt Street to St Augustine's Gates. The street took its name from the church.

Streets off St Augustine's Street
East:
Rose Yard (7–9)
Hindes' Yard (13–15)
Nichol's Yard (also known as Barnes' Court/Yard) (19–21)

Bushel Yard (27–29)*
Nunn's Yard or Court (formerly Minn's yard) (31–33)*
Delph's yard (35–37)*
Prince of Wales Yard (39)
Stone Mason's Yard (39)*
Esdelle Street (51–53)
Catherine Wheel Opening and Catherine Wheel Yard (61)

West:
Pitt Street
Gildencroft
St Augustine's Church Row (near the church)
Wine Coopers' Arms Yard (formerly known as Wine Coopers' Square) (32–34)
Sussex Street (36–42)
Royal Oak Yard (62–64)
St Martin's at Oak Wall Lane (66–68)
Baker's Road (leads to the junction of St Martin's Road and Oak Street)

Exact location unknown:
Luke's Yard*

Buildings on St Augustine's Street
City wall
St Augustine's Gate, also known as St Austin's gates, were demolished in 1794. There was a 'Justing Acre' just inside the walls called Gildencroft; this was the area where the tenants of Tolthorp Manor met to pay their 'geld' or tax. According to Blomefield, the city used Gildencroft as a place for public exercise, including tilts, tournaments and 'justing' (or jousting), and the Buthills were 'cast up' there and used for crossbow shooting. There was also a leper house (called the Infirmary) outside St Augustine's Gate; it was dedicated to the Blessed Lady and St Clement, and the lepers were buried in St Clement's Churchyard in Colegate. At the Dissolution, the infirmary became a hospital for the poor.

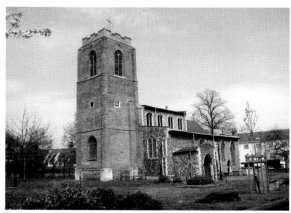

St Augustine's Church. (Photograph by author)

Churches
St Augustine's Church has a redbrick steeple tower that was built in 1687 as a replacement for the one that fell down 10 years earlier. Because of the colour of the tower, the congregation became known as the 'red steeplers'. The church was restored in the 1880s by R.M. Phipson, who also added the battlements.

ST BENEDICT'S ALLEY
Sometimes known as St Benedict's Church Alley, ran from St Benedict's Street to 105–11 Pottergate. It was destroyed during air raids in World War Two and has been replaced by a new development called Wellington Green.

ST BENEDICT'S BACK LANE
Ran from 89–91 St Benedict's Street and was destroyed during air raids in World War Two.

ST BENEDICT'S PLAIN
Is the junction where Cow Hill, Willow Lane, Pottergate, Ten Bell Lane and St Benedict's Alley meet. Damocles Court runs off it.

ST BENEDICT'S STREET
St Benedict's Street runs from Charing Cross to the junction of Barn Road/Dereham Road. It was the main entrance to the city from the west until the ring road was built. The street was known as Upper Westwick Street from the 13th century until the mid-18th century, when it became known as St Bennet's or St Benedict's Street; the modern name comes from St Benedict's Church, which was badly bombed during World War Two. The street numbering changed slightly from 1890–1900, when part of the street was demolished to accommodate the trams.

Streets off St Benedict's Street
North:
Coe's or Cox's Yard (19–21)*
Knight's Court and Marsham's Yard (before 21)*
St Laurence Little Steps (before 21)
St Laurence Steps (23)
Maude Gray Court (formerly Self's Yard) (33–35)
St Margaret's Alley (35–37)
St Margaret's Street (37–39)
Barlow's Court (47)*
Queen of Hungary Yard (47–49)
Reeve's Yard (49–51)
St Swithin's Alley (53–55)
Woolgate Court (57)
St Swithin's Terrace (59–61)
Bee Hive Yard (65–67)*
Crown Yard (71–73)*
Mulberry Tree Yard*

Fountain Yard (85–87)*
St Benedict's Back Lane (89–91)

South:
St Gregory's Alley (runs to 27 Pottergate)
Martin's Court (later Pipe Burners' Yard) (4–6)
Lord Howe Yard (6–8)
Green's Court/Yard (8–10)*
St Lawrence Lane (16–18)
Gaffer's Yard (formerly Gaffer's Court and Crow's Yard) (20–22)
Hannant's (or Hannent's) Yard (24–26)
Turner's Court (28–30)*
Prince of Wales Yard (32–34)
St Lawrence Close (formerly St Lawrence School Yard) (36–38)
Grigg's Yard (40–42)*
Mayes' Court (42–44)*
Three King Lane (runs to Pottergate) and Yard (44–46)
Little Plough Yard (56–58)
Plough Yard (58–60)
Hindes' (or Hinds') Yard (68–70)
Ten Bell Lane (78–80)
Cardinal's Cap Yard and Little Cardinal's Cap Yard (84–86)
Adam & Eve Yard (84–86)
Wellington Green (formerly St Benedict's Alley) (94)
Ten Bell Court
Great White Lion Yard and Little White Lion Yard (104–106)*
Wellington Lane (formerly Duck Lane) (110–112)
Griffin Lane (or Yard or Court) (114)*
St Giles' Hill (aka Grapes Hill)

Other streets whose exact locations could not be placed include:
Allen's Yard*
Browne's Yard or Court (runs to Pottergate)*
Clark's Yard
Freestone Yard*
Gays' Yard*
Gray's Yard*
Huggins' Row*
Maude's Court*
Middleton's Court
Mowey's Court (runs to St Giles' Hill)*
Mulberry Tree Yard*
Storey's Yard*
Three Turks' Yard*

Buildings on St Benedict's Street
City Wall
St Benedict's Gate was also known as Heaven's Gates

St Benedict's tower remains. (Photograph by author)

because it was next door to Heigham Gates (or Helgate) and was also the start of the pilgrim path to Walsingham. The gate was also once known as Westwic (sic) Gates or Porta de Westwyck and there was a gallows outside the gate. When Henry VI visited the city in June 1448, he entered the city by St Benedict's Gate, which had been decorated specially for him. The gate was demolished in 1793 by John de Carle and Philip Barnes, although the south side was left with its hinge pin. The air raids of April 1942 blew the wall away and left the remains of the gate sitting on the edge of a crater, so the last bit had to be demolished. According to Blomefield, there was an almshouse near St Benedict's Gate – a hermitage inside the gate, and a leper house (known as St Bennet's Hospital) on the outside.

Churches
St Benedict's Church dates from the 15th century. It was repaired and re-roofed in the 1860s for a cost of £180. It was badly bombed in World War Two and only the tower remains; the area around it was redeveloped as housing in 1972. According to Blomefield, there was once an orchard on the west side of the churchyard.

St Gregory's Church dates from the late 14th century. It has bosses in the porch showing St Gregory teaching music, and also has what Pevsner describes as one of the best wall

War damage in St Benedict's Street, picture courtesy of Norfolk County Council Library and Information Service.

paintings in the country: these are of the fight between St George and the Dragon, on the west wall of the north aisle, and were hidden until June 1861, when workmen moved the church organ to clean the wall. The *Norfolk Chronicle* reported that 'the figures are life-size and the colours and drawing exceedingly good'. The church also had the only spire in Norwich apart from the cathedral; its leadwork was cast in 1597, but the vane and spindle blew off in a storm in January 1806; part of the spire fell down in 1840 and it wasn't replaced. The church has been redundant since 1974 and is in the care of the Norwich Historic Churches Trust; it is now a music and drama centre.

St Gregory's Church (from Pottergate). (Photograph by author)

St Laurence the Martyr's Church was recorded before the conquest, and according to Blomefield it stands on the spot where herrings used to be landed. It was once known as St Lawrence at Quay as the churchyard originally led down to the river; most of the churchyard has been lost due to road-widening. The current church dates from 1472 and replaces an earlier one pulled down in 1460. Over the west door, there is a carving of St Lawrence being grilled to death on the orders of the Roman emperor Decius, and one of St Edmund tied to an arrow with Danes shooting arrows at him. The church had a new tower in 1468–79; according to Blomefield, in 1448 there were three devotees or women vowing chastity, known as the Sisters of St Laurence, living in a tenement by the churchyard. In 1643 the altar rails were pulled down and the painted windows were defaced, and in 1710 the east end of the chancel was blown down and repaired. There was a very strange incident on 6 January 1866 when George Nobbs, a shoemaker of St Martin at Oak, turned on every burner of the gas. The churchwarden's lad was overcome by the fumes before he could open a window; but there was no damage and magistrates dismissed the case as Nobbs was simple and didn't realise what the consequences of his act would be. The church has been

St Laurence's Church. (Photograph by author)

redundant since 1974, and in the early 1980s the church was in danger of collapsing.

St Margaret's Church was restored in 1886. It has been redundant since 1974 and is in the care of the Norwich Historic Churches Trust. It was used as a gym in 1981 but has been unused since the mid-1990s. There are carvings around the entrance showing St Margaret amid branches. According to Blomefield, the Chapel of St Anne was at the end of the south aisle, and the 'barkeres or tanners guild' was kept there.

St Swithin's Church was derelict by 1905, and an anonymous visitor in that year was so moved by the poverty

St Margaret's Church. (Photograph by author)

St Swithin's Church. (Photograph by author)

in the slum areas surrounding the church that he paid for a church hall (built in 1908) and the restoration of the church. The church has been redundant since 1974 and is in the care of the Norwich Historic Churches Trust; it's currently used as Norwich Arts Centre.

Other buildings of note

The Eye Infirmary was founded by Lewis Evans, Robert Hull and Thomas Martineau in 1822 in St Benedict's Plain. In 1854 it moved to new premises in Pottergate and moved again in 1913 to St Stephen's Road, opposite the Norfolk and Norwich Hospital.

People linked with St Benedict's Street

Sir Peter Seaman, a brewer who was mayor in 1707, was knighted in July 1712 and was also a Colonel of the city company. He lived in a house near St Lawrence's Pump. When he died in 1715 he was buried in St Gregory's; his coffin was reportedly 7ft 1in long.

Events at St Benedict's Street

St Benedict's Street has suffered badly from fires; on 19 August 1815 there was a fire at Hubbard's cabinet makers, near St Lawrence's Church. The *Norfolk Chronicle* said that the house was a 'sheet for fire'. Six houses were destroyed, including those of Mr Blake the pawnbroker, Mr Stannards the pork butcher and Mr Taylor. The heat was so intense that houses on the opposite site of the road caught light, and the wood yards of merchants Mr Coleman and Mr Walker were threatened. However, by 7pm the blaze was out; and one of the West Norfolk Militia (who attended the fire) had his eyes burned in the blaze. Three years later, Griffiths' tool maker's shop (next to St Gregory's Church) was destroyed by fire; and the most recent fire on the street was at Pinocchio's Restaurant in 2004.

There was a very strange incident here on Christmas Eve 1899 when Horace Alfred Cox fired three shots at Ellen Parker in a café on St Benedict's Street. He missed her, so he shot himself in the head and died in the Norfolk and Norwich Hospital.

The street was very badly bombed during air raids in 1942. By 1944 most of the ruined buildings were cleared away, the roads were re-laid and the water mains were repaired. The street was given a 'facelift' in 1960, similar to Magdalen Street, and the areas between Wellington Lane and Neale's Square were replaced by modern housing in the 1970s.

ST CATHERINE'S PLAIN

Runs from Surrey Street to Finkelgate, was formerly open land in front of St Winwaloe's Church, which King Stephen gave to the nuns of Carrow. The church was rededicated to St Catherine. Streets running from St Catherine's Plain include: Alderson Place; Gloucester Place; Kensington Row.

ST CLEMENT'S ALLEY

Runs from 16 Colegate to Fye Bridge Street. St Clement's Court runs off it. John Aldrich, a grocer who was mayor in 1558 and 1570, lived in a house off St Clement's Churchyard. The house became the Sun and Anchor pub, then a weaving factory for Custances, then a warehouse for C. and F. Bolingbroke, and then a labour exchange by 1938.

ST CLEMENT'S COURT

Runs off St Clement's Alley.

ST CRISPIN'S ROAD

Runs from Barn Road, across the river, to the roundabout by Barrack Street. It was named after the patron saint of shoemakers. It was built in 1971 to lead to the Anglia Square shopping centre, and is also the flyover above Magdalen Street. According to historian Brian Ayers, St Crispin's Road contains the earliest concrete urinal in the world (this was formerly on Oak Street).

Streets off St Crispin's Road

North:
Oak Street
Talbot Square
Quaker's Lane
Botolph Street (runs to St Augustine's Street)
Upper Green Lane (runs to Edward Street)

South:
Calvert Street (runs to Colegate)
St George's Street
Oak Street

ST ETHELDREDA'S CHURCH ALLEY

182 King Street, takes its name from the church and leads to Mariner's Lane.

ST FAITH'S LANE

St Faith's Lane runs from 98 Prince of Wales Road to 25–26 Tombland. It was formerly known as Mountergate Street (which, confusingly, used to be St Faith's Lane), and was a major road in mediaeval Norwich, running from King Street along the boundary of the Close to Tombland. In Victorian times, when there were vinegar works on Recorder Road, it was known as Vinegar Lane. In the 19th century, Keymer's Vauxhall Gardens (pleasure gardens) ran between St Faith's Lane and the river – this may have been on the site of Browne's Meadow, where Sir Thomas Browne (see Hay Hill) had the garden admired by the diarist Evelyn.

Streets off St Faith's Lane

The Close (3–5)
Cathedral Street (formerly Cathedral Street North) (8–10)
Brown's Buildings
Horse Fair
Recorder Road
Stuart Gardens

Events at St Faith's Lane

In October 1829 there was a fire at Squire, Hills & Son's distillery; £2,000 of damage (over £120,000 in today's money) was caused.

ST GEORGE'S ALLEY

Also known as St George's Church Alley in 1793 – not the same as the Tombland Alley. Runs between Muspole Street and 76–82 St George's Street.

ST GEORGE'S CHURCH ALLEY

Is a former name for Tombland Alley; it takes its name from St George's Church in Tombland.

ST GEORGE'S PLAIN

Colegate, runs in front of the tower of St George's Church in Colegate to the entrance of the former Norvic shoe factory.

ST GEORGE'S MIDDLE STREET

Former name for St George's Street.

ST GEORGE'S STREET

St George's Street runs from St Andrew's Hall Plain; it originally ran to 42 Botolph Street but now runs to St Crispin's Road. Part of St George's Street was formerly known as Blackfriars Street or Blackfriars Bridge Street (after the bridge at the end), then as Gildengate (as it led to the Gildencroft), and another part was known as St George's Middle Street or just Middle Street. Different bits of the street were even known by different names at the same time, and the road numbering switched fairly often! Since the Inner Ring Road development, the section on the other side of St Crispin's Road (from approximately 128 St George's Street) is now known as Botolph Street.

Streets off St George's Street

East:
Snowdon's Yard (21)*
Colegate (31–37)
Lowe's Yard (41–43– runs to 2–10 Calvert Street)
Cross Lane (57–59 – runs to 22 Calvert Street)
St Crispin's Road
King's Head Lane (before 63 – runs to Calvert Street)
Green's Lane (89–91) originally ran to Calvert Street; now known as Upper Green Lane, leading from St Crispin's Road to Edward Street
Anchor Yard (or Crown & Anchor Yard) (107 – runs to 98–102 Calvert Street)*
Appleton's Court (111)*

West:
Red Lion Yard (14–18)
Bray's Yard (26–28)*
Symond's Yard (formerly St Simon's Yard) (30–32)*
Water Lane (48–52) (Little Water Lane runs off this)
Gun Wharf (52–58)
Merchant's Court
Two Quarts Court or Yard (70–72)
Colegate (74–82)
St George's Alley (76–82 – runs to Muspole Street)
Alms Lane (88 – runs to Muspole Street)
St Crispin's Road
Little Barrack Yard (114)*
Barrack Yard (114–166)*
Cossey's Court (118–120)*
Stonemason's Yard or Square (120–122)*
Drake's Court (126–130)*
Steward's Court and Steward's Yard (130–132)*
Cherry Tree Yard or Little Cherry Yard (160–162 – ran to Pitt Street)
Burrell's Yard (162 – ran to 49–51 Colegate)*
William the Fourth Yard (may also have been known as Arnold's Yard) (166–168)*
Appleton's Yard (168)*
Hill's Yard (184)*

Other streets whose exact locations could not be placed include:
Arnold's Yard*
Brock's Yard*
Chequers Passage*
Fremoult's Yard
Lawson's Yard*

Buildings on St George's Street

Churches

St Margaret at New Bridge (sometimes known as St Margaret at Colegate) Church stood on the site of Gun Wharf from around 1157. After the Black Death wiped out much of its congregation in 1349, the parish was joined to St George's Colegate and the church became a hermitage.

St Olave the King and Martyr (commonly called St Tooley's) stood near Cherry Alley. According to Blomefield, in 1289 the church had an anchorage inhabited by Margaret and Alice. The church was repaired in 1504; the parish was joined to St George's Colegate in 1546 and the church was demolished. The churchyard ran along the side of St Tooley's Lane, which had become known as Cherry Alley by 1700.

Other buildings of note

The Art School on the east side of St George's Street was built as the Technical Institute in 1899 by W. Douglas Wiles.

Blackfriar's Bridge, also known as St George's Bridge or New Bridge, was originally a wooden bridge during the reign of Henry IV. It was rebuilt in 1483 then rebuilt again in stone in 1586. The current stone bridge was built in 1783, designed by Sir John Soane – who also designed the gaol at the castle from 1789–93, then became architect to the Bank of England. The cast-iron railings on the bridge were added in 1820.

Blackfriar's Bridge. (Photograph by author)

St Andrew's Workhouse – this was part of the remains of the old Blackfriars Church. According to *White's Directory* of 1845, the building was repaired and new buildings were added in 1802 extending down to the river, so by 1845 there were 'accommodations for about 600 paupers'. Part of the workhouse was the infirmary (aka the Leper Hospital outside St Augustine's gates), which accommodated 130 men and women over the age of 65; next to this, in a new building, was the 'Asylum for Pauper Lunatics'. The workhouse was run by

a Court of Guardians following an Act of Parliament in 1712, however, the assessment of the poor rates caused 'much dissatisfaction among the merchants, manufacturers and shopkeepers, due to a mixture of an economic depression, an increased population, and poor management by the Court of Guardians.' A new act was passed in May 1827 to alter the constitution of the Guardians, and it was reformed again in 1831.

According to *White's Directory* of 1845, there was a 16ft-high alder tree 'growing out of the wall of a building' on St George's Street.

People linked with St George's Street

John Crome, the landscape artist, was probably born in King Street where his parents kept the Griffin tavern, and lived at 89 St George's Street – the site is now buried underneath the ring road. Crome was the errand boy of Edward Rigby (see Rigby's Court) at the age of 11 then in 1783 became apprenticed to the coach and sign painter Francis Whisler in Bethel Street, where he learned to prepare colours and do simple designs. He taught drawing to the Gurney family (including Elizabeth Fry) and was one of the founders of the Norwich School of Painters. He founded the Norwich Society with his friend the painter Bob Ladbrooke, which aimed to study art; however, they fell out over how the proceeds from the exhibitions should be used. Ladbrooke wanted to spend it on casts so that members of the society could study them; Crome wanted to spend it on monthly or fortnightly suppers for the society. Legend has it that Crome's dying advice to his son John, also a painter, were 'John, my boy, paint, but paint for fame; and if your subject is a pigsty – dignify it!'

John Martin, anchorite, lived in the Church of St Margaret at New Bridge in 1429.

Events on St George's Street

St George's Street saw a tragic case in September 1844, when there was an inquest at the Dove. Lucy Thorpe, who had taken lodgings there, assured the landlady that she was not pregnant (although she had a two-year-old and was a single mother). On Tuesday 10 September she gave birth to a baby when her landlady's 15-year-old daughter was there. The girl heard a cry and then a 'gurgle' and told her mother – who called the doctor. When the surgeon, Mr Dashwood, examined the baby's body, he said that the baby had been strangled. The jury's verdict was wilful murder.

There was a major fire on the street on 17 June 1928, when the paint and oil store of Gunton Sons & Dyball, opposite the Technical Institute, caught fire. Although it wasn't a windy day, the way the building was constructed (to allow fumes to escape) meant that draughts fanned the fire; the *Eastern Daily Press* described the building as full of 'blood-red flames and belching masses of choking smoke'. Amazingly, the factory was saved! Similar luck was in store for the potato warehouse on 15 May 1973 – the building had a 100ft frontage and it took 30 firemen to subdue the blaze, but the potatoes were mainly intact – apart from a bit of smoke damage.

ST GILES' HILL
Former name of Grapes Hill. Mowey's Court runs from here to the south side of St Benedict's Street.

ST GILES' STREET
St Giles' Street runs from the junction of St Peter's Street and Guildhall Hill at the corner of the Market Place to Grapes Hill. The street's original name was Lower Newport Street but later took its name from the church.

Streets off St Giles' Street
North:
Lower Goat Lane (before 1)
Upper Goat Lane (5–7)
Chestnut or Chesnutt's Court (formerly Schumach Court) (15)
Freeman's Court (formerly Cannell's Court) (29–31)
Fisher's Lane (39–41 – runs to Pottergate)
Iselin's Court (45)*
Willow Lane (runs to Cow Hill) (53a–55)
Cow Hill (runs to 92–94 Pottergate) (73–5)
May's Court (formerly Hayes' court) (83–85 – or 5–6 Upper St Giles)
Wellington Lane (runs to 110–112 St Benedict's Street) (97–99, or 13 Upper St Giles)

South:
Cleveland Road
Low's Yard (12)*
Tuck's Court (24–26)
Rigby's Court (52–54)
Bethel Street (66a–68)
Bateman's Court (72)
Hales' Court (72–74)
Fox's Court (76)
Cock Yard (80–82)
Gunn's Court (82a–84)

Exact location unknown:
Bennett's Yard (near Bethel Street)*
Harrison's Court*

Buildings on St Giles' Street
City Wall
St Giles' Gate was originally known as Newport Gate, reflecting the street's original name. It was the main entrance from the west of the city, and the road led to Cambridge, Ely, Huntingdon and Peterborough. At one point there was a leper house nearby. The gate was pulled down in 1792.

Churches
St Giles' Church dates from 1420 and has the tallest parish church tower in Norwich at 120ft. It was selected as the site for a fire beacon in 1549. The soldiers at Britannia Barracks (Norwich Prison) also used it to practise semaphore signalling. The church was first lit with gas on 15 January 1860.

St Giles' Church. (Photograph by author)

Other buildings of note
Churchman House was built by Thomas Churchman the worsted weaver. His son Thomas added the front range in 1751. The building was used as the Norwich High School for Girls in 1875 until it moved to the Assembly House in 1877. It was restored in 1990 at a cost of £400,000 and is now the Norwich Register office.

Churchman House. (Photograph by author)

Gladstone House, 28 St Giles' Street, was mayor John Harvey's house.

The Hippodrome or 'Grand Opera House' was built in 1903 and demolished in 1966; the site is now a car park.

The Masonic Hall, 17 St Giles' Street, was built in 1907 by Albert Havers for the Norwich Masonic Association. It contains the Masonic Temple and Banqueting Hall.

The Salvation Army building was the site of Brown's Hotel; musicians who played at the Hippodrome stayed there. According to *White's Directory* of 1890, the building was put up as a rink 'during the roller-skate mania' – this was November 1876. The skating rink cost £9,000; it was 103ft long and 55ft wide, and had a promenade gallery and smoking rooms as well as an outer rink on Bethel Street. However, by May 1877 the craze had died down and the managers had to introduce entertainment acts. The first ones were, according to the *Norfolk Chronicle*, 'a couple of clever bicyclists and a troupe of performing dogs'. The rink reopened in September 1877 as 'the Vaudeville Theatre of Varieties'; but on 14 March 1982 the memorial stone of the Salvation Army HQ was laid by George White, and the building opened on 30 October.

People linked with St Giles' Street

Sir Frederick Bateman, physician, lived at 70 St Giles' Street. James Bennett, watchmaker, lived at St Giles' Gates; he invented an instrument to perform the 'trepan' operation. His obituary in 1845 said that he was the first man who made an electrical machine in Norwich and 'could dissect an eye very beautifully'.

William Burt, an upholsterer and auctioneer who was mayor in 1820, lived at 49 St Giles' Street; his house was later rebuilt by the brewer Richard Bullard.

Thomas Churchman, worsted weaver, was mayor in 1749. He laid out the elms in Chapelfield Garden in 1749 and built Churchman House. His son Thomas, who was mayor in 1761, was knighted by George III following an address congratulating the king on his marriage.

John Hammond Cole, a bank clerk, was mayor in 1811. He was the Distributor of Stamps from 1793 until his death in 1829; he lived at 36 St Giles' Street and the Stamp Office was at his house.

Sir Peter Eade, physician and historian, was mayor in 1883, 1893 and 1895. He lived in Churchman House and, together with F. W. Harmer, was responsible for the layout of Chapelfield Gardens, the gardens around the Castle and the city's acquisition of Mousehold Heath.

Sir William Foster Bt, solicitor, was mayor from 1844–45. He lived at Upper St Giles' Street and his legal offices (listed as Fosters, Burroughes & Robberds in *White's Directory* of 1883) were also in St Giles'. He was made a baronet in 1838.

John Harvey, mayor in 1792, lived at 28 St Giles' Street (also known as Gladstone House). He commanded the

Norwich Light Horse Volunteers in 1797 and revived the tradition of horse racing on Mousehold Heath. Although he was a leading partner in Harvey & Hudson's bank, he also introduced shawl weaving to Norwich in 1791; in September 1822 2,631 journeymen weavers collected money to buy him a silver vase.

William Herring, a manufacturer who was mayor in 1796, lived at 48 St Giles' Street (now the YMCA). During Herring's mayoralty in May 1797, Nelson presented his sword to the city.

Elias Norgate, a surgeon who was mayor in 1785, lived at 35 St Giles' Street.

In February 1866 F. W. Windham died at the Norfolk Hotel on St Giles' Street from 'an obstruction of the circulation by a clot of blood in the pulmonary artery'. He had come into a huge inheritance in 1861, but the *Norfolk Chronicle* says he led an 'ill-spent life' and 'dissipated' the lot; although he had rooms at the Norfolk Hotel, he spent most of his time at one of the city's 'low public-houses'.

Henry Woodcock, a surgeon and dentist, was mayor from 1849–51 and paid for the clock and clock turret on the Guildhall. He lived at 70 St Giles' Street.

Events at St Giles' Street

There have been several fires in St Giles' Street; on 1 April 1775 a chimney fire from Mr Fielding's spread to the house of glover Benjamin Hugman, opposite the Curriers Arms. During the fire, someone stole a box from him containing 'plate, rings and cash' worth £30 (around £2,500 of today's money). On 23 May 1852 there was a serious fire at the Norfolk Hotel, which lost its roof and a few of the rooms; afterwards, the Watch Committee held an inquiry into allegations of a deficiency in the water supply and inefficiency of the engines. Rather more nastily, on 3 May 1890 there was a fire at H. Cole Furnishing shop, which resulted in the contents of the shop being destroyed – which might not have happened if a mob hadn't impeded the work of the fire brigade. And in September 1920 there was a fire at Neale's Coachmakers, where all the workshops were destroyed and the damage was estimated at £2,000.

In July 1823 there was an advertisement about an exhibition at Mrs Chestnut's in St Giles' Street of 'a machine exemplifying perpetual motion'. It was claimed that the machine 'has been going since it was invented, upwards of seven years'; the mayor was suspicious, investigated it and banned it as a fake.

Workmen sinking a well near the gates on 23 December 1823 discovered vaults 'running in all directions at a depth of 35 feet' – these were the chalk mines, which have led to the collapse of parts of the road in the 'golden triangle' area between Earlham Road and Unthank Road, Victorian developments outside the City Wall. The most famous hole in the road was probably when it opened up under the front of a double-decker bus.

The *Daylight* was published at 26 St Giles' Street, and landed its printer in a lot of hot water. On Valentine's Day 1883 solicitor Joseph Stanley horsewhipped the *Daylight's* printer Edward Burgess in London Street for publishing 'certain statements' in the *Daylight* – he was fined a mere shilling, showing that the jury's sympathies lay with Stanley rather than the printer. This opened the gates for more complaints against Burgess; a week later, E. Field and Co claimed they'd been libelled by the *Daylight*, but lost the case. On 24 February artist Arthur Ventnor was in the dock for breaking the windows of the *Daylight* after they exhibited a caricature of him; the city recorder said that Ventnor had had considerable provocation and would be sentenced to be imprisoned for 3 hours – but as he'd already spent more than that time in the dock, he would be discharged and the *Daylight* should pay the costs of prosecution. Finally, on 24 April there was another libel case from Lewin Samuel, a clothier of St Giles' Street; the *Daylight* claimed that he and his brother were moneylenders and extorted over 150% interest for small loans. Halfway through the case – after a lot of dirt had been aired –Samuel suddenly decided to withdraw.

St Giles' Street was bombed during World War Two, and Sir Frederick Bateman's house (70 St Giles' Street) was destroyed in an air raid in June 1942. The furniture store next door to it was rebuilt but was demolished in the 1960s when Cleveland Road was built.

ST GILES' TERRACE
58–60 Bethel Street, runs from opposite the Coach and Horses pub in Bethel Street. The painter Joseph Stannard lived at St Giles' Terrace; he studied with Crome's friend Robert Ladbroke. He specialised first in portraits and then moved into painting landscapes; he was commissioned by Thomas Harvey to paint the Thorpe Water Frolic. He

St Giles' Terrace. (Photograph by author)

married the artist Emily Coppin (who painted as Mrs Joseph Stannard) and died in 1830 from tuberculosis.

ST GREGORY'S ALLEY
St Gregory's Alley runs from 27 Pottergate to St Benedict's Street; it takes its name from St Gregory's Church (see St Benedict's Street). In 1783 it was known as St Gregory's Churchyard.

Streets off St Gregory's Alley
On the north side, the street has included:
St Gregory's Lower Alley.

ST GREGORY'S LOWER ALLEY
Runs from St Gregory's Alley. It included St Gregory's Church Road (under the chancel of the church); Golden Cross Yard* and Charing Cross.

ST HELEN'S SQUARE
19 Bishopgate.

ST HELEN'S WHARF
Bishopgate, near the Adam & Eve pub, is used as a car park.

ST JAMES' CLOSE
112 Barrack Street, takes its name from the church and was built between 1935 and 1941. (Following the street renumbering, it's now at 154 Barrack Street.)

ST JAMES' PALACE YARD
44–54 or 109 Barrack Street. The yard was lost 1883–90.

ST JOHN'S STREET
Runs from 36–38 Mountergate; it originally ran to 41–43 Rose Lane on the north and St Ann's Lane in the south but is now a cul-de-sac. It contains Parmentergate Court and the Rose Lane car park.

ST JOHN STREET (MADDERMARKET)
St John Street (Maddermarket) runs from 7 Pottergate to St Andrew's Street. The street was known as Maddermarket from the early 13th century but became St John's Street (or St John Maddermarket) from the mid-18th century. The maddermarket – where the red dye from the madder root was sold – was at the north end of the churchyard.

Streets off St John Street (Maddermarket)
Farnell's Yard or Court (runs between the church and chapel at 3–4 St John's Alley)
St John's Alley
Golden Lion Yard (15)*

Buildings on St John Street (Maddermarket)
Churches

St John the Baptist's (Maddermarket) Church was originally dedicated to the Holy Trinity and St John the Baptist and was sometimes known as St John at Pottersgate (sic); there was a church there from before the Conquest, but the present church dates mainly from the mid-15th century. The church was restored in the mid-1860s at a cost of £1,200, and after a gas explosion in September 1876 it had to have a new roof. During choir, the vicar (Revd H.L. Rumsey) noticed an escape of gas, and was turning off the

St John the Baptist's Church, Maddermarket. (Photograph by author)

St John's Pump. (Photograph by author)

gas (with a lit taper in his hand) when 'a brilliant flame shot across the north side of the nave'. The choir wasn't hurt, but Revd Rumsey was thrown several yards and was shaken by the experience. St John's Church was used briefly as a Greek Orthodox Church and is now redundant. There is still a parish pump at the bottom of the churchyard called St John's Pump.

Other buildings of note

Maddermarket Theatre was founded in 1911 by Walter Nugent Monck (see Ninham's Court). The building was formerly a Roman Catholic chapel, a baking powder factory and a Salvation Army citadel, but was opened as the Maddermarket Theatre in September 1921.

Maddermarket Theatre. (Photograph by author)

People linked with St John Street (Maddermarket)

Robert Rugge (or Rugg) was a mercer who was mayor in 1545 and 1550. According to Blomefield, he was an oppressive mayor. He lived opposite St John Maddermarket; the cellars are below the building known as Trevor Page & Co in 1938.

John Terry was a mercer and merchant who was mayor in 1523; he lived in a house opposite St John Maddermarket.

Events on St John Street (Maddermarket)

In 1599 Will Kemp had a row with Shakespeare about who was the more popular. He ended up claiming that he could morris dance his way from London to Norwich in just nine days, and backed himself at odds of 3 to 1. He set off from Whitechapel on the first Monday in Lent with Tom Slye on pipes and drum, his general servant William Bee and George Spratt as referee; not including the resting time in between dancing (which amounted to about a month), he won the bet. Though he embarrassed one Norwich girl when, at the end of his dance, he lept over the wall of the churchyard at St John Maddermarket and landed with one foot on her skirt – and her petticoat came off! The mayor presented Kemp with £5 'in Elizabeth Angels' (around £628 in today's money) and an allowance of 40 shillings a year, as well as making him a freeman of the merchant venturers. Kemp wrote of his journey in *Nine Daies Wonder*; and 400 years later the 127-mile route was danced as a morris relay – with no rest days, and the morris clubs knocked a day off Kemp's time.

ST JOHN'S ALLEY
Is the section of St John Street running beneath the tower of St John's Church past the Maddermarket.

ST JULIAN'S STREET
St Julian's Street originally ran from 37 Thorn Lane to Horns Lane. It was flattened in World War Two and is now part of Rouen Road. It took its name from the church.

Streets off St Julian Street
North:
St Julian's Church Alley (now St Julian's Alley) (15)

South:
Crusoe Street (led to Garden Street) (18–20)*

Buildings on St Julian's Street
Churches
St Julian's Church was, according to Blomefield, founded before the Conquest and given to the nuns of Carhoe (Carrow) by King Stephen; the east part of the churchyard

Norman arch at St Julian's Church. (Photograph by author)

had an anchorage where an 'ankeress or recluse' lived. The house was demolished at the Dissolution but the foundations could still be seen in Blomefield's time. It's thought that the church was originally dedicated to Julian the Hospitaller, patron saint of ferrymen, and Saint Julian of Norwich took her name from the church. Julian's cell fell down in the 16th century, and the east end of the chancel fell in during April 1845; the church was restored later that year at a cost of £500. The church was badly bombed during air raids in June 1942 and was rebuilt in 1953 by the architect A.J. Chaplin. The reconstruction includes a Norman doorway, which was originally part of the Church of St Michael at Thorn, and three Anglo-Saxon windows. The bell that was blown out of the tower in Word War Two was repaired, named Gabriel, re-hallowed and put back in the tower on 5 January 1993.

St Julian's cell, St Julian's Church. (Photograph by author)

People linked with St Julian's Street
Julian of Norwich was the author of *Revelations of Divine Love*, which was the first book published by a woman in English. She may have been educated at Carrow Abbey and became an anchoress at about the age of 30, after having 16 visions in May 1373. She lived according to the 'Ancren Riwle' of recluses, which meant she was allowed to have a servant, could eat two meals a day (which should not include flesh or lard) and could keep a cat.

Events at St Julian's Street

Rather gruesomely, in June 1819 a grave was opened in St Julian's Churchyard. The grave was that of a woman who had died of smallpox and been buried within 48 hours of her death. The newspapers reported grimly, 'it was suspected that she had been buried alive'.

ST JULIAN'S ALLEY

Sometimes known as St Julian's Church Alley, runs from King Street to Rouen Road (formerly St Julian Street, where it was crossed by Horns Lane).

ST LAURENCE LITTLE STEPS

Runs from 21 St Benedict's Street to the south side of Westwick Street, and takes its name from the church next door.

ST LAURENCE STEPS

Runs from 23 St Benedict's Street to the south side of Westwick Street, and is a flight of 30 steps next to the church. John Gudgeon, a shuttle-maker who was reported to be 'eccentric and whimsical', died at his home there in April 1836, aged 37.

ST LAWRENCE CLOSE

36–38 St Benedict's Street (formerly St Lawrence School Yard 1883–90), takes its name from the church.

ST LAWRENCE LANE

Runs from 51 Pottergate to 16–18 St Benedict's Street. It takes its name from the church and was known as St Laurences Lane from the mid-14th century, although Sandred and Lingström mention that it was also known as Shouldhams Lane in the late 15th century, which they identify with John de Shuldham, a bailiff during Richard II's reign who owned the houses on the west of the street.

A tragic incident occurred in February 1817; Elizabeth Pope, aged 83, was alone in her apartment 'over the portico' of the church and accidentally set herself on fire when she stooped to stir the fire and a candle she was holding caught her clothes. She died from her burns.

A rather unsavoury incident occurred there in April 1840, when sickly children were taken to a woman near St Lawrence's to be 'cut' because they had a 'supposed disease called the spinnage'. She charged parents 3d to cut through the lobe of the child's right ear and make a cross with the blood upon the child's breast and forehead. She did the same thing on the following Monday with the child's left ear, then repeated it on the right ear on the following Monday.

ST LAWRENCE SCHOOL YARD

Former name of St Lawrence Close.

ST MARGARET'S ALLEY

35–7 St Benedict's Street, takes is name from St Margaret's Street.

ST MARGARET'S STREET

St Margaret's Street runs from 37–39 St Benedict's Street to 57 Westwick Street. The street takes its name from the church (see St Benedict's Street), but was known as Nether Westwick Lane in the mid-18th century.

Streets off St Margaret's Street

South:
Bakers' Arms Yard*

Exact location unknown:
Arnold's Yard*

ST MARTIN AT BALE COURT

28 Cattle Market Street, is an early 21st-century development, which takes its name from the former Church of St Martin at Balliva.

ST MARTIN'S AT OAK WALL LANE

Runs from 182–184 Oak Street to 66–68 St Augustine's Street. It takes its name from the City Wall and the Church of St Martin at Oak, and was known as 'Under the Walls St Martin at Oak' before 1890. Henry Fuller, who was the mayor in 1544, was the first mayor to hold his inaugural feast in St Andrew's Hall. He lived in Fuller's Hall in St Martin's at Oak Wall Lane, which was demolished during slum clearances before 1938. Ebenezer Place originally ran from here to Sussex Street.

ST MARTIN'S LANE

St Martin's Lane originally ran from 68–70 Oak Street to 26–28 Pitt Street; the Pitt Street end has been truncated by the Inner Ring Road and it is now a cul-de-sac. The street was called Horlane in the 13th century (possibly meaning 'dirty lane'; Sandred and Lingström also suggest it may be from the 'harstone', which marked the parish boundary). Although it was known as Whore's Lane in the 18th century, it was a corruption from 'Horlane' as that wasn't the red light district of the city. The street became known as St Martin's Lane by the mid-18th century, taking its name from the nearby St Martin at Oak Church.

Streets off St Martin's Lane

North:
Butcher's Yard or Square (3)*
Quaker's Lane (47–59 – now off St Crispin's Road)
Maltzy Court (now off St Crispin's Road)

South:
Springfield's Yard or Court (34)
Fox & Goose Yard (46)

Exact location unknown:
Leach's Yard*

ST MARTIN AT PALACE PLAIN

St Martin at Palace Plain runs from 37 Palace Street to 23 Bishopgate. The street takes its name from St Martin's Church and the bishop's palace. At one point, it was known as St Martin's at the Palace-Gate, as it stands opposite the north gate to the bishop's palace. In the early 14th century it was known as Bichil. Sandred and Lingström suggest this is either 'bitch hill' or 'beak hill', meaning a promontory, as ships were unloaded there at one point. It became known as St Martin's Plain by 1783 and finally St Martin at Palace by 1830.

Streets off St Martin at Palace Plain
The street has included:
White Lion Lane (8)
World's End Lane (10)*
Whitefriars (12)
Beehive Yard (18)*

Buildings on St Martin at Palace Plain
Churches
St Martin at Palace Church was recorded by name in

St Martin at Palace Church. (Photograph by author)

Domesday as there was a church there dedicated to St Martin before the Conquest; archaeological excavations showed Norman foundations and at least one former timber church on the site. Lord Sheffield and 35 of his followers who were killed during Kett's Rebellion in 1549 were buried here. The upper part of the tower collapsed in 1783; it was rebuilt without the top storey and was restored

in the 1800s. During restoration work in August 1851, the north aisle collapsed; luckily, 16 workmen escaped unscathed. The church was rebuilt and reopened in May 1852. The church has been redundant since 1974 and is in the care of the Norwich Historic Churches Trust. It has been used as the Norfolk Probation Centre since 1990.

Other buildings of note
Alnwick Gate, also called Bishop's Palace Gate, leads to the Bishop's Palace and the Bishop's House in the Close. It's named after the Bishop of Norwich who started building it, but he moved to Lincoln in 1436 and left it unfinished. Bishop Lyhart added the doors. Elizabeth I came to the city on horseback on 16 August 1578 as part of her 'progress' through the county. She stayed for a week at the Bishop's Palace, where she was entertained by various pageants and (according to *White's Directory* of 1845) 'dined publicly in the north aisle of the cathedral cloister, and often went… to witness wrestling and shooting on Mousehold Health'.

Cotman House was built by Samuel Pye in 1767 on the site of the White Swan. In 1823 the painter John Sell Cotman moved here and set up a 'School for Drawing and Painting Water-colours: terms one guinea and a half the quarter'. He stayed there until 1834, when he was evicted because he spent more than he earned! The house fell into ruin and was threatened with demolition in 1937; Mrs Russell Colman bought the building and gave it to the Norwich Amenities Preservation Society for restoration.

Cotman House. (Photograph by author)

The mullioned window at 10 St Martin at Palace Plain was originally from a mediaeval house which formed part of the Beehive pub and may have belonged originally to the Calthorpe family. The Beehive was demolished in 1962 but the window was dismantled and moved into number 10.

People linked with St Martin at Palace Plain
John Sell Cotman, painter, was baptised at St Mary Coslany Church and lived at Cotman House from 1823.

Oriel at 10 St Martin at Palace Plain. (Photograph by author)

John Thompson, city lamplighter, died at the age of 62 in February 1811; he was buried at night under the lamplights of his 'brethren of the ladder and torch', and thousands assembled on the plain to see him to his final rest.

Events on St Martin at Palace Plain

One of the biggest events at St Martin at Palace Plain was Kett's Rebellion in 1549. Robert Kett, a landowner in the nearby village of Wymondham, joined the rebels in tearing down his own enclosure fences and led them to Norwich. Kett and his followers sent the king a list of 29 requests – as well as stopping enclosure (where rich men put fences round common land), they wanted weights and measures standardised throughout the country, they wanted ineffective priests sacked and rich priests made to teach the poor children. In their own words, they wanted 'all bond men made free, for God made all free with his precious blood shedding'. The city refused to reach a truce with Kett, so he attacked Bishop's Bridge and Norwich fell to the rebels, who camped on Mousehold Heath.

Kett's rebels held strong against the Earl of Northampton's army and there was a huge battle in Bishopgate, when Lord Sheffield was killed. The rebels were finally beaten by the Earl of Warwick's troops and a team of German mercenary knights. Kett and his brother William were hanged – William from the steeple at Wymondham Abbey, and Robert from the walls of Norwich Castle. Though, in 1949 Norwich citizens recognised that Robert was fighting for social and economic justice and placed a tablet on the castle 'in reparation and honour'.

Unrest in the city spilled over to St Martin at Palace Plain again in January 1850. Female factory hands, upset at a change in their working hours, broke the windows of Mr Douglas's house with snowballs and waylaid him on the plain. The *Norfolk Chronicle* reported that he took refuge in a neighbouring office 'to save himself from being stripped naked'.

St Martin at Palace Plain has also seen some major fires. On 29 June 1776 fire started at the premises of cabinet maker Samuel Cooper and burned down his house and that of William Woods in less than an hour. The houses of George Gibbs and Cave Burridge were also destroyed. In 1822 chandlers Staff & Chamberlin were destroyed by fire. H.F. Butcher's paper and mill-board factory met the same fate on 5 January 1858, as did Frazer's sawmills on 15 March 1865, with £4,000 worth of damage being caused (the equivalent of nearly a quarter of a million pounds in today's money). There was also a huge fire on 6 August 1897, when Cullingford's paper mills went up.

Gasworks were built at St Martin's Plain in 1858; when the gas company expanded in 1880, part of World's End lane was pulled down. The gasworks were demolished in 1970.

ST MARY'S ALLEY

St Mary's Alley originally ran from 16–18 St Mary's Plain to 6 Pitt Street but now runs to Duke Street. It takes its name from St Mary Coslany Church (see St Mary's Plain). Part of the area was known as Soutergate Street in 1783 (after the shoe industry there); it became Southgate Street from 1845–83 and St Mary's Alley by 1890.

Streets off St Mary's Alley

The street has included:
Bell Yard (3–4)
Bantam's Yard (formerly Benton's Yard) (5)

People linked with St Mary's Alley

Thomas Osborn Springfield, clockmaker and crape manufacturer, was mayor in 1829 and 1836. He was the first mayor under the new Municipal Government Act; at the time, political corruption was the norm, and John Harvey noted that Springfield gave away £6,000 in bribes (over £386,000 in today's money) to secure his nomination. He lived in St Mary's Alley; in 1938 his house was known as the headquarters of the Boot and Shoe Operatives. His original business was making clocks in Colegate, but after 1819 he set up the crape factory of Springfield Son and Nephew, silk merchants, in St Mary's. He died in 1858; his obituary in the *Norfolk Chronicle* says that 'during his career he won and lost several fortunes' because of silk market fluctuations. They added that he was a very sharp politician and went in to win, so 'many of his victories were, doubtless, most costly' – but they also said that in his private life he 'exhibited many good traits [and] was never unamiable nor ungenerous'.

ST MARY'S PLAIN

St Mary's Plain runs from the junction of Duke Street and

Muspole Street to 40–42 Oak Street. It was known as Soutergate (from the shoemakers) and then Colegate in the 14th century; by the mid-18th century it was known as St Mary's Plain, taking its name from St Mary Coslany Church.

Streets off St Mary's Plain
North:
Rosemary Lane (9)
White Bear Yard (formerly Marine Store Yard) (29–31)

South:
St Mary's Alley (18)
Newbegin's Yard (later Atkinson's Yard) (18–24)*
Hen & Chickens Yard (28)*

Buildings on St Mary's Plain
Churches
St Mary's Coslany Church has the oldest structure in the city – its tower dates from 1070, though the nave was rebuilt in 1477. According to *White's Directory* of 1890, it has the oldest mural inscription in the city, in Norman French: 'I Tomas de Lingcole a done a cet auter sirge e un liape e la rente de Colegate' (i.e. he gave the altar a candle and a lamp). The church has been hit by several floods over the years; in October 1762 the water was 3ft deep inside the church, and almost the same in November 1770 despite the churchyard being banked up from the inside. In February 1785 the churchyard was overflowed within 12 hours and the church was more than 2ft deep in water; the following year, water overflowed the churchyard again and the south door was bricked up to keep the water out of the church. The painter John Sell Cotman was baptised here in 1782, fellow artist John Crome married here 10 years later and the printer Luke Hansard was also baptised here. Drovers used to pen their cattle in the churchyard here overnight before market day, and the church was derelict by 1906. It was

St Mary's Coslany Church. (Photograph by author)

restored but has been redundant since 1975 and is in the care of the Norwich Historic Churches Trust; it has been a craft centre since 1985.

St Mary's Baptist Church was a new chapel built under Joseph Kinghorm, enlarged in 1839 and 1886 but badly damaged by a fire in September 1939 – it was restored and reopened in 1940 but gutted in an air raid in June 1943.

Other buildings of note
Pykerell's house is one of the five original thatched houses left in the city following the 1507 fires. It was once known as Pilgrim's Hall, then became the Old Rosemary Tavern.

Pykerell's House. (Photograph by author)

People linked with St Mary's Plain
Tomas de Lingcole was a tanner and city bailiff who died in 1298. According to the inscription in St Mary's Church, he gave a wax taper and a lamp to the altar of the Holy Trinity. Thomas Pykerell (or Pickarell) was mayor in 1525, 1533, and 1538. He lived in a house on the corner of St Mary's Plain and Rosemary Lane (then known as Little Helsden Lane East).

Events at St Mary's Plain
There was a tragic accident in December 1896 at St Mary's silk mills (Hinde's factory) when 15-year-old Leonard Ostler Delves turned round carelessly and his clothes caught in the machine he was using and pulled him into it. The inspectors said that the machines were very safe, and the verdict was accidental death.

ST MICHAEL AT PLEA'S ALLEY
Later known as Church Alley or Church Walk, runs from the south side of Prince's Street to Redwell Street.

ST MICHAEL AT PLEA'S COURT
South side of Prince's Street, is a new development (the building also houses Eversheds solicitors). It takes its name from St Michael at Plea's Church nearby.

ST MICHAEL'S SQUARE
8–10 Thorn Lane, was lost by 1947.

ST MILES' ALLEY
Runs from 59 Colegate to just before 12 Oak Street (Coslany Street before 1890). Chantry Yard runs off it.

ST PAUL'S OPENING
Originally ran from 31 Peacock Street to Church Street (aka Barrack Street). Since the damage during the war and the Inner Ring Road development, St Paul's Opening runs off Blackfriars Street (formerly Peacock Street). Jolly Sawyers' Yard ran off it.

ST PAUL'S SQUARE
Originally ran from Church Street (aka Barrack Street) to Cowgate. It now runs from Willis Street and has been truncated by St Crispin's Road. The half-timbered houses there (called a 'rookery of disgraceful tenements' in *White's Directory* of 1883) were demolished. The area may have been known as Norman's Lane near St Paul's Church in 1783 and as Spitalfields in 1830.

ST PAUL'S TERRACE
19–21 Barrack Street, appears to be lost by 1964.

ST PETER'S COURT
80 King Street, is a new development; it takes its name from the Church of St Peter Parmentergate, nearby.

ST PETER'S COURT
Former name for Rackham's Court, 23 St Peter's Street.

ST PETER'S ALLEY OR STEPS
33–34 Market Place, takes its name from the church.

ST PETER'S STREET (MANCROFT)
St Peter's Street runs from 39 Market Place to 25 Bethel Street. In the 13th century it was known as 'Overrowe', and by the 18th century it was called Upper Market Street, as it was the top of the market place; it took its present name in the 19th century from St Peter Mancroft Church.

Streets off St Peter's Street (Mancroft)
East:
Pope's Head Yard (7)*
Bennett's Court (also known as Graham's Court) (9–11)*
Wounded Hart Street or Lane (13–15)*
Rackham Court (formerly St Peter's Court) (23)*
Swan Yard (27)*
Mancroft Yard (33)*
White Hart Yard (39)*

West:
Page's Yard (10)*

Exact location unknown:
Day's Court or Yard*
Western's Court*

Buildings on St Peter's Street
Churches
St Peter's (Mancroft) is actually dedicated to St Peter and St Paul. According to Blomefield, the name 'Mancroft' comes from 'Magna Crofta' or 'great croft', land which was attached to the manor house (in this case, the castle). At 180ft long and with a steeple 146ft high, St Peter's is the biggest parish church in city. According to Blomefield, the parish grew to the point where the churchyard had to be enlarged in 1367, as there wasn't enough room to bury the parish dead. The present church was built in 1430–55 on the site of a Norman church and was restored in 1851–56 by Phipson. There were originally houses on the north and south side of the church, but they were cleared away in 1882. The church has a peal of 12 bells, and the first true peal of changes (5,040) was rung in 1715. According to *White's Directory* of 1890, 'in the vestry is a curious old coloured carving in alabaster of nine female saints', including St Margaret holding down a dragon; there is a similar carving of male saints in St Stephen's Church. In 1880 workmen discovered

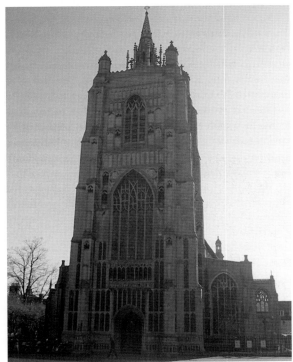

St Peter Mancroft Church. (Photograph by author)

a vault with 12 earthen jars laid on their sides, with their mouths open to the vault. Nobody knew what they were for, but similar jars have been found at Fountains Abbey.

People linked with St Peter's Street

Thomas Aleyn, a grocer who was mayor in 1450, was buried at St Peter Mancroft. In his will, he gave 50 marks to make a new pillory for the market, and a covering for corn to be sold under.

Richard Ballys, a grocer who was mayor in 1489, lived in the area.

Michael Beverley, a grocer who was mayor in 1692, is though to have lived at 25 St Peter's Street.

John Browne, who was mayor in 1798, was an ironmonger, ironfounder and colourman; his business was located at 19 St Peter's Street. The house was pulled down in April 1935.

Thomas Turner, who was mayor in 1699, owned the Black Swan in St Peter's Street.

Charles Weston, a banker and brewer, was mayor in 1772. He established one of the first provincial banks in the country in January 1756, in a court at 5 Upper Market (St Peter's Street). During his mayoralty, the City Waits were abolished. In 1801 Weston's son won £15,000 (over £700,000 in today's money) in the Irish Lottery; he'd bought a ticket the previous year but didn't check it until May 1801! Weston's bank then became Charles Weston & Co; however, the bank had closed by 1811.

Events at St Peter's Street

St Peter's Church was where Nelson's victories were celebrated in the city. The news that Nelson had destroyed the French fleet in Aboukir Bay reached Norwich on 2 October 1798 and the bells of St Peter rang all day. On 13 October Mr and Mrs John Berry gave a ball at the Assembly House in honour of Nelson and his captain Edward Berry (John's brother). On 22 October the bells were rung again, and this time the French tricolour was flown from St Peter's tower with the Union Jack over it.

The vault of St Peter Mancroft Church was opened in February 1806 for the first time in over 30 years – and a live bat was found there; the newspaper report described it as 'of a greyish colour' and said it had probably been there in a torpid state since the last time the vault was opened. In March 1816 it was opened again; this time, three bats were discovered, 'entirely covered with mould and dust', and one of them 'immediately took flight'.

The Swan, as well as being a theatre, held exhibitions; in April 1819 two of the 'exhibitions' were of Master Sewell, the Lincolnshire gigantic youth, who at the age of 13 weighed 18 stone, and Miss Elenor Fitzjohn, Queen of the Dwarfs, who was 30in high and weighed 27lbs at the age of 19.

February 1805 saw a strange case in the city; a woman who had eloped with a horse dealer was found by her husband in a house in St Peter Mancroft. She refused to return to her husband, and the horse dealer offered to buy her for £5 (worth around £250 today – very insulting!). In an act very similar to that of Hardy's Mayor of Casterbridge, the husband put a halter round his wife's neck and sold her to the horse dealer.

In May 1811 there was a fire at R&S Culley, grocers, which also burned down the top two stories of Mr Freeman's house. The *Chronicle* said that 'there was a large quantity of sugar, upwards of sixty chests of tea, and other articles on the premises, and the column of flame that rose up from them was truly awful'. The Pope's Head pub just about escaped, but the cost of damage was estimated at £5,000 (around £228,000 in today's money). There was also a fire at shoe manufacturer's Willis & Southall on 21 May 1879, causing £1,000 worth of damage.

A particularly nasty event happened on 20 November 1876; William Nelson was severely injured when a gas pipe charged with gunpowder exploded in the street, and he died the following day. The mayor offered a reward to find out who did it, but the whole event was shrouded in mystery.

ST SAVIOUR'S ALLEY

Runs from 17–19 St Saviour's Lane to Magdalen Street; it was known as St Saviour's Back Street in 1783 but had become St Saviour's Alley by 1883.

ST SAVIOUR'S LANE

St Saviour's Lane originally ran from 45–47 Magdalen Street to 22 Peacock Street; now it runs to Blackfriars Street. It was known simply as 'the lane leading to Rotten row' in the early 18th century. By the mid-18th century it was known as St Saviour's Lane, taking its name from St Saviour's Church.

Streets off St Saviour's Lane

North:
St Saviour's Alley (17–19)

South:
Campling's Yard or Square (20–22)*

People linked with St Saviour's Lane

Jeremiah Ives, a merchant who was mayor in 1756, lived at 24 St Saviour's Lane. He was known as Justice Ives or Jeremiah Ives the Elder, to distinguish him from his cousin (also called Jeremiah Ives), who was his business partner. John Whitaker Robberds, a Worsted manufacturer who was mayor in 1814, revived the Guild festivities. He died in his home at 24 St Saviour's Lane in 1837.

ST SIMON'S COURT
South side of Elm Hill, takes its name from St Simon and St Jude's Church. The yard apparently ran to Waggon & Horses Lane.

ST SIMON'S YARD
Former name for Symond's Yard.

ST STEPHEN'S BACK STREET
St Stephen's Back Street runs from 24 Coburg Street. In 1825 there were oil works in St Stephen's Back Street, which were sold to the British Gas Light Company. George Allen built a large factory in St Stephen's Back Street in 1857; in November 1860 he pioneered the manufacturing of elastic cloth in the city.

Streets off St Stephen's Back Street
All the yards ran to St Stephen's Street.
Lock's Court (6–16)*
Wade's Court (24–26)*
Pipe Burners' Yard (26*
Shoulder of Mutton Yard*
Unicorn Yard or Alley
One Post Passage or Alley
Malthouse Road (formerly St Stephen's Church Lane – eventually both streets became known as Malthouse Road)

ST STEPHEN'S CHURCH LANE
11 Rampant Horse Street, became known as Malthouse Lane.

ST STEPHEN'S PLAIN
Runs from 3 Westgate. It was known as Tuns Corner (from the Three Tunnes inn) in the 17th century and as Bunting's Corner (after Bunting's department store, now the Marks & Spencer's building) in the 20th century. Alden's Court runs off it, exact location unknown.

ST STEPHEN'S SQUARE
99–101 Chapel Field Road. Elizabeth Bentley, author of *Tales for Children in Verse,* lived at 45 St Stephen's Square.

ST STEPHEN'S STREET
St Stephen's Street runs from Rampant Horse Street to the junction of St Stephen's Road, Queen's Road and Chapelfield Road. It was originally known as Nedeham Street in the mid-13th century (which Sandred and Lingström say means 'poor homestead'), and became St Stephen's Street in the late 17th century, taking its name from the church. It was once the principal entrance to the city from the south.

St Stephen's Street. (Photograph by author)

Streets off St Stephen's Street
North:
Andrew's Yard or Court*
Malthouse Yard (6)*
Barwell's Court (formerly Goodman's Yard) (10 – leads to Malthouse Road)
Day's Yard (near 16)*
Stockings' Court (24–26)*
One Post Alley (also found as One Post Passage) (26 – leads to Malthouse Road)
Unicorn Alley or Yard (28 – also appears to lead to Malthouse Road)
Magnet Square (28)*
Loyalty Court (formerly Sardinian Court) (34–36)
Duke of Wellington Yard (42–44)*
Pipe Burners' Yard or Row (44 – led to St Stephen's Back Street)*
Wade's Court or Yard (also known as Bullard's Yard – led to St Stephen's Back Street) (50–52)*
Shoulder of Mutton Yard (52–54)*
Lock's Court (60–64)*
Swan Yard (64)*
George Yard (64)*
Trumpet Lane and Yard (68–72)*
Coburg Street (72–74)

South:
Surrey Street (7–9)
The Archway (formerly King's Head Yard and then Hunt's Yard) (25–27)*
Browne's Court (also known as Mansfield Yard or Pipemakers' Yard) (39–41a)*
Wild's Court (41a)*
Crown & Angel Yard (41–43)*
Wheatsheaf Yard (51–55)*
Rose Yard (57–59)*
Bull Lane (69–71)

Exact location unknown:
Factory Yard*
Gowing's Passage*
Norgate's Court*
Plain Yard*

Buildings on St Stephen's Street
City Wall
St Stephen's Gate (also known as Nedeham Gate) was the principal city entrance from the south. In 1549 it was decorated with the quartered remains of Kett's rebels (see St Martin's Plain), and in 1578 Elizabeth I entered the city by this gate. It was one of the first of the city gates to be demolished in 1793. According to Blomefield, there was a hermitage in a room over the gate. There was a gibbet just outside it in 1561, located in the Town Close area.

Other buildings of note
The Norfolk and Norwich Hospital was founded in 1771; it was the first modern general hospital in Norfolk. It was built between 1771 and 1775 on new ground outside the City Walls. As well as pioneering gallstone surgery, it was one of the first English hospitals to use anaesthetic and antiseptic. A new wing was added in 1802, and the hospital was redesigned in the 1880s by Edward Boardman. The tower blocks were added in 1965 and the Maternity Block in 1966–68, followed by the Main Block in 1971–74. Many of the buildings were demolished in 2003 after the hospital moved to Colney, and the areas has been redeveloped as housing.

Ranelagh Gardens – also known as Victoria Gardens, Quantrell's Garden's and Finch's Gardens – were sited in the space between St Stephen's Road to the railway and Queen's Road to Victoria Street. As well as pleasure gardens, there was a skittle alley, a bowling green and a Pantheon where there was a circus every Christmas. Parson Woodforde wrote about them in his diary; he visited them in June 1780 to see the fireworks display. Other highlights at the gardens were balloon ascents by Mr Sadler in 1815 and the feats of Townshend the walker in June 1824 (and John Mountjoy in June and July 1840). In December 1841 there was roller skating in the gardens – the skates, which were 'on two iron wheels', were invented by J. Ayton of Norwich. In 1849 the site was bought by the Eastern Union Railway Company and turned into a railway station.

St Stephen's Hospital was a leper house which was sited just outside St Stephen's Gate.

People linked with St Stephen's Street
James Keymer was the surgeon and apothecary at the Bethel Hospital for over 50 years. As an 'accoucheur' (male midwife) he delivered 8,000 children, and his obituary in 1830 said that he often attended three and four generations of the same family in succession.

Events at St Stephen's Street
The Thetford turnpike opened in 1767. The first stone of the new paving was laid on 7 February 1807; and in June 1815 the newspaper reported that St Stephen's pit was about to be removed – 'a long and justly complained-of nuisance'.

There were some major fires on the street; on 24 September 1774 a fire was caused at Mr Hines the cord spinner's by someone taking a candle to the hemp room to look for something they'd lost; the entire stock was destroyed. September wasn't a good month for St Stephen's Street, because on 2 September 1780 the chimney at Bolingbroke & Yallop's cutlers set fire to the thatch and destroyed three houses.

On 31 March 1863 boxers Mace and King had hired St Stephen's Gates Circus for a match; they were so popular that the place was overcrowded and the staging of the seats collapsed. Many people were severely bruised and shaken, and one man broke his leg. On a happier note, on 16 January 1869 Jolly & Son coach builders on St Stephen's Streets arranged to supply 'the celebrated bicycle velocipede', popular in Paris, at cost of 8 guineas. The first long bicycle journey in Norwich was made on 30 March 1869 by Mr B.W. Jolly; he cycled from Norwich to Yarmouth in 2 hours 30 mins, including a 15-minute stop at Acle. The Velocipede Club was established in April 1869 and put on an exhibition of machines at the Corn Hall.

When the Victoria Railway Company in Queen's Road (where Sainsbury's supermarket is now) wanted a grander approach to the station in 1915, they suggested widening St Stephen's Street. The suggestion was resisted; however, the street was flattened during air raids in June 1942, and the street was rebuilt and widened between 1953 and 1963.

ST SWITHIN'S ALLEY
Runs from 53–55 St Benedict's Street to 77–79 Westwick Street, along the tower of St Swithin's Church, and has been referenced as St Swithin's Lane from the 14th century. The Hampshire Hog Yard runs off it.

ST SWITHIN'S TERRACE

Now St Swithin's Road, runs from 59–61 St Benedict's Street to 95–97 Westwick Street. It takes its name from the church.

ST SWITHIN'S WHARF

90–92 Westwick Street, took its name from the church.

ST VEDAST STREET

Runs from 61–63 Prince of Wales Road to 52–60 Rose Lane; it was formerly known as Cathedral Street South. It took its name from St Vedast's Church, which was sited at 8–12 St Vedast Street. The church dated from before the Conquest and was dedicated to the Flemish saints Vaast and Amand. The parish was added to St Mary in the Marsh in around 1272, and to St Peter Parmentergate in around 1562. The church was demolished in 1540, and according to Blomefield the bells were sold in 1541 to Mr Codde. When a house on the street was pulled down in 1896, archaeologists found a Scandinavian-type churchyard cross there dating from around AD 920.

SACKVILLE PLACE

44–48 Magdalen Street, was cut through in 1974 and made into offices.

SADD'S YARD

Coslany Street, exact location unknown. *White's Directory* of 1845 lists William Sadd, gentleman, and Mrs Margaret Sadd as residents of Sadd's Yard in Coslany Street. Ineson's rag and bone merchants were there in 1856; there was a bad fire on 31 May 1856, where Ineson's was destroyed along with Fisher's building workshop and Turner's paint shop – and that was also the end of the yard.

SADDLER'S or SADLER'S YARD

115–119 Oak Street. *Robson's Commercial Directory* of 1839 lists James Sadler as the landlord of the Old Crown in Oak Street. The yard was lost 1935–41.

SAINTS' COURT

Runs from 43–45 All Saints' Green to 30–40 Surrey Street, and is a modern development which takes its name from the church.

SALTER'S COURT

Former name of Beckham's Yard, 116–118 Magdalen Street. The yard was lost by 1964.

SAMSON AND HERCULES COURT

14 Tombland, exact location unknown. The court takes its name from the figures of Samson and Hercules outside the court, which was open as far back as 1783; the court itself has since been closed in.

SANDLING'S FERRY

Former name for Pull's Ferry, the Close.

SARDINIAN COURT

Former name of Loyalty Court, St Stephen's Street.

SAW MILL YARD

On the south side of Fishergate, may have taken its name from the Saw Mills pub, which is recorded at Fishergate in 1856. The 1905 Ordnance Survey map also shows Porter's saw mill nearby; the mill burned down in 1904 and the yard was lost. Sexton's boot factory was built on the site.

SAW MILL YARD

13–15 Oak Street (Coslany Street before 1890). The yard was lost 1941–47.

SAY'S YARD

42 Barrack Street. The yard was lost 1935–41.

SCHOLAR'S COURT

14 Oak Street, is built on the site of Eight Ringers' Yard and Sun Yard.

SCHOOL LANE

Used to run from St Andrew's Street to Pottergate, but now runs from Bedford Square to Parsonage Square/Lower Exchange Street. It was originally called Cockey Lane in the 13th century, after the watercourse that ran there; then Crouch Lane in the 16th century from St Crouch's Church; then Hole-in-the-Wall Lane in 1830 after the pub. By 1890 it had become School Lane. There was an infant school in Hole-in-the-Wall Lane from 1836; *White's Directory* of 1845 said that 100 children attended it.

Events on School Lane

On 14 August 1886, George Harmer visited the home of Henry Last, an elderly carpenter, in School Lane. Harmer bludgeoned Last to death, stole his money and left his body covered under a pile of sacks. Harmer was arrested in London four days later, tried in Norwich in November, and was hanged on 13 December 1886; he was the last man hanged at Norwich Castle.

SCHOOL YARD

North side of Barrack Street, exact location unknown. *White's Directory* of 1845 lists St James' Infant School, established in 1837–38, in Barrack Street; it was known as the National School by 1890 and the yard was lost 1890–96.

SCHOOL YARD

11 Calvert Street, took its name from the Presbyterian Board School (later the Council School). The yard was lost 1935–41.

SCHOOLROOM YARD

Crookes Place, exact location unknown.

SCHUMACH COURT

Former name of Chestnut Court, St Giles' Street.

SCOLES GREEN

Scoles Green (formerly Scholes Green) ran from the corner of Globe Lane and Rising Sun Lane. According to historian Mark Knights, Scoles Green was named after a school established by the Carmelites.

Streets off Scoles Green

Wilde's Yard (also known as Blazeby's Buildings) (1–2)*
Prospect Road and Prospect Place (3)
Market Lane (6–8)*
Stepping Lane (8–13)
Bedford Yard (14–15)*
Globe Yard (after 15)
Ivory Square (exact location unknown)

People linked with Scoles Green

Robert Ladbrooke, artist, lived at Scoles Green and died there at the age of 73 in 1842. Ladbrooke was one of the founder members of the Norwich School of Artists, and was a close friend of John Crome – though they did fall out about whether money should be spent on dinners or artists' models. (Crome voted for dinner – and won!)

SCOTT'S COURT/YARD

45 Timberhill. *White's Directory* of 1883 lists William J. Scott, furniture broker, at Timberhill.

SCOTT'S YARD

119–121 Ber Street. *Robson's Commercial Directory* of 1839 lists F. G. Scott, coachmaker and wheelwright, at Ber Street.

SEELEY'S COURT

116–120 Pottergate. *White's Directory* of 1845 lists William Seeley, pork butcher, at Pottergate.

SELF'S YARD

33–35 St Benedict's Street, is now Maude Gray Court.

SEVEN STARS YARD

141–143 Barrack Street, was named after the Seven Stars pub, which is recorded at 143 Barrack Street from 1760. The pub closed in 1908 and the yard was lost 1935–41.

SEVERN'S COURT OR YARD

16–18 Cowgate. *Harrod & Co's Directory* of 1877 lists the landlord of St Paul's Tavern at 20 Cowgate Street as Samuel Severn. The yard was lost 1935–41.

SEXTON'S YARD OR COURT

28–38 Calvert Street. *Peck's Directory* of 1802 lists Jos Sexton, Shawl Manufacturer, at 46 Snailgate Street (the name for Calvert Street at that time). The yard was lost 1883–90.

SHALDER'S COURT

Bank Street. *Pigot's Directory* of 1830 lists William Shalders, currier – and tantalisingly mentions that he was the 'patentee of the expressing fountain'. The yard was lost by 1839.

SHAVE'S YARD OR COURT

16 Colegate. *White's Directory* of 1883 lists William Shave, brushmaker, at Colegate. It was known as Shaw's Yard in 1830 when Benjamin Crotch, camlet manufacturer, had a factory there.

SHAW'S YARD

16 Colegate – see Shave's Yard.

SHERBORNE PLACE

Runs from the north side of Mariner's Lane; it originally ran to 182 King Street but now runs only to Rouen Road.

SHIBLEY'S COURT

1–3 Fisher's Lane, is referenced in *White's Directory* of 1890 but was lost by 1941.

SHIP YARD

108 Cowgate, was named after the Ship inn, which is recorded at 106 Cowgate from 1830. The pub was apparently there from the 15th century and was reputed to be Sir John Falstolfe's house (better known as Falstaff in Shakespeare's *Henry V*.) The yard was lost 1935–41.

SHIP YARD

168 King Street, was named after the Ship inn, which is recorded at 168 King Street from 1760. There was a lintel above the main door of the Ship with the carving 'Princes In' (sic), which may have belonged to the Prince's inn in Tombland. The pub closed in 1969; in 1970 it was converted into two houses. This may run to the Old Ship Yard at 32 Thorn Lane.

SHIP YARD

32 Thorn Lane, may run to Ship Yard at 168 King Street.

SHORTEN'S YARD

17 Rising Sun Lane. *Harrod & Co's Directory* of 1877 lists Robert Shorten, baker, at Rising Sun Lane. The yard was lost by 1941.

SHOULDER OF MUTTON YARD

54–56 St Stephen's Street, was named after the Shoulder of Mutton pub, which is recorded at 54 St Stephen's Street from 1760. The pub closed in 1892 and the yard was lost by 1925.

SHRIMPLING YARD

Former name of Beckham's Yard, 116–118 Magdalen Street. *Pigot's Directory* of 1830 lists Daniel Shrimplin (no g), silk and yarn throwsterer, at Magdalen Street. The yard was lost by 1964.

SHUTTLE YARD

Pitt Street, exact location unknown.

SILVER ROAD

66–68 Barrack Street. It was renumbered 128–130 in 1964.

SINGER COURT

Calvert Street, is a new development near St Crispin's Road.

SKEYGATE

Former name for Horn's Lane.

SMITH'S YARD

121 Oak Street. *Harrod & Co's Directory* of 1877 lists Samuel Smith, Whitesmith, at Oak Street. The yard was lost 1935–41.

SNOWDON'S YARD

21 St George's Street. *White's Directory* of 1883 lists Henry Snowdon, draper. On 12 October 1887 the drapery buildings were destroyed by fire, with damage estimated at £12–15,000 (around a million pounds of today's money).

SOMAN'S YARD

16–20 Fishergate. *White's Directory* of 1883 lists Soman, Son & Co, Boot Manufacturers. The yard was lost by 1964.

SOUP OFFICE YARD

4–6 Fishergate. *White's Directories* of 1845 and 1883 lists the Norwich Soup Society at Fishergate. *White's Directory* of 1845 says that the charity was established in 1840 to give the poor nutritious soup at a low price in winter. The yard was lost by 1925.

SOUTH YARD

Lower Westwick Street, exact location unknown.

SOUTHERN COURT

East side of Lady's Lane; this may also have been known as Sotheron's Buildings in the 19th century. *White's Directory* of 1845 lists Mrs Margeret Sothern (sic) as a resident of Lady's Lane. The court was lost when the new library was built in the 1960s.

SOUTHGATE LANE

King Street, is a footpath which runs from the west side of King Street to Bracondale, past the remains of St Peter Southgate Church.

SOUTHGATE STREET

Former name of St Mary's Plain.

SOVEREIGN WAY

A footpath at 58 Magdalen Street, which runs to Anglia Square, was built in the late 1960s.

SPENCER'S YARD

Horn's Lane. *Robson's Commercial Directory* of 1839 lists Mr Spencer, surgeon, nearby at King Street. The yard was lost 1890–96.

SPORTSMAN'S YARD

141–143 Barrack Street, was named after the Sportsman pub, which was originally recorded at 139 Barrack Street by 1830 and was rebuilt at 108 Barrack Street. It was known as the Jolly Sportsman from 1922–39 and closed in 1992, though the yard seems to have been lost somewhere between 1935–41.

SPRINGALL'S COURT

42–44 Bethel Street, is listed in *White's Directory* of 1883 as Sizeland's Yard. *Robson's Commercial Directory* of 1839 lists Adam Sizeland, dancing master, at Bethel Street. Mrs Matilda Springall, resident at 42–44 Bethel Street, is listed in a later directory. The yard was lost by 1912.

SPRINGFIELD'S YARD OR COURT

34 St Martin's Lane. *Robson's Commercial Directory* of 1839 lists Springfield & Filking, silk merchants, at St Martin's Lane. The name had changed to Springfield & Co by 1883 and *White's Directory* of 1883 and *Kelly's Directory* of 1890 also locate the city laundry in the yard. The court appears to have been lost by 1941, although the laundry is still listed there in 1947.

STAFF OF LIFE YARD

51–53 Fishergate, was named after the Staff of Life pub, which is recorded at 51 Fishergate from 1830. The pub closed in 1891 and the yard was lost by 1941.

STAMP OFFICE YARD or COURT

See Old Stamp Office Yard.

STANNARD PLACE

West side of Calvert Street (near St Crispin's Road).

STAR & CROWN YARD

20 Timberhill, was named after the Star & Crown pub, which is recorded at 20 Timberhill (formerly Orford Hill) from 1806; it may have been known as the Rose & Crown pub in 1760. It became known as the Crown & Star and the license was transferred in 1933. The building was severely damaged during an air raid in April 1942 and the site is now part of the Castle Mall development.

STAR YARD

8–9 Haymarket, was named after the Star inn, which is recorded at 10 Haymarket from 1760. The pub closed in 1894 and the yard appears to be lost by 1925.

STARLING PLACE

24 Coburg Street. *White's Directory* of 1854 lists Lt. Col. Parlett Starling nearby at 4 the Crescent.

STARLING ROAD

9–35 Magpie Road.

STATION ROAD

Runs from just before 83 Oak Street to the south side of Westwick Street; it took its name from the City Station. The road was lost by 1975.

STEAM PACKET YARD

Stepping Lane, was named after the Steam Packet pub, which is recorded at 92 King Street (on the corner of Stepping Lane) from 1824. The pub closed in 1931 and became a butcher's shop.

STEPPING LANE

Originally ran from 8–13 Scoles Green to 90–92 King Street; nowadays it runs from Norman's Buildings off Rouen Road to King Street. It was known as Tofts Lane in the early 14th century after Adam de Toftes, a bailiff in the late 13th century, then as Cockerell Lane (which Sandred and Lingström say is probably from Peter Cockerel, a French merchant who was probably a poultry dealer). It became known as Stepping Lane from the 18th century, which Sandred and Lingström suggest may be from a personal name, possibly Philip Stebbing. Steam Packet Yard ran off Stepping Lane. The area is being redeveloped at the time of writing, including a development of flats called Morgan House (named after the brewery sited between there and King Street) and another development known as Stepping Lane Court.

STEPPING LANE COURT

See Stepping Lane.

STEWARD'S COURT AND YARD

130–132 St George's Street. *Harrod & Co's Directory* of 1877 lists G.F. Steward, boot and shoe manufacturer, at Middle Street (aka St George's Street). The yard was lost 1935–41.

STEWARD'S YARD

South side of Bull Close. *Harrod & Co's Directory* of 1877 lists George Steward, baker, at Bull Close. The yard was lost 1883–90.

STEWARDSON'S YARD

42 Barrack Street. The yard was known as Crotch's Yard before 1900 and was lost 1935–41.

STEWARDSON'S YARD

North side of Bull Close Road. *Pigot's Directory* of 1830 lists George Stewardson, printer, just round the corner in Magdalen Street; his yard could have backed on to Bull Close Road. The yard was lost 1890–96.

STRANGERS' COURT

Formerly Emms Yard, is a modern housing development at 17–21 Pottergate.

STOCKINGS' COURT

24–26 St Stephen's Street. *White's Directory* of 1883 lists Matthew Bane Stockings & Son, grocer's, at 22 St Stephen's Street and Stockings & Saunders, butchers, at number 26. The yard was lost by 1960.

STONE MASON'S YARD

39 St Augustine's Street. *White's Directory* of 1883 lists Henry Hammond, stone mason, at St Augustine's Street; A.J. Woods, stone masons, are also listed there in 1941 and 1960. The yard may have been known as Prince of Wales Yard at one point.

STONEMASON'S YARD OR SQUARE

120–122 St George's Street. *White's Directory* of 1883 lists John Miller, joiner and builder, at St George's Street. The yard was lost 1935–41.

STOREY'S YARD

St Benedict's Street, exact location unknown. *Pigot's Directory* of 1830 lists Robert Osborne, coal dealer, at the yard.

STRIKE'S YARD

102–108 King Street, was lost by 1896 and became part of the site of Morgan's Brewery.

STUART ROAD

236–238 King Street, takes its name from James Stuart (see James Stuart Gardens). It was built 1925–35.

STUART'S COURT

West side of Recorder Road.

STUMP'S CROSS

60–62 Magdalen Street.

SUFFOLK ARMS YARD

119 Oak Street, was named after the Suffolk Arms pub, which is recorded at 119 Oak Street from 1842. The landlord, Fredrick Scotter, died in 1881 after falling accidentally from a cart. The pub closed in 1907 and the yard was lost.

SULTZER'S OR SUTZER'S COURT

61–63 Botolph Street. John Sultzer, a magistrate in the 1860s, had a manufacturing business on St Augustine's Street. The yard was lost in the mid to late 1960s for the Anglia Square development.

SUN YARD

14–26 Oak Street (formerly Coslany Street) sounds as if it should take its name from a pub, although no pub called the Sun was recorded in the area. The yard was lost in slum clearances in the 1930s and Scholar's Court is now on the site.

SURREY GROVE

46–48 Surrey Street, was lost by 1964.

SURREY MEWS

Off Rodney Street (aka Upper Surrey Street, later All Saints' Green). *Pigot's Directory* of 1830 lists livery stables there. The yard was lost by 1883.

SURREY STREET

Surrey Street (Surry Street in 1783) runs from 7–9 St Stephen's Street to the junction of Queen's Road and Finkelgate. In the 13th century, the part of the road between St Stephen's Street and All Saints' Green was originally called Great Newgate, and the section between All Saints' Green to St Catherine's Plain was known as Little Newgate. Sandred and Lingström suggest that the name came about because it was 'new' in comparison with other streets (as with New Mills Yard). The name changed to Surrey Street in Tudor times, when the Earl of Surrey lived there. The part of the road between All Saints Green and Queen's Road has been known as Upper Newgate, St Winwaloes Street, St Catherine's Lane, St Catherine's Street and Surrey Road. Upper Surrey Street was also known at one point as Rodney Street.

Streets off Surrey Street

On the west side, the street has included:
Bignold's Court or Yard (13–15)*
St Catherine's Close
All Saints' Green (35–37)
Carlton Terrace and Gardens

On the east side, the street has included:
Boar's Head Yard (2)*
Anchor Yard (18)*
Quantrill's Court (also known as Miller's Court) (22–24)*
All Saints' Green (36–38)
Saints' Court (30–40 – runs to 43–45 All Saints' Green)
Surrey Grove (46–48)*
Chapel Loke (56–58)
Butcher's Alley (58)

Other streets whose exact locations could not be placed include:
Taylor's Court

Buildings on Surrey Street

Bignold's Court was originally on the site of the old bus station. The house was famous for its glass-houses, grape vines, fig trees and magnolias.

The Norwich Union Building was built by George Skipper in 1903–04. There are two statues on the outside: Bishop Talbot of Oxford, who established the Amicable Life Insurance Office, and Sir Samuel Bignold.

Surrey Court was the home of Henry Howard, the Earl of Surrey. He'd just finished building it in 1547 when Henry VIII executed him for treason – though the charge was false. The building was sold to the Wodehouse family. It became a school in the 1870s (attended by Ralph Mottram – see Bank Plain), then Norwich Union bought it, and George Skipper built the Norwich Union building on the site.

Surrey House was built in 1800; George Skipper adapted it in 1907. The marble inside it was originally meant for Westminster Cathedral but was delivered too late, so Skipper persuaded Norwich Union to buy it.

People linked with Surrey Street

Lt Col Charles Edward Bignold, who was mayor in 1894, was born in Surrey Street. He was the secretary of the Norwich Union Fire Office, and died in May 1895 of a sudden haemorrhage.

Samuel Bignold, the son of the founder of Norwich Union, was mayor in 1833, 1848–49 and 1853; he was the first mayor since 1616 to hold office three times and lived in Surrey Street. As well as being the secretary of the Norwich Union Life Office and Fire Office, he set up a bank in 1827; although the Norfolk and Norwich Joint Stock Banking Co failed nine years later, there was no loss to clients. He also formed the Norwich Yarn Co in 1836 to help unemployment among the poor; the building became part of Jarrolds printing works. He laid the foundation stone of Norwich Free Library. He was knighted in May 1854 when he presented Queen Victoria with an address giving the Corporation's support during the Crimean War.

Thomas Brightwell was a solicitor but also interested in science; he wrote a treatise on infusoria (single-celled animals or protozoa which live in water). In 1821 he became a Fellow of the Linnaean Society; he also gave a collection of insects to the Norfolk and Norwich Museum.

John Daniel was mayor in 1407 and 1417. Together with his brother William, he built almshouses for the poor of St Stephen's parish on the site of 12, 23, 25, and 27 Surrey Street.

Henry Francis was an attorney and proctor who lived at 4 Surrey Street. He was mayor in 1824; at his dinner as sheriff in September 1820, 130 guests ate a 130lb turtle at the Assembly Rooms.

Henry Howard, Earl of Surrey, was a soldier, courtier and poet. He translated Virgil's *Aeneid* into blank verse.

Dr Sydney Long, founder of the Norfolk Naturalists Trust, lived at 31 Surrey Street. He was born at Wells, Norfolk, but after taking his degree at Caius College, Cambridge and studying at University College Hospital, he moved back to Norwich. He was a physician in the Norfolk and Norwich Hospital and the Jenny Lind Hospital for 40 years.

John Manning, who was the physician of the Norfolk and Norwich Hospital for more than 30 years, died at his house in Surrey Street in March 1806.

John Morse, mayor in 1781 and 1803, was a brewer of porter – a dark beer brewed from charred malt. He lived in a house on St Catherine's Close. *White's Directory* of 1890 refers to a strawberry tree that was 20ft high in the garden of his old house.

William Peter Nichols was the surgeon of the Norfolk and Norwich Hospital for 22 years. Edward Copeman said that Nichols had the best average of successful cases in 'lithotomy'.

John Patteson, a wool stapler (from the firm Patteson & Iselin), was mayor in 1766. On 28 September 1766 there was a riot and he had to read the Riot Act; he left his chain of office with his sister-in-law, his mayoress, telling her to take care of it as he wasn't sure if he'd come back alive. The eight ringleaders of the riot were sentenced to death. He built a house in Surrey Street in 1765, and it cost so much that it's said he burned the bills so nobody would know just how extravagant he was!

John Patteson, nephew of John Patteson above, came to live with his uncle at the age of nine following his father's death. He was mayor in 1788 but his bank failed in 1819 and his wool business was also a failure. This, coupled with his love of lavish hospitality (he was the first person in the city to drive a private chariot), meant he had to sell some of his possessions to cover his debts; he sold 208 paintings at Christie's and received £2,349, and sold the house on Surrey Street to Samuel Bignold. He ended up moving to a house near St Helen's vicarage on Bishopgate.

Richard Peete, a master carpenter and cabinet maker, was mayor in 1775. He lived at 33 Surrey Street then moved to Cutler's Row (35 London Street).

Sir James Edward Smith was the son of a merchant who became a botanist; he was born in a house in the Market Place (now the Sir Garnet Wolseley pub) and lived at 29 Surrey Street, where he charged people 2 guineas to attend his lectures on botany and zoology. He could only study botany as part of a medical degree, so he studied first at Edinburgh and then at Leyden in Holland. He became friendly with Sir Joseph Banks, Captain Cook's botanist. In 1792 Smith instructed the Queen and Royal Princesses in botany at Windsor; he was knighted in 1810. He borrowed £1,000 from his father to buy Carl Linnaeus's botanical collection from his widow and founded the Linnean Society. His contemporary Harriet Martineau (see Gurney Court) called him 'not pedantic and vulgar like the rest, but weak and irritable'.

John Venning had worked in Russia as a merchant's rep; he founded a school for poor Russian children and became very friendly with the Russian Imperial Family.

Events at Surrey Street

In August 1843 there was a major thunderstorm and hail. The first floors and cellars of houses in Surrey Street, St Stephen's Street, Rampant Horse Street, the Market Place and London Street were flooded, and ice lay 4–5ins deep. The audience in the theatre couldn't get out because of the water, and the river at Bishop's Bridge rose a foot in five minutes. There was another bad storm the following day and again five days later; in September the newspapers reported that total losses from the storm came to £30,770, 2s 3d (nearly £2 million in today's money).

There was a tragic incident at 12 Surrey Street in March 1922 when fire broke out at Frederick George's greengrocery shop. Frederick escaped by climbing through his son's window and was rescued from the roof; sadly his wife Emily, his 21-year-old daughter Winifrid and his 16-year-old son Sidney died from smoke inhalation.

SUSSEX STREET

Sussex Street runs from 154–156 Oak Street to 36–42 St Augustine's Street. It was laid out in 1821–24 over part of the Gildencroft.

<<insert picture: filename sussex street>>

<<caption>>
Sussex Street. (Photograph by author)

Streets off Sussex Street
North:
Howard Terrace (27)
Eagle Opening (31–35)
Ebenezer Place (formerly Ebenezer Terrace) (43–45)

South:
Cross Lane or Street (40–42)
Chatham Street (62–64 – runs to Gildencroft)

SUTTON'S YARD

77–79 Magdalen Street, was also known as Woolcombers' Arms Yard by 1900. *Harrod & Co's Directory* of 1877 lists Henry Sutton, draper, Robert Sutton, furniture broker, and Robert Sutton senior, picture frame maker, at Magdalen Street. The yard was lost by 1964.

SWAN LANE

Runs from 14–16 Bedford Street to 27–29 London Street. It was called Rackey Lane in the 14th century (which Sandred

The sign of the swan at Swan Lane. (Photograph by author)

and Lingström say is from Robert de Rackheythe, who had a house there) but became known as Swan Lane in the 19th century, after the White Swan inn, which is recorded at 8 Swan Lane from 1760 and closed in 1859. Its last licensee was Jem Mace, a champion bare-knuckle fighter. Mace, a Whig, was beaten at the age of 19 by John 'Licker' Pratt who kept the Hampshire Hog (see Hampshire Hog Lane). Mace won the British Championship in 1862, fighting against King, after a 43-round fight. He lost the title in a return match, but he claimed it again and kept it for seven years. He was buried in Anfield Cemetery, Liverpool.

SWAN YARD

68–70 King Street, was named after the Swan pub, which is recorded at 70 King Street in 1830. The yard was lost for the City Hall development in the early 1930s.

SWAN YARD

178–180 Oak Street, was named after the Swan with Two Necks pub, which is recorded at 180 Oak Street from 1806. The pub closed in 1865 and the building was sold to the Norwich Co-op Industrial Society. The yard was lost by 1964.

SWAN YARD

64 St Stephen's Street, was named after the Swan with Two Necks pub, which was illustrated by Ninham in 1791 between the George and Lock's Court. The pub is listed there from 1830; it closed in 1869 and became a pawnbroker's shop. The yard was lost by 1883.

SWAN YARD

27 St Peter's Street, was named after the White Swan, which is recorded at 31 St Peter's Street from the 15th century. The pub was a theatre before Thomas Ivory built New Theatre in 1757 and was the headquarters for the Norwich Company of Comedians from 1730. According to *Chase's Directory* of 1783. the freemasons lodge met there on the first Wednesday in the month from May 1774. It was demolished in the 1960s so the car park could be built in front of the library.

SWEEP'S YARD

Magdalen Street, exact location unknown.

SYMOND'S YARD

30–32 St George's Street, was formerly known as St Simon's Yard. The yard was lost 1912–25.

SYNAGOGUE STREET

Ran between 37–39 Mountergate and St Ann's Staithe Lane. It took its name from the synagogue that was built there in

1848. The whole area was badly bombed in World War Two – the synagogue was flattened – and the street no longer exists.

TABERNACLE STREET
Former name for Bishopgate.

TALBOT SQUARE
Is a block of flats formerly on 90–96 Oak Street but now off St Crispin's Road.

TALBOT YARD
108–10 Oak Street. *Pigot's Directory* of 1830 lists Ann and Jane Talbot, dressmaker & milliners, at Oak Street.

TAWLER'S COURT
Magdalen Street, exact location unknown.

TAYLOR'S COURT
Surrey Street, exact location unknown. *White's Directory* of 1845 lists the private house of Adam Taylor, solicitor, at Surrey Street.

TEN BELL COURT
Runs from St Benedict's Street to 83–87 Pottergate/north side of Ten Bell Lane, and is a development of flats built around the remains of St Benedict's Church by Edward Skipper in 1971–76. The area was previously St Benedict's Church Lane and leads off Ten Bell Lane.

TEN BELL LANE
Tell Bell Lane runs from 95–97 Pottergate to 78–80 St Benedict's Street. The street was originally called Hollegate in the 13th century (which Sandred and Lingström says is because the street was probably hollowed out by rain) then St Swithin's Lane in the 18th century. It took its present name in the 19th century from the Ten Bells pub, which is recorded at 96 St Benedict's Street from 1760 (later 78 St Benedict's Street).

Streets off Ten Bell Lane
South:
Ten Bell Court (runs to Wellington Green)

North:
Willett's Court (6)
Ford's Yard*
Trowse Yard (14–16)*
Plough Yard (14)*
Browne's Yard or Court (16–18)*
Ten Bell Yard*

Exact location unknown:
Atkins's Yard

TEN BELL YARD
North side of Ten Bell Lane after number 18. The yard was lost by 1890.

THATCHED HOUSE YARD
Rampant Horse Street, exact location unknown. The yard took its name from the Thatched House pub, which is recorded at Rampant Horse Street from 1811 and closed after 1851; the yard was lost with it.

THEATRE SQUARE
10 Theatre Street.

THEATRE STREET
Theatre Street runs from the end of Rampant Horse Street to the junction of Chapel Field East and Chapel Field North. The street used to be known as Chapel Field Lane in the 16th century but was renamed after the theatre by 1800.

Streets off Theatre Street
On the north side, the street has included:
Church Street (former name for William Booth Street) (1)
Butcher's Court or Yard (9)*
Fromanteel's Court (13)*
Lady's Lane (17–19)*

On the south side, the street has included:
The Chantry, Chantry Court, Theatre Square (after 10)
Assembly House Yard (near the Assembly House)*

Buildings on Theatre Street
The Assembly House is built on the site of St Mary Chapel of the Fields and still contains a brick vaulted cellar, which may have been part of the original building. The College of St Mary was dissolved in 1544 and the buildings were granted to Miles Spencer, the last dean of the college. The buildings were then known as Chaply-field House. Sir Henry Hobart bought the house in 1609; it was enlarged by Sir Thomas Ivory in 1754–55, and the Hobarts leased it to the city as an Assembly House in 1753. It remained an assembly house until 1856, when dancing master Frank Noverre had a ballroom built there. The ballroom was converted to the Noverre cinema in 1950 by Rowland Pierce (who also designed the City Hall); the cinema was opened in 1950 and closed in 1922. Shoe manufacturer Henry Sexton bought Chapelfield House and restored it at a cost of £70,000 in 1950 then presented it to the city.

St Mary Chapel of the Fields was founded as a hospice by John le Brun in 1248. It became a college in 1278, and its

Assembly House, Theatre Street. (Photograph by author)

chapel was supposedly even bigger than the Church of St Peter Mancroft. The chapel was closed at the Dissolution in 1544 and became the site of the Assembly House.

Theatre Royal – also known as the 'New Theatre' – was built by Thomas Ivory in 1757 and opened the following year. It was pulled down and a new one was built in 1826. It was destroyed by a massive fire in June 1934, but a new theatre was built and opened in 1935. The theatre was refurbished in 1991.

Events at Theatre Street

The Assembly Rooms and the theatre were two of the most popular showplaces for exhibitions and events during the 19th century. At the Assembly Rooms, exhibitors included: Signor Antonio (known as 'Il Diavolo Antonio') with an exhibition of gym exercises, feats of strength, juggling and fantoccini (marionettes); Madame Tussaud in 1825; Madame Persiani, Signor Negri, Signor Rubini and Signor Puzzi in September 1840 – who, together with Lizst, who played at the Assembly Rooms on the preceding day, were reviewed as some of the 'greatest performers of the present day'. On 16 March 1863 Professor John Henry Pepper

lectured at Noverre's Rooms on Optical Illusions' it was the first time the city had seen 'Pepper's Ghost'. This particular illusion is still used in the theatre today; glass or a mirror is set into a box and turned at a 45-degree angle to the viewer; by clever lighting, an image of an actor off-stage will appear as a ghostly image on the mirror. When the lights are dimmed again, the actor disappears. In January 1876 the first 'Spelling Bee' was given at Noverre's Rooms, presided over by mayor J. H. Tillett; according to Mackie, this was a very popular entertainment for a few months but was short-lived.

At the theatre, in May 1804, the tightrope performer Richer appeared to 'the theme of general admiration'; rather less well received in April 1828 was the performance of Ching Lau Lauro, 'the celebrated posture master and buffo from Drury Lane'. According to the *Norfolk Chronicle*, 'no viler tissue of nonsensical stuff could be foisted on the patience of an insulted audience', who hissed all the way through – even though he allegedly swallowed his own head! Tom Thumb (Charles Stratton), introduced by Mr Barnum, had a much better reception in July 1844. Famous actors who appeared at the theatre in the 19th century include Charles Kemble, Fanny Kemble, Edmund Kean and Eliza O'Neill. Fred Phillips, while playing Rob Roy in April 1851, fell from a 'fictitious precipice' and broke his leg and ankle so badly that surgeons had to amputate under the knee. The operation 'was borne with heroic fortitude', and in July 1853 he became landlord of the Boar's Head in Surrey Street.

Theatre Street has also been the victim of fires. On 22 June 1934 there was a massive fire at the Theatre Royal, described as 'one of the fiercest fires ever seen in the city' – the theatre acted as a kind of wind tunnel and the building was gutted within a couple of hours. In September 1940 a 1,000lb delayed bomb fell on the street opposite number 4 – but it didn't explode and was defused and dug out. Some of the houses were cleared away in the 1950s and 1960s, and the street was widened in 1964. There was another fire on 12 April 1995, this time at the Assembly House; more than 100 firemen fought the flames, and the roof was rebuilt. The Assembly House was reopened on 14 February 1997.

THOMPSON'S FERRY

157–175 King Street. *Harrod & Co's Directory* of 1877 lists William Thompson as boat builder and licensee of the Steam Packet pub, which is recorded at 191 King Street from 1822; the pub became the Ferry Boat in 1925. Edward's Ferry is listed at the same location in 1890, and it's now ABC Wharf. See also Wright's Ferry.

THOMPSON'S YARD

37–39 Fishergate. *Robson's Commercial Directory* of 1839

lists John Thompson, bricklayer, at Fishgate Street (aka Fishergate).

THOMPSON'S YARD

Rampant Horse Street. *Harrod & Co's Directory* of 1877 lists Thompson & Sons, coppersmiths and braziers, with a factory at Rampant Horse Street.

THORNS' YARD

Was the first yard on the west side of Duke Street. *White's Directory* of 1883 lists Robert Thorns, Ironmonger, at Duke Street. The yard was lost by 1890.

THORN LANE

Thorn Lane originally ran from 28 Ber Street to 100 King Street; now it's truncated by Rouen Road. The street was known as Sandgate in the mid-13th century but took its current name in the late 17th century from the Church of St Michael at Thorn (see Ber Street).

Streets off Thorn Lane

South:
Freeman's Buildings (17)
Bartholomew Street (25–27 – led to Horns Lane)*
Garden Back Lane (27–31)
Garden Street (31–33 – led to Horns Lane)*
Carpenters' Arms Yard (33)*
Wells Court (33–35)
Foundry Yard*
St Julian Street and St Julian's Alley (after 37 – led to Horns Lane)

North:
St Michael's Square (8–10)*
Toper's Square
Paradise Place
Curtis Buildings (18)*
Middle Square (20)*
Lower Square (22)*
Morris's Court or Tooley Yard (24–26)*
Commerce Yard/Court (30)*
Market Lane (26–28)*
(Old) Ship Yard (32)

Exact location unknown:
Matthews Yard*
Mint Yard*

THOROUGHFARE YARD OR ROAD

Runs from 27 Fishergate to 13–15 Magdalen Street. According to local historian George Plunkett, there were major slum clearances here in 1936.

THOROUGHFARE YARD

Runs from Bedding Lane to Quayside.

THREE KING LANE

Runs from 44–46 St Benedict's Street to 79–81 Pottergate. It was originally called Bachouse in the early 14th century as it was the area where the bakers worked in the city; according to Sandred and Lingström, a bakery was excavated there. It then became St Margaret's Lane in the mid-14th century (as it stands opposite St Margaret's Churchyard), and finally Three King Lane in the 19th century after the Three Kings pub. The Three Kings pub was recorded at 46 St Benedict's Street from 1763; the pub was damaged during an air raid in April 1942 and was closed in 1968. Three Kings Yard was just off the lane, as was Hipper's Yard.

THREE TUNS COURT

Formerly Tuns Yard, 60 King Street, was named after the Three Tuns pub, which is recorded at 60 King Street from 1761. The pub closed in 1969.

THREE TURKS' YARD

St Benedict's Street, was named after the Three Turks pub, which is recorded at 6 Lower Westwick Street (aka St Benedict's Street) from 1760 and closed some time after 1886. The yard was lost then, too.

THROCKMORTON YARD

On the west side of Magdalen Street, next to Bailey's Yard, is a car park built in the mid to late 20th century.

TIGER YARD

43–47 Fishergate, was named after the Tiger pub, which is recorded at 47 Fishergate from 1760. The pub closed in 1936 and was demolished in 1938.

TILL'S COURT

71 Ber Street, former name of Brooke Place.

TILLETT'S YARD

47–49 Botolph Street, was also known as Fountain Yard. *White's Directory* of 1883 lists John Tillett, butcher, at Botolph Street.

TIM'S YARD

9–11 Oak Street (Coslany Street before 1890) – alternate name for Tuns Yard. The yard was lost 1935–41.

TIMBERHILL

Timberhill runs from Orford Hill to the junction of Golden Ball Street, All Saints Street and Ber Street. The street was

Timberhill. (Photograph by author)

originally called Durnedale in the early 14th century, which Sandred and Lingström say is obscure but has been suggested as meaning 'hidden or secret dale', then Old Swine Market Hill at the end of the 13th century because the Swine Market used to be held near there. In the early 16th century it was called Timberhill or Timberhill Street, after the timber market.

Streets off Timberhill

West:
Palmer's Yard (19)
Lion & Castle Yard (23)
Scott's Yard/Court (45)

East:
Osborne Square (or Osborn's Yard) (10–12)*
Mounser's Yard (14–16)*
Star & Crown Yard (20)*
Grout's Thoroughfare (24–26)

Exact location unknown:
Grout's Court*
Horseman Square*
Nelson Tavern Yard*

Buildings on Timberhill

There was a Baptist Chapel on Timberhill, but it was demolished some time after 1960.

People linked with Timberhill

Nicholas Bickerdyke was the mayor in 1696. Dean Prideaux said that Bickerdike 'hath approved himself the wisest man in ye city'. Bickerdyke owned a messuage and little tenement next to the Castle Dyke, which he gave to the Boys' and Girls' Hospitals; the property is now known as the Gardeners' Arms pub.

Catherine Maude Nichols was the president (and founder) of the Woodpecker Sketch Club, held at 6a Timberhill. She was the first woman fellow of the Royal Society of Painter-Etchers in London and wrote novels as well as painting (including *A Novel of Old Norwich* in 1886).

Events at Timberhill

On 10 May 1783 fire broke out at the premises of plate glass grinding and carpenter Mr Godman at 28 Timberhill; the premises were burned down but luckily the fire didn't spread. In June 1895 Frederick Miles was indicted for murdering his wife on Timberhill; he pleaded extreme provocation and was sentenced to 9 months' imprisonment. At the end of the 19th century, the ironmonger's shop next to the Bell Hotel was taken down to give the trams access to Bank Plain. The castle gardens and some of the castle mound were taken away.

Timberhill was also the scene of tragedy. On 9 January 1928 there was a severe fire at Leveridge Bros, sweet manufacturers and warehousemen. Three girls were trapped and overcome by fumes when fire broke out in the matchbox room; one window overlooked Star & Crown Yard, and residents could see one of the terrified girls at the window. Sadly, Mary Ann Elizabeth Trowse, Blanche Emma Jefferies and Violet Maud Granados perished in the fire.

Timberhill suffered heavy damage during air raids in June 1942.

TIMME'S ROWE

Former name for London Street.

TODD'S YARD

14 Whitefriars Street. *Harrod & Co's Directory* of 1877 lists W.H. Todd, wholesale candle manufacturer and soap merchant, at the City candle works on Whitefriars Bridge. The yard was lost by 1896.

TOLL'S COURT

Ran from Little Orford Street (aka Orford Place) to Brigg Street. *Peck's Directory* of 1802 lists George Toll, Glass and China Warehouse, nearby at 12 Haymarket. The court was lost by 1883.

TOMBLAND

Tombland runs from 6 Prince's Street to the junction of Upper King Street and Queen Street. The street name dates from the late 13th century and means 'empty space' – it was the market place of the town before the Conquest.

Streets off Tombland

The street has included:
Prince of Wales Yard
Kerrison's Yard (3–4)
Prince's Street (6)
Tombland Yard (near no 7)
Tombland Alley (formerly St George's Church Alley) (13)
Samson and Hercules Court (14)
Waggon & Horses Lane (17)
Wensum Street (17)
Palace Street (20)
St Faith's Lane (25–6)

Buildings on Tombland

Churches

St George's Tombland was once called St George at the Gates of the Holy Trinity. It was built in the mid-15th century, and there is thought to be a plague burial pit there. The tower was repaired in 1645, and the church was restored from 1879–86. Francis Blomefield, to whom any historian of Norwich owes an enormous debt, was the curate there. (See Willow Lane.)

St George's Church, Tombland. (Photograph by author)

St Michael Tombland was originally sited at 23 Tombland and was the richest church in the city at Domesday. It was founded by the Earls of East Angles along with a royal palace, which was sited to the south end of chapel yard and the south end of Tombland, leading from the monastery gates to the castle ditch. It was destroyed in the 1090s when the Cathedral Close was constructed, and a stone cross with an 'image of St Michael' on the top was placed on the site of the chapel. This was known as 'St Michael's Cross' and marked the boundary between the church and the city. The area became known as Ratton-row in the 13th century – which Sandred and Lingström suggest is from 'rat-infested' – Blomefield says it was divided into four houses. One of these belonged to the Papinjay (sic) family, who later called it the Popinjay (sic) inn. The area was excavated in Victorian times, and the site was partly destroyed when public lavatories were built there in 1871.

Other buildings of note

Augustine Steward's House at 14 Tombland is a Tudor prefab – the oak beams of the house are actually numbered! It was built in 1549 for Augustine Steward (see below), and during Kett's Rebellion (see St Martin's at Palace Plain) it was used as the headquarters for Lord Northampton's army and then for the Earl of Warwick's army. The house was restored around 1900; the roof was rebuilt after a fire in 1944, and it was restored again in 1962 and 1991–94. It has been used as a butcher's, a broker's, a book shop and a coffee house; it was used as the tourist board office in the 1980s and then as an antiques centre. There is apparently an underground passage running between the house and St George's Church.

Augustine Steward's House. (Photograph by author)

The Erpingham Gate to the cathedral was built by St Thomas Erpingham around 1420, after the victory at Agincourt in 1415 (where he led the English archers). Erpingham was instrumental in getting the charter for Norwich.

The Ethelbert Gate was built by parishioners as part of their reparation for the the 1272 riot (see Close); the Black Death intervened so the building wasn't done until around 1316–20. The upper chamber of the gate was used as St Ethelbert's Chapel.

Edith Cavell's monument – Edith Cavell was a nurse from Swardeston who was executed in World War One by the Germans for helping Allied soldiers to escape from Belgium. Her last words were 'I am glad to die for my country,' but she was far from bitter about her fate; she'd told Revd Stirling Gahan, 'Standing as I do in view of God and Eternity, I realise that patriotism is not enough. I must have no hatred and no bitterness towards anyone.' After the war, her body was exhumed and returned to Norwich, and she was buried in Life's Green at the cathedral.

Samson and Hercules House dates from the mid-17th century and is named after the figures in its portico. It was rebuilt by Christopher Jay, and the enamelled figures of Samson and Hercules stood there until 1789, when they were removed to the inner court. In 1889 the antique dealer Charles Cubitt found them and restored them. The building has been the YWCA (opened by the Duchess of York – the Queen Mother – in 1924), a swimming pool, a social centre and a dance hall. There are Norman arches in its basement. It was damaged by fire in 1948 but was restored in 1952–55. According to Blomefield, the house was owned by Sir John Falstolf, then by the Countess of Lincoln, and then during Henry VII's reign it was owned by the Duchess of Suffolk, who used it as city house for herself and her family.

People linked with Tombland

John Anguish, who was mayor in 1635, lived at Tombland.

William Browne, a draper who was mayor in 1630, lived in Samson and Hercules House.

Robert Dixon, artist, studied at the Royal Academy but settled in Norwich in 1800; he died at his home in Tombland in October 1815.

Sir Thomas Erpingham was Henry IV's chamberlain and led the English archers at Agincourt in 1415. He built the Erpingham Gate as thanksgiving. He lived in St Martin at Palace Plain and was buried in the cathedral after his death in 1428.

Jeremiah Ives (jnr), who was mayor in 1786 and 1801, lived at 26 Tombland. In January 1802 he gave a ball in honour of the short-lived peace.

Christopher Jay, a draper who was mayor in 1657, rebuilt Samson and Hercules House. Charles II promised him a knighthood but didn't actually give it to him, and Jay died in poverty in 1677.

Robert Marsh, a worsted weaver who was mayor in 1731, lived at 25 Tombland. He was an alderman of the city for 47

Erpingham Gate, Tombland. (Photograph by author)

Ethelbert Gate, Tombland. (Photograph by author)

years. He also founded Robert Marsh & Co, which ran a stage wagon from Tombland to the Bull inn at Bishopsgate twice a week.

James Nasmith, a linen draper who was mayor in 1743, lived at 24 Tombland, he became a waggoner and owned a coach, which ran between London and Norwich.

Nicholas Norgate was a mercer who was mayor in 1564. He owned the 'Mayden's Hed' (or Maid's Head) and lived there. After his death in Christmas 1568, his will gave land outside Magdalen Gates for the citizens to lay their compost on.

Augustine Steward was a mercer (cloth merchant) who was deputy mayor during Kett's rebellion, when the mayor Thomas Codd was in the hands of the rebels; his house on Tombland was used as the headquarters for the Earl of Northampton. Steward was mayor in 1534, 1546 and 1556 and usually signed his name 'Awsten Styward'. He reconstructed the Guildhall, restored Pettus House in Elm Hill after the 1507 fire and bought St Andrew's Hall for the city. He was known as 'a good and modest man, beloved of rich and poor'.

Samuel Warkhouse, who was mayor in 1698, owned the Maid's Head and various shops in Tombland.

Events at Tombland

In March 1507 a fire started near the Popinjay inn and spread from Tombland all the way through to St Andrew's, completely destroying Rotten Row.

Until 1744, Tombland was the site of the Tombland Horse Fair. According to Blomefield, fairs were held on Tombland on Good Friday, Whitsuntide and Trinity. The Tombland Fair moved to the Castle Meadow in 1818; it moved back again after the alterations to the cattle market in 1860. Attractions included Hugh's theatre, wild Indians and the Hottentot Venus.

There was a serious fire on 11 June 1978 at Ethelbert House (then known as Boswell's); it took nearly 60 firemen to subdue the blaze and the damage ran into tens of thousands of pounds.

TOMBLAND ALLEY

Formerly known as St George's Church Alley, runs from 26 Prince's Street to 13 Tombland. Horatio Nelson, probably the most celebrated admiral in British history, was a pupil of Norwich School in the 1760s and is thought to have lived at Tombland Alley. He destroyed French sea power in victories at the Nile, Copenhagen and Trafalgar. In February 1797 he sent a sword to the Mayor of Norwich, which belonged to a Spanish admiral that Nelson had killed in the battle of St Vincent; five months later, he lost his right arm and had to learn to write again.

Tombland Alley. (Photograph by author)

TOMBLAND YARD

Near 7 Tombland, was named after the Tombland Stores pub, which is recorded at 7 Tombland from 1883 (formerly the Army & Navy Stores). It was renamed the Edith Cavell in 1914 in honour of our famous nurse.

TOOLEY STREET

Pitt Street – former name of Cherry Lane.

TOPER'S SQUARE

On the north side of Thorn Lane (between 10 and 18), was named after the Jolly Topers pub, which is recorded at 2 Thorn Lane from 1806; it was renamed the Topers Tavern in 1822–89, and then the Duke of Fife from 1890. The pub closed in 1914.

TOWLER'S COURT

24–26 Elm Hill. *White's Directory* of 1845 lists shawl manufacturers Towler, Campin, Shickle and Matthews at Elm Hill.

TROWSE YARD

14–16 Ten Bell Lane. *Kelly's Directory* of 1912 lists Christopher Trowse, working tailor, at 10–14 Ten Bell Lane. The yard was lost during slum clearances in 1938.

TRUMPET YARD and TRUMPET LANE

68–72 St Stephen's Street, were named after the Trumpet pub, which is recorded at the corner of St Stephen's Street and Coburg Street from 1760. The pub was damaged during an air raid in April 1942. The building and lane were demolished during the 1960s redevelopment of the area, and the pub was rebuilt in 1964; the yard was lost around the same time. The pub was renamed Swifts in 1983 and closed in 1989.

TUBBY'S YARD

28–34 Muspole Street. *Pigot's Directory* of 1830 lists John

Tubby, baker, nearby at Cross Street. The yard was lost by 1925.

TUCK'S COURT

King Street, exact location unknown. *Chase's Directory* of 1783 lists John Morphew, attorney at law, in the court. The court appears to be lost by 1830.

TUCK'S COURT

Is listed in the street directories at both 24–26 St Giles' Street and 76 St Giles' Street. *Pigot's Directory* of 1830 lists James Tuck, confectioner, however, it is more likely that the name came from a family of solicitors. *White's Directory* of 1883 lists Algernon D. Tuck, solicitor, and Charles E. Tuck, JP, at 76 St Giles' Street.

People linked with Tuck's Court

William Rackham, who was mayor in 1821, was a solicitor at Simpson & Rackham in Tuck's Court, St Giles'. The author George Borrow also served his articles here.

Charles Edward Tuck, who was mayor in 1864–65, was a solicitor in Tuck's Court.

TUNS YARD

9–11 Oak Street (formerly Coslany Street), was named after the Tuns pub, which is recorded in the parish of St Mary from 1806 – the location varies between Coslany Street, Oak Street and Church Street (due to Victorian renaming!). The pub closed some time after 1864 and the yard was lost 1935–41. It was also known briefly as Tim's Yard in 1900.

TURNER'S COURT

28–30 St Benedict's Street (formerly Upper Westwick Street). *Robson's Commercial Directory* of 1839 lists John Turner, hairdresser, at St Benedict's Street.

TURNER'S SQUARE

After 15 Rose Lane. *Pigot's Directory* of 1830 lists Nicholas Turner, baker, at Rose Lane. The square was lost by 1964.

TURRELL'S YARD

149 Ber Street. *White's Directory* of 1845 lists James Turrell, shopkeeper, at Ber Street. The yard was also known as Tyrrell's yard, and was lost 1947–60.

TWIDDY'S COURT

34–36 Ber Street. *Pigot's Directory* of 1830 lists Rosetta Twiddy, shopkeeper, at Ber Street. The yard was lost 1935–41.

TWO BREWERS' YARD

52–54 Calvert Street, was named after the Two Brewers' pub, which is recorded at 54 Calvert Street from 1760; the pub closed some time after 1830 and the yard was lost by 1960.

TWO BREWERS YARD

149–51 Magdalen Street, was named after the Two Brewers pub, which is recorded at 151 Magdalen Street from 1822. It was renamed the Viking Stores in 1957 and closed in 1961.

TWO QUARTS COURT or YARD

70–72 St George's Street, was named after the Two Quarts pub, which is recorded at 70 Bridge Street (aka St George's Street) from 1762; in 1842 the pub was also known as the 'Mermaid and Fountain and Three Quarts'. It closed in 1907.

UNICORN ALLEY or YARD

Runs from 28–30 St Stephen's Street to St Stephen's Back Street. It was named after the Unicorn pub, which is recorded at 28 St Stephen's Street from 1836. The pub was closed in 1940 for the war, but was damaged during an air raid in April 1942. It reopened in 1943 but closed in 1955 and was demolished. The yard appears to be interchangeable with One Post Alley in the directories from 1941.

UNICORN YARD

39 Oak Street (formerly Coslany Street), was named after the Unicorn pub, which is recorded at 39 Oak Street from 1761 and closed in 1968. According to *Chase's Directory* of 1783, the freemasons lodge met at the Unicorn on the second and fourth Monday of the month from 1749.

UNION STREET or PLACE

53 Chapel Field Road.

UNTHANK'S COURT

Near 2 Rampant Horse Street. *Chase's Directory* of 1783 lists William Unthank, corn merchant, salesman and perukemaker, at 2 and 3 Rampant Horse Street, and William Unthank jnr, attorney, at 2 Rampant Horse Street. The court was lost by 1830.

UPPER GOAT LANE

Upper Goat Lane runs from 5–7 St Giles' Street to 20–22 Pottergate. It was originally known as Stonegate (from the 13th century), which Sandred and Lingström interpret as meaning the stony street', as the first known orders to pave Norwich streets weren't until the early 15th century. It became known as Goat Lane by Cleer's map of 1696. The Old Goat pub is listed at Goat Lane from 1802 – the Young Goat pub was also listed there in 1830. The Old Goat closed after 1861.

Roads off Upper Goat Lane
Malthouse Yard (6–10)*
Warner's Yard (10–12)*

Buildings on Upper Goat Lane
The Friends' Meeting House was built in 1825–26 by J.T. Patience on the site of the old meeting house, which was demolished in 1825. The Meeting House was opened for public worship in October 1826, but the building may not have been as thorough as it should have been, because a large part of the premises next door (which had been built on the site of the old almshouses) fell down a week later 'with a tremendous crash'.

People linked with Upper Goat Lane
John Reynolds, Sheriff in 1796, lived in Upper Goat Lane.

UPPER GREEN LANE
Runs from Edward Street to St Crispin's Road. Cherry Lane leads from here to Botolph Street.

UPPER KING STREET
Runs from the end of Tombland to the beginning of Prince of Wales Road.

UPPER YARD
1–5 Coslany Street – see Gent's Yard and Abbs' Court.

VALENTINE SQUARE
Wellington Lane, exact location unknown. *White's Directory* of 1845 lists William Valentine as a resident nearby at Ten Bell Lane. St Giles' Infant School is listed in the area by 1890.

VARNISH YARD
46 Ber Street. *Chase's Directory* of 1783 lists Edward Varnish, butcher, at 46 Ber Street. The yard was lost by 1830.

VAUXHALL STREET
19–21 Chapel Field Road, was named after the Vauxhall Gardens pub (later the Vauxhall Tavern), which is recorded at Union Place (later 47 Vauxhall Street) from 1830. The pub was destroyed during an air raid in 1941 and was rebuilt in 1959; it was renamed the Wrestlers in 1998, then Dixie's, then Slippery's.

VINEGAR LANE
Is the former name for the Tombland end of St Faith's Lane during the 1870s, and the name came from the distillery that was located there from 1762. It was known as Sevecote Rowe from the 13th century (which Kirkpatrick suggests means 'seven-cottage row') and the name gradually changed from Cote to Cole by the mid-18th century then became Vinegar Lane.

WADE'S COURT
8 Bank Street. *Harrod & Co's Directory* of 1877 lists Robert Wade, hairdresser, at Bank Street; *White's Directory* of 1883 lists Francis Joseph Wade, hairdresser, at Bank Street.

WADE'S COURT OR YARD
50–52 St Stephen's Street, ran to St Stephen's Back Street. *White's Directory* of 1883 lists Mrs Hannah Wade of Scott & Wade, drapers, at St Stephen's Street. The court was also known as Bullard's Yard and was lost by 1960.

WAGGON & HORSES LANE
Runs from 19 Elm Hill to 17 Tombland (at the junction with Wensum Street), and was known as Hundegate in the 14th century, Prynce inne (or Prince's inn) Lane in the 15th century, the Lane by the Elm in the 16th century, Elm Hill Lane by the 17th century and Elm Lane by the 18th century. It became Waggon & Horses Lane in the 19th century and takes its name from the Waggon & Horses pub, which is recorded at 17 Tombland from 1771. The pub was renamed the Louis Marchesi in 1976 after the founder of the Round Table movement (see London Street). The pub closed in 2004 and reopened as the Take Five Café and Bar.

WAGGON & HORSES YARD
17–19 Coslany Street, was named after the Waggon & Horses pub, which is recorded at 23 Coslany Street from 1845 (previously known as the Jolly Dyers from 1811). The pub was closed in 1923 and the yard was lost by 1941.

WALES SQUARE
58–60 Prince of Wales Road, runs behind the Belmont Hotel. According to local historian George Nobbs, the Victorian houses there were pulled down in the 1970s.

WALES YARD
Pump Street (off Buffcoat Lane).

WALLER'S YARD
East side of Peacock Street (near 33). *Kelly's Directory* of 1890 lists Matilda Waller, grocer. The yard was lost by 1896.

WALL LANE
64–66 Barrack Street, takes its name from the City Wall. The lane was lost 1935–41.

WALL LANE
152 Magdalen Street, was known as Under the Walls in

1883. It takes its name from the City Walls, and runs approximately along the line of the walls.

WALPOLE GARDENS
Formerly Walpole Street, 45–47 Chapel Field Road.

WARMINGER COURT
28–64 Ber Street, is a new development of retirement flats built in 2005. It takes its name from A.H. Warminger, waste paper merchant, who owned the site.

WARNER'S YARD
10–12 Upper Goat Lane. *Harrod & Co's Directory* of 1877 lists Warner and Co, coppersmiths and brass founders, nearby at 2 St Giles' Street. The yard was lost by 1925.

WATER LANE
36 Colegate, runs down to the River Wensum – hence the name. Little Water Lane runs off it.

WATER LANE
36 Fishergate – former name of Hansard Lane.

WATER LANE
48–52 St George's Street.

WATER LANE
See River Lane, Barrack Street.

WATERMAN YARD
142–144 King Street, was named after the Waterman Tavern, which is recorded at 142 King Street (the corner of King Street and Horns Lane) from 1806. At one point the landlord was a barber, and there was a sign above the pub which said 'Roam not from pole to pole but step in here /Where nought excels the shaving but the beer'. The pub closed by 1961 and the yard was lost 1964–70.

WATERMAN'S YARD
50–52 Westwick Street, was named after the Waterman Tavern, which is recorded at 50 Lower Westwick Street from 1830. The pub had closed by 1897. However, the name lives on in an early 21st-century housing development on the site.

WATLING'S COURT
Formerly Watling's Yard, 12 Cow Hill, was named after carrier Charles Watling. Charles Frederick Watling was born in Norwich; he started his career as a stable boy. By 1890 he was driving a parcel delivery cart, and he took over Globe Parcels Express when it went bankrupt in 1915. He always ran his business with horses rather than cars. He became a magistrate in 1934 and was Lord Mayor from 1937–38.

WATSON'S BUILDINGS
55 Rose Lane.

WATSON'S COURT
64 King Street. *Harrod & Co's Directory* of 1877 lists the house and offices of Frederick Elwin Watson, solicitor, in King Street.

WATSON'S YARD
108–110 King Street and 71–73 King Street. *Pigot's Directory* of 1830 lists Edward Watson, coal merchant, at King Street. *Harrod & Co's Directory* of 1877 lists Gilbert P. Watson, chemist, at King Street. The yard at 71–73 was lost 1890–96 and the yard at 108–110 was lost 1883–90.

WATSON'S YARD
122–24 Ber Street, was also known as Knight's Yard from 1883–1900. *Harrod & Co's Directory* of 1868 lists William Watson, newsagent and shopkeeper, at Ber Street. The yard was lost 1925–35.

WATTS' COURT
Runs from 55 Bethel Street to 10 Chapel Field North. It was named after merchant John Langley Watts, who was mayor in 1774 and lived at 61 Bethel St (near to the court). He was the first mayor of Norwich to have two Christian names.

WEAVER'S LANE
Runs from 32–33 Market Place to the back door of houses in the Haymarket. The churchyard was once on the other side of the lane. The last pub on Weaver's Lane was the Suffolk Hotel, which was demolished in 1905. According to Blomefield, the lane was once called 'Cobler's Rowe' as it was originally the shoemakers' section of the market. Later, Kirkpatrick says the country linen weavers had their stalls here on a Saturday.

WEBB'S YARD
1438–42 Magdalen Street. *Pigot's Directory* of 1830 lists William Webb, rope and twine maker, at Magdalen Street.

WEBSDALE COURT
15-17 Bedford Street.

WEBSDALE YARD
135–139 King Street. *White's Directory* of 1883 lists James Websdale, grocer, at 135 King Street; by 1912 the firm's name had changed to Websdale Bros, Grocers. The yard was lost by 1925.

WEBSTER'S COURT
12 Peacock Street. The yard was lost 1935–41.

WEEDS SQUARE

7 Bishop's Bridge Road. *White's Directory* of 1883 lists shopkeeper Mrs Mary Ann Weeds near there.

WELLINGTON GREEN

Runs between Wellington Lane/Pottergate and 94 St Benedict's Street. It was a new development designed by Edward Skipper after the destruction of St Benedict's Alley in World War Two and takes its name from Wellington Lane. The area was originally Neale's Square.

WELLINGTON LANE

Wellington Lane runs from 97–99 St Giles' Street (or 13 Upper St Giles) to 110–112 St Benedict's Street; the section between St Benedict's Street and Pottergate was known as Duck Lane until after World War Two. The lane was named after the Duke of Wellington pub, which is recorded at 16 Wellington Lane from 1830 (though the building dated from 1647). It was closed in 1930 and the cottages there were flattened during air raids in April 1942.

Streets off Wellington Lane:

Bell's Yard (2)*
Baker's or Bailey's Yard (12)*
Valentine Square*
Wellington Green (runs to St Benedict's Street)
Wellington Square (ran to Pottergate)*

WELLINGTON SQUARE

Ran from Wellington Lane to 108 Pottergate; it took its name from the lane rather than from the pub. It was destroyed during World War Two and has been replaced by Damocles Court and Copeman Street.

WELLINGTON YARD

42 St Stephen's Street, was named after the Duke of Wellington pub (formerly the Marquis of Wellington), which is recorded at 42 St Stephen's Street (on the corner of Pipe Burners' Row) from 1822 and was closed in 1908.

WELLS COURT

33–35 Thorn Lane.

WENSUM STREET

Wensum Street runs from 17 Tombland to the beginning of Fye Bridge Street. It was called Cookerowe (Vicus Cocorum) in the 13th century because it was the area of the city where the cookshops were; then it became known as part of Fye Bridge Street in the early 19th century and finally Wensum Street from 1830, named after the river. There was once a circulating library at number 18, belonging to Martin Crocket.

Streets off Wensum Street

The street has included:
West side:
Mandell's Yard (2)*
De Caux's Court (near 4)*
Elm Hill (10–12)
Roache's Court (formerly Rice's Court) (14)
Ribs of Beef Yard (24)
Barnard's Yard*

East side:
Flower's Court (13)
Quayside (27)

Buildings on Wensum Street

The Maid's Head hotel is thought to have been built on the Norman foundation of the Bishop's palace; according to historian Walter Rye, there is the capital of a Norman pillar in the cellar and also a deep stone well in the courtyard. It used to be called the Molde or Murtel Fish and became known as the Maid's Head in 1472. According to *Chase's Directory* of 1783, the freemasons lodge met at the Maid's Head on the third Tuesday of the month from 1748. The first regular stagecoach to London (known as The Norwich Machine) set out from here in 1762; the trip cost a guinea and took 15 hours. The stagecoach continued until the

Anguish's door at the Maid's Head Hotel, Wensum Street. (Photograph by author)

railways took over in 1856. One of the visitors to the Maid's Head was 'Dr' Graham, who ran the Temple of Health in Pall Mall; his servant girl was dressed rather skimpily, and turned out to be Emma Hart (Lady Hamilton)! It was also a favourite haunt of the painter Alfred Munnings.

Events at Wensum Street

In 1747 mayor Robert Harvey was permitted to set the churchyard wall of St Simon and St Jude's Church back by 3ft, as carriages were getting stuck there.

WESTERN'S COURT

Upper Market (aka St Peter's Street), exact location unknown. *Robson's Directory* of 1839 lists F.C. Taylor, solicitor, there. The yard appears to be lost by 1845.

WESTLEGATE

Westlegate runs from St Stephen's Plain to All Saints Green. It was originally called Needham in the late 13th century (presumably because it was an extension of St Stephen's Street) but became Wastle-gate or Wastelgate in the mid-14th century. It took its name from 'wastel' bread, which was made from fine white flour; according to Blomefield, the 'wastel or wheat-bread market began at Wastle-gate to Hay-market'. It was a very narrow lane until 1925; at one point, according to local historian A. P. Cooper, a cottage on the point of collapse was shored up by a post across the street at second-storey level!

The Barking Dickey, Westlegate. (Photograph by author)

Streets off Westlegate

The street has included:
City of Norwich Yard (5)*
All Saints Alley (runs to Lion and Castle Yard) (20–22)

Buildings on Westlegate

The Barking Dickey (currently Carsaccio's) at 20 Westlegate is one of the five original thatched houses left in the city after the 1507 fires. It took its name from the pub sign when it was called the Light Horseman; the sign was painted so badly that the horse looked like a cross between a dog and a donkey (known as a 'dickey' in local dialect).

The Glass Tower was the first tower block in the city; it was built in 1960–61 by Chaplin & Burgoine.

Events at Westlegate

In July 1838 there was a sensational case of bodysnatching at Westlegate. Mary Maxey claimed that George Perowne – a vet who was her late husband's employer – took her husband's body from the house. She saw it at his surgery, with the heart cut out and the body 'hacked about'. When she took friends with her to remove the body for burial, Perowne drove them out of his yard with a gun, saying that he'd paid for the body 16 years ago. Perowne was too drunk to appear at the court hearing, but later said he bought Mr Maxey's body during the deceased's lifetime and had cut it up in the interests of science; even though he was a vet, he was also a member of St Bartholomew's Hospital, which was why he needed to study human anatomy. He was committed for trial at the assizes, but in the end the case was dropped.

WESTWICK STREET

Westwick Street runs from Charing Cross to the site of the old Westwick Gates at Heigham Street (now Barn Road). It was originally called Nether Westwick Street in the late 13th century, then in the 14th century it became Letestere Rowe (Dyer's Row), because the dyeing industry was centred there, and then Westwick Lane and Lower Westwick Street in the late 18th century. According to Blomefield, the name is derived from the fact that the city stands on the western 'wic' or winding of the river.

Streets off Westwick Street

South:
Bakers' Arms Yard*
St Laurence Steps
St Laurence Little Steps
Helgate Court
St Margaret's Street/Alley (before 57)
Peel Yard (69)*
Pipe Yard (73–75)*

St Swithin's Alley (77–79)
Alefounder's Yard (off Browne's Yard) (83)*
St Swithin's Terrace (95–97)

North:
Robert Gybson Way
Coslany Street (leading to Coslany Square) (26)
Anchor Quay (leads to Coslany Street)
Waterman's Yard (50–52)
Holmes' Yard or Court (58)*
Balloon Yard and Wharf (62)*
Drum Yard (64–66)*
Cowling's Yard (68–70)*
Barker's Yard (74–86)*
Baker's Yard*
Butler's Yard*
St Swithin's Wharf (90–92)*
New Mills Yard (98)
Little Eagle Yard (100–110)*
Eagle yard (110–112)*

Exact location unknown:
Aborne's Yard*
Coleby Place*
English's Yard*
Fair Flora Yard*
Filbey's Yard*
Jermy's Yard*
Mason's Yard*
Nowhere Yard (south)*
Roger's Yard*
Station Road (south, ran to Oak Street)*
South Yard*

Buildings on Westwick Street
City Wall
Heigham Gate (also known as Helgate) was sited at the entrance to Westwick Street. It was too narrow for anything larger than a small cart to pass through the postern, and it was removed before 1792.

Other buildings of note
Gibson's Conduit; this was built by Robert Gibson (see below) in 1576 when he was granted the rights to an old well in the parish of St Lawrence on the condition he 'conveyed the water in a conduit or cock of lead to the public street for the convenience of the common people, and should maintain the same'.

People linked with Westwick Street
John Croshold lived in Robert Gibson's old house next to St Laurence's pump. He was apprenticed as a worsted weaver

Gibson's Conduit, Westwick Street. (Photograph by author)

but traded as a mercer and hosier; he was mayor in 1663. Robert Gibson (or Gybson) was a brewer who was sheriff in 1596.

Carpenter Thomas Rutland lived on Westwick Street; the *Norfolk Chronicle* reported on 17 December 1864 that he had invented 'a very ingenious means of communication between the passengers and guard in a railway train'; apparently it alerted the guard and the driver, and the signal showed which carriage it came from.

Events at Westwick Street
In 1603 Robert Gibson had a huge fight with the mayor. During an outbreak of the plague, the mayor asked everyone to remove their drapes. Gibson didn't. The mayor commanded him to remove them. Gibson retorted 'I would see who dare pull them down'. The mayor's reply was, 'That dare I.' He did so and, following their row, Gibson was no longer allowed to be an alderman or have the freedom of the city.

Westwick Street has been hit by fire several times. On 23 September 1855 there was a fire at F.W. Waters' steam flour mills; the damage was estimated at £4,000 (nearly £500,000 of today's money), including the building, 200 sacks of flour and 'much valuable machinery'. On 13 March 1866, there was a boiler explosion at the brewery of Arnold & Wyatt; tragically, engine driver William Whitworth was killed when his body was 'hurled into the beck containing six quarters of boiling wort'. And on 11 November 1932 Maidment's shoe factory fire (known as the Aethelda factory) went up; the fire started at 9pm on the Friday evening and the *Eastern Daily Press* reported that 'the whole skyline of Norwich was silhouetted against a red glow deeper than a sunset' – it was even visible from Christchurch Road! Firemen were worried that Cushion's timber yards in Barn Road would be involved, but luckily they'd fireproofed their roof.

WHEATSHEAF YARD

51–55 St Stephen's Street, was named after the Wheatsheaf pub, which is recorded at 51 St Stephen's Street from 1822 and closed by 1867. The yard was lost 1947–60.

WHIP & NAG YARD

3 Pitt Street, was named after the Whip & Nag pub, which was recorded as the Whip & Egg pub at 3 Pitt Street from 1760. The pub was damaged during an air raid in April 1942 and was closed in 1960; the yard was lost at the same time.

WHITE BEAR YARD

29–31 St Mary's Plain, was formerly Marine Store Yard; it became known as White Bear Yard by 1925. Presumably it took its name from a pub, but I can find no records of a White Bear.

WHITE ENTRY YARD

15–17 Bull Close. The yard was lost 1935–41.

WHITE HART YARD

6–8 Ber Street, was named after the White Hart pub, which is recorded at 6 Ber Street from 1763. The pub was closed in 1940 for the war, but was damaged during air raids in 1942 and was never reopened. In January 1809 resident Robert Fenn died at the age of 75; his obituary said he 'possessed great skill as a marksman and had the best method of training dogs'.

WHITE HART YARD

39 St Peter's Street, was named after the White Hart pub, which is recorded at 39 St Peter's Street as far back as 1546 but closed by 1915.

WHITE HORSE YARD

145–149 Barrack Street, may have taken its name from a pub, though I can find no record of a White Horse pub in Barrack Street. The yard was lost 1925–35.

WHITE HORSE YARD (and LITTLE WHITE HORSE YARD)

13 Botolph Street, was named after the White Horse pub, which is recorded at 84 Magdalen Street (which backs onto it) from 1760. The yards were lost in the mid to late 1960s for the Anglia Square development.

WHITE HORSE YARD

84–86 Magdalen Street, was named after the White Horse pub, which is recorded at 84 Magdalen Street from 1760. The pub was closed in 1955 and the building was demolished.

WHITE LION LANE

8 St Martin's at Palace Plain, was named after the White Lion pub, which is recorded at 8 Palace Plain from 1760 (though the building dates from the 16th century). The pub was renamed the Wig & Pen in 1985 when the new Magistrates' Court opened. On 18 November 1775 there was a fire in the lane at shoemaker Ezekiel Delight's premises – but the *Norwich Mercury* reported that it was 'put out in time' so there was no major damage.

WHITE LION STREET

White Lion Street runs from 30 Market Place (at the junction of Gentleman's Walk and Haymarket) to Red Lion Street. It was originally called Selaria or Saddlegate in the mid-13th century (after the saddle-makers), then Lorimer's Row in the 14th century (after the the larrimers, who made harness straps), Bridlesmith's Row and Spurrier's Row. It was known as the Lyon Lane in the early 17th century, and White Lion Street in the 19th century after the White Lion pub, which is recorded at 10 White Lion Street from 1760. The pub was renamed the Haymarket Stores in 1914 and closed in 1974. York Alley (or Passage) ran from here to Castle Meadow (originally to Orford Hill before it was cut through for the trams).

WHITE LION YARD

135–137 Magdalen Street, was named after the White Lion pub, which is recorded at 135 Magdalen Street from 1760. The pub closed in 1962 and the yard has become known as Hartley's Yard.

WHITE LION YARD

71–73 Oak Street, was named after the White Lion pub, which is recorded at 73 Oak Street from 1789.

WHITEFRIARS

Runs from 12 St Martin's-at-Palace Plain. It probably took its name from the White Friars, who had a priory there (see Cowgate). The White Friars pub was recorded at 13 Whitefriars from 1822 and was closed in 1902. Whitefriars has two yards: Myhill's Yard (8–10)* and Todd's Yard (14)*.

Remains of Whitefriars priory. (Photograph by author)

WHITING'S COURT

Formerly Clabburn's Yard, 150 Magdalen Street. *Harrod & Co's Directory* of 1877 lists William Whiting, rent collector, at Magdalen Street. The yard was lost by 1964.

WICKHAM'S YARD

193–195 King Street. *Robson's Commercial Directory* of 1839 lists William Wickham, coal dealer, at King Street.

WILD'S COURT

41a St Stephen's Street. *White's Directory* of 1883 lists Frederick Wild, plumber, there. The yard was lost by 1890.

WILDE'S YARD

1–2 Scoles Green, is also listed as Blazeby's Buildings in 1883. *Pigot's Directory* of 1830 lists Robert Wilde, coal dealer and hop dealer, at the corner of Rising Sun Lane and Scoles Green.

WILLETT'S COURT

6 Ten Bell Lane. *Harrod & Co's Directory* of 1877 lists Edward Willett, Nephew & Co, shawl manufacturer, with a factory just round the corner in Pottergate. According to Victorian historian A.D. Bayne, Willets were the first company to manufacture paramattas (a lightweight silk and wool dress fabric) in the city, and were the only company to get an award for their paramattas at the London Exhibition of 1851.

WILLIAM THE FOURTH YARD

166–168 St George's Street, was named after the William IV pub, which is recorded at 108 St George's Street from 1836. The pub closed in 1908. The yard may also have been known as Arnold's Yard and was lost by 1925.

WILLIAM BOOTH STREET

Runs from the junction of Theatre Street and Rampant Horse Street to 18 Haymarket. It was known as Gun Lane until the mid-19th century, and then Church Street. It took its name from William Booth, the founder of the Salvation Army, who first visited the city in September 1882 and told his audience to 'get a drum and rouse Norwich from one end to the other'. Booth was a Methodist minister who believed in preaching but also helping the poor practically, giving them food and shelter. A different William Booth had a circulating library at Brigg Street, according to *Pigot's Directory* of 1830; this library included 'pamphlets' (short books also known as chapbooks) which he lent out at 1d per night.

WILLIAM STREET

27–29 Horns Lane, was a former name of Burleigh Street. See Rouen Road.

WILLIS STREET

Originally ran from 80–96 Cowgate to 75 Peacock Street; now it's a cul-de-sac off Peacock Street. St Paul's Square leads off it.

WILLOW LANE

Willow Lane runs from 53a–55 St Giles' Street to Cow Hill. The name dates from the late 17th century and Kirkpatrick says it comes from the willows that used to grow 'on the S. of it, upon the Wast ground next the Churchyard' – houses were built there by 1720.

Buildings on Willow Lane

The Jesuit Chapel was the first purpose-built Roman Catholic church in Norwich. It was built in 1827–28 to a design by John Patience; in September 1827 the first stone was laid by the Hon and Revd Edward Clifford, and it was opened in September 1829 by Right Revd Dr Weld, bishop of Anycloe. It became a school in 1894–1968 then was converted to offices in the 1990s.

People linked with Willow Lane

Francis Blomefield, who lived at 13 Willow Lane, started writing his history of Norfolk when he was Rector of Fersfield, near Diss. He became the curate of St George's Tombland. As well as writing his five-volume history (to which Norfolk and Norwich local historians owe a huge debt), he discovered the Paston letters at the archive room in Oxnead.

Nathaniel Bolingbroke, a silversmith who had a haberdashery business at 2 Market Place, was mayor in 1819. He lived at 9 Willow Lane. During his mayoralty, he proclaimed the accession of King George IV in Norwich on 21 February 1820.

George Borrow, writer, lived at Borrow House (15 Willow Lane). He originally trained as a solicitor but was fascinated by the life of gypsies and wrote *Romany Rye* and *Lavengro*. He was the one who dubbed Norwich 'a fine old city… view it from what side you will'. He used to carry a tame viper as a pet, so he was known as the 'snake catcher' when he was young; he was also horsewhipped at school for truancy, although he was a keen language scholar and was fluent in 10 different languages before he was 18. He suffered from 'the horrors' and his hair was completely grey before he was 20. From 1826–32 he travelled abroad, possibly to India, and in 1833 he walked to London to get the job with the British and Foreign Bible Society to supervise the printing of the New Testament in Manchu. He then travelled through Spain on a black stallion and was thrown into prison three times and almost shot as a spy. He left the employ of the Bible Society in 1840, married Mary Clarke and went to live at Oulton Broad, where he wrote his novels.

WINDMILL ALLEY
26 Ber Street, was named after the Windmill pub, which is recorded at 24 Ber Street from 1760. The pub was damaged during an air raid in 1942 and was demolished in 1970. The yard was lost by 1960.

WINE COOPERS' ARMS YARD
32–34 St Augustine's Street, was formerly known as Wine Coopers' Square. It was named after the Wine Coopers' Arms pub, which is recorded at 30 St Augustine's Street from 1845. The pub closed in 1936.

WINKLE'S ROW
272–274 King Street.

WINTER'S YARD
82–84 Pitt Street. *White's Directory* of 1883 lists Samuel Winter, baker, at Pitt Street. In *Kelly's Directory* of 1900 the business name had changed to Winter Brothers, bakers, at 86 Pitt Street. The yard was lost by 1970.

WISEMAN'S YARD
Right-hand side of Muspole Street, exact location unknown. *Robson's Commercial Directory* of 1839 lists John Wiseman, engineer, at Muspole Street. The yard was lost 1883–90.

WOODEN ENTRY (or WOOD ENTRY) YARD
34 Pottergate. The yard was lost 1947–60.

WOODHOUSE YARD
5–7 Finkelgate. The yard was lost by 1975.

WOOD'S YARD
7–9 Mariner's Lane. *Hunt's Directory* of 1850 lists Peter Wood, beer retailer, nearby at Ber Street; *White's Directory* of 1854 lists him as the landlord of the Lock and Key, which is recorded at 89 Ber Street from 1806 and closed in 1913. The yard was lost by 1960.

WOOLGATE COURT
57 St Benedict's Street, is a late 20th-century development.

WOOLCOMBERS' ARMS YARD
77–79 Magdalen Street, was formerly known as Suttons Yard in 1883. It was named after the Woolcombers' Arms pub, which is recorded at 79 Magdalen Street from 1867 and closed in 1910. The yard was lost by 1964.

WOOLPACK THOROUGHFARE
Golden Ball Street – see Woolpack Yard, 9 Golden Ball Street.

WOOLPACK YARD
46 Botolph Street, was named after the Woolpackers pub, which is recorded at 46 Botolph Street from 1802. The pub closed in 1907 and the yard was lost with it.

WOOLPACK YARD AND THOROUGHFARE
9 Golden Ball Street, was named after the Woolpack pub, which was listed there from 1760. The building was originally sited on the corner of Timberhill but was rebuilt in 1938 slightly further back from the road and away from Timberhill.

WOOLPACK YARD
Runs from 2 Muspole Street to 51 Colegate. It was named after the Woolpack pub, which is recorded at 2 Muspole Street from 1760.

WORLD'S END LANE
10 St Martin's at Palace Plain, was named after the World's End pub, which is recorded at 6 World's End Lane from 1830; the pub closed in 1907. The British Gas Light Company built extra gasworks on World's End Land in 1851 to supplement the works they built opposite Bishop Bridge in 1830 at a cost of nearly £40,000. Sir Thomas Erpingham's house (see Tombland) stood at the end of World's End Lane but was pulled down in 1858.

Streets off World's End Lane
Porter's Yard (6)*
Brickwood's Buildings (location unknown)*
Great Yard (location unknown)

WOUNDED HART STREET/LANE
13–15 St Peter's Street, was named after the Wounded Heart

pub, which is recorded at Upper Market Street (aka St Peter's Street) from 1760. The street was known as Cosyns Lane in the early 14th century (which Sandred and Lingström suggest is from John Cosyn, a bailiff in 1307 who had a house there) and Herlewynes Lane from the late 14th century (after linen draper John Herlewyne, who also had a house there). The street became Wounded Heart Lane by 1720. The pub changed its name to the Wounded Hart in 1845 and to Kitcheners Arms in 1915; it closed in 1928. The yard was lost for the City Hall development in the early 1930s.

WRESTLER'S YARD

44–46 Barrack Street, was named after the Wrestler's pub, which is recorded at 58 Barrack Street from 1760. It closed in 1935 and the yard was lost 1935–41.

WRIGHT'S COURT

43–45 Elm Hill. *Pigot's Directory* of 1830 lists John Wright, 'Bombasin, crape manufacturer, camlets & silk', near here.

WRIGHT'S COURT

After 10 Fisher's Lane, is referenced in *White's Directory* of 1890 but was lost by 1964.

WRIGHT'S FERRY

157–175 King Street. *White's Directory* of 1883 lists Charles Wright, boatbuilder, at King Street. See also Thompson's Ferry.

WRIGHT'S FOUNDRY YARD

29–31 Muspole Street. *White's Directory* of 1883 lists George Godfrey (late Wright), iron and brass founder.

WRIGHT'S YARD

157 Ber Street. *Pigot's Directory* of 1830 lists Wright & Cattermoul, bricklayers, at Ber Street. The yard was lost 1935–41.

YARN MEWS

53–55 Cowgate, is a new development that was on the site of Finch's Yard. It takes its name from the industry in the area in the 19th century (St James' Yarn Mill).

YORK ALLEY or PASSAGE

Runs from 2–4 Castle Meadow (originally from 1 Orford Hill) to White Lion Street. It was known as Castledyck Lane in the 16th century (as it clearly led to the castle ditches at that point), but became York Alley by the early 20th century. The modern name comes from the York Hotel, which is recorded as the City of York pub from 1760 at the Castle Ditches (later 2 Castle Meadow). The York Hotel closed in 1964.

ZIPFEL'S COURT

111–113 Magdalen Street, takes its name from a family of watchmakers. *Pigot's Directory* of 1830 lists John Zipfel, watchmaker, and *Harrod & Co's Directory* of 1877 lists C. Zipfel and C. Zipfel junior at Magdalen Street. The yard may have been known as Lipfield's Yard at one point.

Bibliography

Ayers, Brian *English Heritage Book of Norwich*, BT Batsford Ltd, London, 1994, ISBN 0713475684.

Barringer, Christopher (ed) *Norwich in the Nineteenth Century*, Gliddon, Norwich, 1984, ISBN 0947893008.

Beatniffe, R. *Norfolk Tour*, Cockey Lane, Norwich, 1773.

Beckley, Rene *Ancient Walls of East Anglia*, Terence Dalton Ltd, 1979, ISBN 090096393X.

Blomefield, Francis *The History of the City and County of Norwich, Part II*, London, 1806.

— *Essay towards a topographical History of the County of Norfolk, Part III*, London, 1806.

Browne, P. *The History of Norwich, from the Earliest Records to the Present Time*, Norwich, 1814.

Campbell, James *Historic Towns Series – Norwich*, The Scholar Press in conjunction with The Historic Towns Trust, 1975, ISBN 0859671844.

Chase, William *Compleat History of the Famous City of Norwich, from the Earliest Account to the Present Year, 1728* Norwich, 1728.

Claxton, W. H. *Record of Local Events in Norwich from 575 to 1904*, Norwich, 1904.

Cluer, Andrew and Michael Shaw *Former Norwich*, Archive books, Attleborough, 1972.

Cooper, A.P. *The Changing Face of Norwich*, Norwich, 1948.

Cotman, Alec M. and Francis W. Hawcroft *Old Norwich – a collection of paintings, prints and drawings*, Jarrold & Sons, Norwich.

Cozens-Hardy, Basil and Ernest A. Kent *The Mayors of Norwich 1403 to 1835*, Jarrold & Sons, Norwich, 1938.

Day, James Wentworth *Norwich Through the Ages*, East Anglian Magazine Ltd, 1976.

Gibbs, Michael *English City Companion: Norwich*, Harraps, 1991, ISBN 024560256.

Goreham, Geoffrey *Georgian Norwich*, Norwich, 1972.

Hudson, Revd William MA FSA *How the City of Norwich Grew into Shape*, Norwich, 1896.

Jewson, C.B. *The Jacobin City, a Portrait of Norwich in its Reaction to the French Revolution 1788–1802*, Blackie & Son, 1975, ISBN 0216898749.

Kirkpatrick, John, Dawson Turner (ed) *History of the Religious Orders and Communities and of the Hospitals and Castle of Norwich, written 1725*, Norwich, Stevenson and Matchett, 1845.

Knights, Mark *The Highways and Byways of Old Norwich*, Jarrold & Sons, Norwich, 1887.

Lane, Richard *The Plains of Norwich*, Larks Press, Norwich, 1999, ISBN 0948400773.

Nobbs, George *Norwich, City of Centuries*, George Nobbs Publishing, Norwich, 1972.

Palgrave-Moore, Patrick *The Mayors and Lord Mayors of Norwich 1836–1974*, Elvery Dowers Publications, Norwich, 1978.

Peart, Stephen *What Happened to the Cinema Near You?* Northacres, Strumpshaw, 1996, ISBN 0951719203.

Pevsner, Nikolaus and Bill Wilson *The Buildings of England – Norfolk 1: Norwich and North-East*, Penguin, London, 2nd edition 1997, ISBN 0140710582.

Plunkett, George A.F. *Disappearing Norwich*, Terence Dalton Ltd, Lavenham, 1987, ISBN 0861380578.

— *Rambles in Old Norwich*, Terence Dalton Ltd, Lavenham, 1990, ISBN 0861380789.

Riddington Young, John *The Inns and Taverns of Old Norwich*, Wensum Books, Norwich, 1975, ISBN 0903619180.

Rye, Walter *The Parish of Heigham*, Roberts & Co, Norwich, 1917.

Sandred, Karle Inge and Bengt Lingström *The Place Names of Norfolk, Part I*, The English Place-Name Society, 1989, ISBN 0904889157.

Solomons, Gerald *Stories behind the Plaques of Norwich*, Capricorn Books, Norwich, 1981.

Spencer, Noel and Arnold Kent (revised by Alec Court) *The Old Churches of Norwich*, Jarrolds, Norwich, 1990, ISBN 0711705445.

Tanner, Norman P. *The Church in Late Mediaeval Norwich 1370–1532*, Pontifical Institute of Mediaeval Studies, Toronto, Canada, 1984, ISBN 088840669.

Veriod, Bryan S. *A History of the Norwich City Fire Brigade*, Norwich, 1986, ISBN 0951195808.

Wicks, Walter *Inns and Taverns of Old Norwich*, Norwich, 1925.

EAA 51: East Anglian Archaeology, Report no. 51, 1991 – The Ruined and Disused Churches of Norfolk, editor Peter Wade-Martins, Norwich, 1991, ISBN 0905594037.

Directories consulted:
Chase's Directory: 1783
Harrod & Co's Directory: 1868, 1877
Hunt's Directory of East Norfolk and Part of Suffolk: 1850
Kelly's Directory: 1896, 1900, 1912, 1925, 1935, 1947, 1960, 1965, 1970–71, 1975
Peck's Directory: 1802
Pigot's Directory: 1830
Robson's Commercial Directory: 1839
White's Directory: 1845, 1854, 1883, 1890

Websites I found particularly helpful:
Historical Directories (http://www.historicaldirectories.org) – gave me access to some directories not available at the library.
Norfolk Pubs (http://www.norfolkpubs.co.uk/) – this was invaluable for tracing the beginnings and endings of some of the pubs, particularly when I couldn't find the information in the directories.